A SPY IN THE ENEMY'S COUNTRY

A SPY IN THE ENEMY'S COUNTRY

The Emergence of
Modern Black Literature

BY DONALD A. PETESCH

University of Iowa Press

Iowa City

University of Iowa Press, Iowa City 52242
Copyright © 1989 by the University of Iowa
All rights reserved

Printed in the United States of America
First paperback printing, 1991

Typesetting by G & S Typesetters, Austin, Texas
Printing and binding by Thomson-Shore, Dexter,
Michigan

Library of Congress Cataloging-in-Publication Data
Petesch, Donald A.
   A spy in the enemy's country: the emergence of
modern black literature / by Donald A. Petesch.—
1st ed.
      p.   cm.
   Bibliography: p.
   Includes index.
   ISBN 0-87745-223-7, ISBN 0-87745-322-5 (pbk.)
   1. American literature—Afro-American authors—
History and criticism.   2. Afro-Americans—
Intellectual life.   I. Title.
PS153.N5P45   1989   88-37391
810'.9'896073—dc19   CIP

For Natalie

CONTENTS

PREFACE

RECENT HISTORIOGRAPHY has revealed an intricate network of relationships, attitudes, perceptions, emotions, and expressions in the nineteenth-century world of the master and the slave. Over the past twenty to thirty years, new kinds of evidence—such as oral accounts and slave narratives—have been considered in an attempt to develop a fuller understanding of a "peculiar institution" that grew, and prospered, in democratic America for over two hundred years. The effect has been to see the institution through the eyes of the slave, not simply through the eyes of the master. This viewing has helped to reveal a world more complex than Ulrich Phillips's 1918 depiction of plantations as "schools," to reveal a world closer to that imagined by Wendell Phillips, "when the lions [would write] history." In this world black culture and the black family are more complex than had been believed; the human element has been restored to the abstraction "slave"; people suffer, grow, ponder, and dream; and slaves, with the depth and complexity of other people, emerge in the literature.

In the field of black literary criticism, complementary developments are occurring as "the canon" is broadened to include more black literature, as course offerings in black literature increase in number, as the rhetorical qualities of black literature are explored. Increasingly, the power to define—as understood by such diverse nineteenth-century figures as Wendell Phillips and Lewis Carroll— is viewed as an aspect of power. From this perspective, the "grand theorists" of American literary criticism (either those who view the American novel, irrespective of race, as the expression of a romance tradition in literature or those who see the quintessential protagonist as an American male, separating himself from society and developing in the wilderness, on the river, or on the ocean) are seen to limit our grasp of both the breadth and depth of American literature, just as historians such as Phillips limit our understanding of the complexity of American slavery. Apart from ignoring the content of other fine literatures, the exclusiveness of these approaches is seen to narrow our understanding of even "the canon"—of its relationship, for example, to both its historical and its social contexts.

In Part One I examine the literary, historical, and social contexts within which the emerging black literature took root. It was a nineteenth-century world, with definite assumptions regarding the form and content of matter admitted into the "world of letters," or, more intimately, into the world of the drawing rooms. It was a world that publicly denied the existence of difference while indulging in racism and class division. In sum, it was a world where, following the Civil War, there was no appropriate written form (only the underground of oral lore) for the expression of the black experience. These conditions encouraged certain qualities in the literature, qualities which have persisted as racism has persisted: (1) a collective point of view; (2) the mimetic mode; (3) a sensitivity to the play of power; (4) a consciousness of the fragility of the self; (5) a predilection for the moral imperative; and (6) a recurrence of the tactic of masking.

The preoccupation with identity and the self, among the writers considered in Part Two, grows out of the pressures explored in Part One. The portrayal, for example, of injured selves profoundly reflected black experience in the period. Those black writers who began to shape the written literature were intensely concerned with the self and with the "look" of the white "other." Their writings form a unique record of the consciousness of a people, taking form within a social order that often denies that consciousness and, at times, even their very selves. The literature that developed was a literature of dissimulation, of masking, of self-hatred, of racial ambivalence, and even, for some writers, a literature of passing, of disappearance.

This book began at Johns Hopkins University, where I was a National Endowment for the Humanities Post-Doctoral Fellow in Afro-American Studies. I am indebted to Professor David Donald, then director of the Institute of Southern History, for selecting me for this fellowship, for stimulating my interest in history, and for encourag-

ing me in the direction of my research. The other major figure behind this book is my wife, Natalie, whose fiction I have always
cherished.

The institutional support of the National Endowment for the Humanities was invaluable, providing me with a year's research in a
stimulating environment. The University of Pittsburgh provided me
with a travel grant, which permitted me to examine slave documents and slave narratives at the Chicago Historical Society, the
New York Historical Society, the Schomburg Collection of the New
York Public Library, the Columbia University manuscript collection, the Library of Congress, the Widener Library, the Schlesinger
Library, and the Boston Public Library. The staffs at these libraries
were always helpful. Two secretaries in the English Department at
the University of Pittsburgh, Patricia M. Renkiewicz and Susan L.
Berovik, worked long hours typing this manuscript; and Annette
Galluze, executive secretary for my department, organized the many
details that made the preparation of the manuscript possible. I am
particularly grateful for all their help.

PART ONE

CHAPTER ONE

Introduction

FREDERICK DOUGLASS—hesitant and embarrassed, "prevailed upon" by a friend—spoke before an antislavery convention in Nantucket, Massachusetts in August 1841. The impression he created on that occasion was recalled later by abolitionist William Lloyd Garrison: "After apologizing for his ignorance, and reminding the audience that slavery was a poor school for the human intellect and heart, he proceeded to narrate some of the facts of his own history as a slave, and in the course of his speech gave utterance to many noble thoughts and thrilling reflections."[1] The act of standing before that audience transformed Douglass's life (the private fugitive slave became the public Frederick Douglass: abolitionist speaker, autobiographer, statesman, adviser to presidents), but it also provided a metaphor for important differences between black and white writing, differences which must be considered in any generalizations about the nature of American literature.

Audiences were accustomed to writings about slaves. Charles Osborn's antislavery journal the *Philanthropist* appeared in Ohio in 1817, to be followed by other antislavery periodicals, including *Freedom's Journal*, the first black newspaper, established in 1827. And they were accustomed to hearing about slaves; by 1836 "there were seventy lecturers in the field, drawn largely from the ministry, theological seminaries, and colleges."[2] But here was the word literally made flesh: a former slave telling his own story. Garrison was so impressed by Douglass that he joined with others in urging him to become active in the abolition movement, and Douglass, though legally a fugitive slave, agreed. As an agent for both the Massachusetts and American Anti-Slavery Societies, Douglass subsequently recounted, before many audiences, facts from "his own history as a slave," and in 1845 he published the classic account of his experiences, *Narrative of the Life of Frederick Douglass*.[3]

This early stress upon mimesis grew out of the needs of the abolitionists for a literature of reportage. People wanted to know, What is slavery really like? What is peculiar about the "peculiar institution"? Is the relation of master to slave benign or evil? In the 1830s and 1840s, with their experience of indentured servants and bound apprentices (recall the questions put to Benjamin Franklin and Huckleberry Finn) and the "wage slavery" identified with the rise of the mills and factories (recall Melville's "The Tarturus of Maids"), such questions were not so perverse as they may appear from a contemporary perspective.[4]

What was slavery really like? Both abolitionists and advocates of slavery were concerned with images, with what Walter Lippmann has termed the "pictures in our heads." Under siege from a burgeoning abolition movement that was growing perceptibly more militant (as can be seen most clearly perhaps in the proliferation of the more extreme antislavery manifestations, such as the publication of David Walker's *Appeal* in 1829, the rebellion of Nat Turner in 1830, and the publication of William Lloyd Garrison's *Liberator* in 1831), resistance "at the South" hardened. No longer would men come together, as they still did in the Virginia legislature in 1832, to debate emancipation; no longer would ideas sweep freely through the southern states;[5] no longer would reform of any kind find particular favor—the "isms," it was declared, were creatures of the North.[6] The view of slavery hardened in the South in the 1830s; formerly, it had been viewed as a "necessary evil," now it was to be considered a "positive good," and it was worth at least one's social position to view it otherwise. John C. Calhoun declared in 1837, "But let me not be understood as admitting, even by implication, that the existing relations between the two races in the slaveholding States is an evil:—far otherwise: I hold it to be a good, as it has thus far proved itself to be to both and will continue to prove so if not disturbed by the fell spirit of abolition."[7] George Fitzhugh, the southern sociologist, writing a decade before Marx, will cite many of the sources later employed by Marx in order to excoriate industrial capitalism. In *Cannibals All: or, Slaves Without Masters*, he will argue that northern industrial workers, or "wage slaves," are simply slaves without masters, and that "the negro slaves of the South are the happiest, and, in some sense, the freest people in the world."[8] The slaves' "happiness" will be pictorially represented by lithographs and prints, such as the often-reprinted idyll depicting the happy slaves gamboling and dancing before their slave cabin while the elderly black "uncle" picks at his banjo.[9]

The image of the plantation and the slave in antebellum southern novels was the primary literary form for this depiction of felicity. As Tremaine McDowell has noted, such antebellum southern novelists as John Pendleton Kennedy, Nathaniel Beverley Tucker, and William Alexander Carruthers "omitted almost without exception the unpleasant elements of plantation life." In their portrayals the slave was a paragon of loyalty who even refused freedom when offered. In George Tucker's *The Valley of the Shenandoah* (1824), the field slaves "completely identify themselves with the family as if the crops were their own." But perhaps no writer sounded a more deluded note than Nathaniel Beverley Tucker in this portrait of the self-abasement of an old slave in his novel *George Balcomee* (1836): "As he spoke thus in a tone of reverential affection, I held out my hand to him. He took it, and drawing it strongly downward to accommodate the lowness of his prostration, bowed himself upon it, and pressed it to his lips. I felt a tear upon it, and if an answering tear had not sprung to my eyes, I should not have deserved to be the object of such devotion, as ardent and devoted as it was hopeless."[10] Despite these images of felicity, however, the officials of the Confederacy would never make the mistake of arming their faithful retainers, even during the darkest days of their long struggle.[11]

In the propaganda war, which pitted abolitionist against slaveholder, such images demanded counterimages, and these were best supplied by former slaves: on the public platform, in the pages of slave narratives, or both.[12] Frederick Douglass, Ellen and William Craft, Henry Bibb, Josiah Henson, Anthony Burns, Henry ("Box") Brown, and William Wells Brown were among the former slaves who walked both through the pages of their own narratives and upon the stages of antislavery meetings in hamlets, towns, and cities of the North and the West. They were able to furnish their audiences first-person accounts of a peculiar institution that white anti-slavery speakers could only excoriate from several removes: "In 1842 John A. Collins, an agent for the American Anti-Slavery Society, reported to William Lloyd Garrison: 'The public have itching ears to hear a colored man speak, and particularly *a slave*. Multitudes will flock to hear one of this class speak.'"[13] The Reverend Ephraim Peabody, writing in 1849, observed that "all the theoretical arguments for or against slavery are feeble, compared with these accounts of living men of what they personally endured when under its dominion."[14] Two of the former slaves, Anthony Burns and William Wells Brown, included in their presentations a pictorial element, illustrated panoramas or dioramas of scenes from slave life.[15]

The published narratives of their experiences, which often crystallized their speeches from the public platforms, were widely read:

A large number of the separately printed narratives were issued in pamphlet form, cheaply printed, bound with paper covers and sold for about twenty-five cents. The more lengthy and better bound ones could be had for a dollar or a dollar and a half. *The Interesting Narrative of the Life of Olaudah Equiano, or Gustavus Vassa, the African* (1789) went into at least ten editions by 1837; a Dutch and a German edition are extant. At least six editions of Charles Ball's *Slavery in the United States* were issued between 1836 and 1859. By 1856 *The Narrative of Moses Roper's Adventures and Escape from American Slavery*, first published in 1837, had reached ten editions and had been translated into Celtic. Even so trivial a volume as *The Life of James Mars* (1865) saw eleven editions by 1872. Josiah Henson's narrative reached its six thousandth copy in 1852, having been published in England as well as here in America. By May 28, 1858 advance orders for the "Stowe edition" of Henson's book alone totalled 5,000 copies. In the 1878 edition it is claimed that 100,000 copies of the book had been sold. Indeed, a Dutch translation appeared in 1877 and a French edition in the following year. Within two years after its publication in 1853, *Twelve Years a Slave: The Narrative of Solomon Northup* had sold 27,000 copies. *The Narrative of William Wells Brown* sold 8,000 copies (four editions) by 1849. Needless to say, *The Narrative of the Life of Frederick Douglass* (1845) and *My Bondage and My Freedom* (1855) were widely read. For, according to the Reverend Mr. Peabody, by 1849 Douglass's narrative had "in this country alone passed through seven editions, and is, we are told, now out of print." The 1855 volume was enthusiastically reviewed in the New York *Times* and *Putnam's Magazine* and netted its author a splendid financial return.[16]

Every narrative was another report from the front lines, and these were no "remembrances recollected in tranquillity." These were, as Angelina Grimké characterized an escaped slave's narrative, reports that "came burning from his own lips."[17]

These reports helped to initiate the mimetic quality which has for so long characterized much of black literature. The contentiousness of the times placed an early, formal stress on mimesis.[18] The southern image of the plantation South had to be countered, and who was better qualified? Abolitionist Wendell Phillips wrote in a letter to Frederick Douglass (April 22, 1845): "You remember the old fable of 'The Man and the Lion,' where the lion complained that he should not be so misrepresented 'when the lions wrote history.'"[19] The lions were writing history in the form of the slave narratives. But some accused the lions of fabrication; others said the lions were really men! When *The Narrative of James Williams* (1838) was questioned and James Williams could not be found (his narrative had been "dictated" to Whittier), it was withdrawn from publication.[20] Such an experience, along with its subsequent notice in the southern press, further emphasized authentication of both author and contents: "Narrators were subjected to detailed questioning by committees of knowledgeable people; letters were written to former masters and neighbors for corroboration. A tale so seemingly improbable as the life of Henry Bibb led to an extensive correspondence with white Southerners, all of whom verified Bibb's account—the improbable was the real. Solomon Northup's fantastic experiences were verified by a basketful of legal documents."[21] Some of the principal narratives were prefaced by documents, and the considerable detail regarding the daily life and economy of the plantation South and the slave's role within the institutional structure reflected, in large part, the stress on realistic representation.

Thus, early in American literary history, black literature was exhibiting qualities we tend to identify with "realism" and "naturalism," such as the mimetic representation of the "real world" and the helplessness of the individual in the face of circumstance and situation, while at the same time those white middle-class writers who will later be regarded as most representative of the period were exhibiting those qualities we have tended to identify with the "romantic" consciousness.

Many of the qualities that have characterized black literature have evolved from its early public role—black literature has been the literary equivalent of the commissions of inquiry—as well as from its reflection of the very different sociohistorical experience of blacks in America. In its early public role, its purpose has been to report on the conditions of black life to a hypothetically decent, Christian, democratic audience in the expectation that once that audience was made aware of the gap between democratic, Christian ideals and daily, mundane practice, change would occur. In its reporting to that audience, the voice that literature has employed has ranged from entreaty to anger, but the audience has been presumptively white; it was not until the 1960s and 1970s that a significant group of black writers has emerged that has either ignored or rejected that audience.

In its reflection of the very different sociohistorical experience of blacks in America, black literature has provided glimpses of a world often "undreamt of" by whites, glimpses of "two nations" whose existence long predates the 1969 findings of the Kerner Commission. The two nations actually date from that 1619 Dutch man-of-war that John Rolfe reports docked at Jamestown, discharging, in the process, "twenty negars," the first reported in the British colonies. The black consciousness of the two nations is mirrored in the early spirituals, folk seculars, and slave narratives. That the black consciousness can both mirror and comment is graphically reflected in the folk secular recorded in Frederick Douglass's 1892 autobiography *Life and Times of Frederick Douglass*:

> We raise de wheat,
> Dey gib us de corn;
> We bake de bread,
> Dey gib us de crust;
> We sif de meal,
> Dey gib us de huss;

We peel de meat,
Dey gib us de skin;
And dat's de way
Dey take us in;
We skim de pot,
Dey gib us de liquor,
And say dat's good enough for nigger.[22]

In response to its early public role and to its reflection of the very different sociohistorical experience of blacks in America, certain qualities have emerged and recurred in the literature. (1) The point of view has tended to be collective rather than individual; slave narratives, for example, described what it was like to be a slave, not what it was like to be an individual, romantically perceived. (2) As a report on conditions, black prose early focused on that mundane play of the material and the mannered that Hawthorne in the nineteenth century (and Richard Chase in the twentieth) identified with the novel, rather than the romance, tradition. (3) The content early reflected a relationship of conflict between whites and blacks; scenes involving black-white interaction were often freighted with tension. Violence, either physical or psychological, was always possible. (4) An important result of this relationship has been the recurrence within the literature of the themes of the struggles for freedom and/or identity (self). (5) The literature has often expressed a moral imperative; but since what ought to be so diverges from what is, the literature has tended, also, to deflate myth (national and religious) and to employ irony. (6) The literature early employed, both in form and content, the most effective tactic available to blacks in the face of overwhelming power: masking, which is essentially a strategy for being absent while present.

These qualities in the literature will be considered in chapters 3 through 8, following a discussion of certain tendencies—evaluative, perceptual, emotional—which both influenced white thought in the nineteenth century and helped shape the milieu within which the new black literature developed and emerged.

CHAPTER TWO

Some Motes in the Nineteenth-Century Eye:

On Literary Taste, the Perception of Difference,

and White Images of Blacks

BEFORE CONSIDERING these qualities it is necessary to consider three elements which influenced public perception of, and response to, black literature and the black experience and consequently influenced black literary strategies: (1) the sentimentalizing and idealizing as well as the valuing of certain esthetic principles, in then-current literary theory and practice; (2) the nationalizing, celebratory mode which characterized the public consciousness, illustrated most clearly perhaps in the popularity of oratory, with the resulting tendency to blur the perception of difference; and (3) the images of blacks current in the white mind.

The Literary Taste and the Climate of Propriety

The stress on realism, on the accurate reporting of the verifiable facts of the black collective experience, was opposed by both current theory and practice in literature. William Charvat's *The Origins of American Critical Thought 1810–1835* lists the major features of the developing critical consciousness. He stresses the alliance of propriety and property: "The conservative quarterly critics were more conscious of the gap between the class they represented and the lower classes to whom the weeklies appealed, and it is obvious that the importance which they attributed to their work was partly the result of fears of political disorders among the rising lower classes whose numbers and power constituted a threat to the safety of property which Hamilton and the Federalists had fought so hard to establish." The critical review "felt it a duty to repress any writer who tended to disrupt the political, economic, and moral *status quo*. . . . The announced task of many of the critics was to preserve that social order, and it was implied in the criticisms of the rest of them." Preserving the social order placed the emphasis on restraint, on the curbing of "enthusiasm," on the policing of "good taste." But untune that string and the unlettered clamored at your ear; the un-propertied masses grew restless, as in France: "Not until the unitarians took up the cause of reform did the critics see that change did not necessarily mean a threat to the property of the privileged class, nor that a concern for the condition of the masses meant social leveling."

The preservation of the social order influenced even the response to philosophical pessimism or skepticism. After quoting George Bancroft's 1824 criticism of Goethe, Charvat observes, "Bancroft's attitude was typical of the period. Americans disliked gloominess in literature, and rarely failed to remark on it in their reviews of the Germans, of Byron, and of such of our own poets as indulged in it"—because gloom had social implications: "Most of the critics thought of gloom as a selfish thing, as a product of too much intro-version and a lack of proper social feeling. . . . optimism was felt to be a social necessity, and . . . pessimistic views of life were danger-ous to the social order."[1]

One applied to literature standards similar to those governing admission to one's drawing room. Russell Blaine Nye notes that "George Bancroft . . . counseled American writers to avoid the im-balances, disproportions, and over-enthusiasms of the Europeans in favor of 'moral charm,' 'moral propriety,' and 'earnestness and moral beauty' in art."[2] From such biases follow the strictures against the excesses and questionable morals of European romanticism; such writers as Lord Byron, George Sand, and Eugène Sue were welcome only with reservations. The "beautiful" and the "moral" were com-bined with the "true": "Art is untrue if it falsifies the facts of na-ture; it is doubly so if it deals only with the inconsequential or im-permanent instead of with the highest and most enduring 'truths,' for great art should express 'the most exalted thoughts and kindling aspirations of which human nature is capable!'"[3]

How, in all this moral decorousness, was one to domesticate the content of the black experience? Where patriarchy and the Victorian family, with their mirroring of the ideal and of the status quo, are elements of the approved domestic model, how to assimilate the experience of the black family, subject to the economic, psychological, and sexual violence of whites? Black writers and potential black writers were in possession of a content inappropriate to most possible forms. Slave narratives, for example, stressed, for reasons both of verisimilitude and propaganda, the degradation and victimization so much a part of the peculiar institution. This stress, effective as an antislavery tactic, was unacceptable outside that context, however much the freed slave might still suffer in "freedom." A Frederick Douglass could write, as a fugitive slave, that he had never known a slave who did not bear stripes upon his body, but where was the literary form, apart from the slave narrative, that could contain such an experience, that could domesticate such a troubling, and accusatory, content? The black writer, like Cleopatra's messenger, possessed bad news.

The black experience, in slavery or "freedom," was not the stuff of the literature of the times. An Emerson might write in "Self-Reliance," "Trust thyself: every heart vibrates to that iron string," but the black writer knew it was not *his* "iron string" that could have such a universalizing twang. The stress on uplift and idealization, reflected in Longfellow's 1832 essay in the *North American Review* ("the legitimate tendency of poetry is to exalt, rather than to debase,—to purify, rather than to corrupt"),[4] was not particularly useful to black writers. A Garrison might praise a Douglass's "noble thoughts," but the capacity for such utterances, if it is to be measured by white response to black expression, seems largely to have died out once "freedom" was achieved.

The Celebratory Mode and the Perception of Difference

The nineteenth century was not a century to cherish difference. However, one result of the black experience, in both slavery and "freedom," was to make blacks terribly conscious that they were, if anything, their difference. But where was the audience for difference in a growing nation, one of whose principal claims to the world was that of the elimination of difference? This theme, which has been variously expressed throughout history in such terms as the "melting pot," "rags to riches," "poor boy makes good," and the "American dream" and bodied forth in the experience of such mythic figures as Benjamin Franklin, Andrew Carnegie, and Thomas Edison, is expressed as early as 1616 in the writings of Capt. John Smith, who might be dubbed the first American land developer. Alluding to the hardships in England resulting from the enclosures, rack renting, and inflation, Smith early expressed one of Franklin's later themes: "Here are no hard landlords to rack us with high rents or extorted fines to consume us, no tedious pleas in law to consume us with their many years' disputations for justice. . . . here every man may be master and owner of his own labor and land, or the greatest part, in a small time. If he have nothing but his hands, he may set up this trade and by industry quickly grow rich."[5] This approach to the American experience, with its overtones of the promotional mode, sounds clearly in the text of Crèvecoeur's *Letters from an American Farmer* (1782): "Here are no aristocratical families, no courts, no kings, no bishops, no ecclesiastical dominion, no invisible power giving to a few a very visible one, no great manufacturers employing thousands, no great refinements of luxury. The rich and the poor are not so far removed from each other as they are in Europe. . . . We are all animated with the spirit of an industry which is unfettered and unrestrained because each person works for himself. . . . Here man is free as he ought to be."[6] In a land so well ordered, it is perhaps not surprising that felicity or, more grossly, simple happiness was identified as one of the marks of the American. Crèvecoeur had said, "We are the most perfect society now existing in the world."[7] That peripatetic French observer Alexis de Tocqueville wrote of the America of 1831–32, "it is a hundred times happier than ours. . . . this people is one of the happiest in the world," and President Andrew Jackson declared in his Farewell Address in 1837, "There never have been thirteen millions of people associated together in one political body who enjoyed so much freedom and happiness as the people of these United States."[8] Not surprisingly, perhaps, even a literary figure as wise as William Dean

Howells could make a similar observation. In *Criticism and Fiction* (1891), while comparing British and American fiction, he observed that the "large cheerful average of health and success and happy life" as well as the "more smiling aspects of life" are "the more American."[9]

A country which held such beliefs about its experience, its nature, and its possibilities and which self-consciously felt the need to create itself in the absence of a legendary and historical past makes special demands on the forms of its literary expression. The times favored what historian Daniel J. Boorstin has described as a declamatory literature: a literature rooted in oratory, as reflected in the early Puritan sermons and the Election Day addresses, and finding later expression in the Boston Massacre observances, the Fourth of July orations, the debates (Webster-Hayne, Lincoln-Douglas), the antislavery oratory, the American Lyceum movement, and the sermons of pulpit and revival tent (Lyman Beecher, William Ellery Channing, Theodore Parker, and Peter Cartwright, among others). "As the nation struggled into self-consciousness, the orator—the man speaking to or for or with his community—acquired a mythic role."[10] Tocqueville declared that an American "cannot converse, but he can discuss. . . . He speaks to you as if he were addressing a society."[11] Oratory stressed a commonality of sentiment, the identity of speaker and auditor, a communion of condition and origins, a sharing of tribulations and triumphs, and an ever-imminent and triumphal future. The celebratory mode was the popular mode in the pre–Civil War period, achieving its most intricate expression in the essays of Emerson. The more fulsome examples of the mode have been characterized by Harry Levin: "The rhetoric of the Everlasting Yea, the rhapsody of the eagle-screaming orator, and the note of self-praise have clangorously predominated."[12]

But even after the war, the mode persisted in only slightly altered guise. Unity, not division, was the intent of those great linking metaphors in Walt Whitman. For the Centennial Exposition of 1876, a hymn was written by John Greenleaf Whittier, abolitionist poet and journalist, and a cantata was written by Sidney Lanier, poet and former Confederate soldier. Whittier, the "slave poet," became in the popular imagination the writer of "Snowbound" and "Skipper

Ireson's Ride," and from the evidence of the schoolbooks and an-
thologies it would be increasingly difficult to learn that Whittier
devoted more than ten years of his life to the abolitionist cause,
writing a volume of antislavery poetry and publishing an abolitionist newspaper. Robert E. Lee wrote in a letter to a friend, "I believe
it to be the duty of everyone to unite in the restoration of the country and the re-establishment of peace and harmony."[13] Carl N. Degler has observed that Lincoln's plan, "which his successor Andrew
Johnson adopted, was deliberately lenient to the defeated South in
order that the Union as it was in 1860 might be restored as speedily
as possible."[14] On the literary front, the earlier "battle of the books,"
that contest of images regarding the nature of slavery, was transformed into a celebration of the southern past. The plantation, with
its horrors out of the slave narrative literature, was sentimentalized.
The vision of such writers as Frederick Douglass, Henry Bibb, William Wells Brown, and Solomon Northup was replaced by the songs
of Stephen Foster and the writings of Joel Chandler Harris and others.[15] The difference between blacks and whites dissolved in a celebration of mutuality and sentiment, and the "old times" became the
good times, not to be forgotten.[16]

This ignoring of difference is a tendency that has a long indulged
history in the American experience. It reflects the American willingness to see what is believed. Early examples can be found in the
recurring characterization of America in Puritan writings as a place
that is a "wilderness," "uninhabited," and "uncultivated" (a theme
sounded as late as Crèvecoeur), despite the rather clear presence of
maize-growing Indians; the Indians, however, were not "civil," so,
as savages, their presence was not present.[17]

But probably even more far-reaching in its implications (at least
for non-Indians) than the nonpresence of the very-present Indians
was the ignoring of class differences. Edward Pessen and other historians have probed the various myths of classlessness that have persisted into the twentieth century. On the basis of his own analysis
of tax assessment lists for New York City, Brooklyn, and Boston and
the studies of other historians, Pessen has drawn a picture of an increasing concentration of wealth during the antebellum period, a
concentration quite at variance with the myth of the "age of egali-

tarianism" or the "age of the common man": "During the 'age of egalitarianism,' wealth became concentrated in the hands of an ever-smaller percentage of the population. The trend persisted through-out the 1850s. . . . Far from being an age of equality, the antebellum decades featured an inequality that appears to surpass anything experienced by the United States in the twentieth century." But despite the increasing class division, Pessen observes that from "Tocqueville's time to our own, antebellum America has enjoyed the reputation of being a society marked by an unprecedented eco-nomic equality."[18]

The myth of classlessness in the midst of growing inequality sug-gests the power of ideology. As early as 1829 the Boston Prison Dis-cipline Society reported that 75,000 persons were "annually impris-oned for debt in the United States—more than half of them owing less than twenty-five dollars." Hundreds of private charitable asso-ciations "sprang up in cities during the period to supplement the work of municipal governments in dealing with poverty." Pessen sums up: "Much of the statistical evidence was available at the time, but men convinced that no great disparities existed were hardly disposed to probe the data critically. The era's egalitarian ide-ology fostered roseate notions about the condition of things in America."[19] In an earlier study, *Most Uncommon Jacksonians*, Pes-sen stood in the shoes of labor leaders during the antebellum period to describe the two Americas that emerge when the perspective shifts from the leaders of the community to the leaders of the work-ers: "The picture of American society painted by the Jacksonian la-bor leaders was a grim one indeed, preoccupied as they were with the nation's discordant and unlovely elements. It was very much a minority viewpoint, since most of their eminent contemporaries saw a very different social landscape, marked by comparative equality and widespread abundance."[20]

This selective seeing will shape the nation's response to the con-dition of blacks in America in the hostile post-Reconstruction pe-riod. As we shall see, hardly anyone in the decades following Recon-struction will stand in the black man's shoes. And even blacks will mask their presence or, perfecting the ultimate form of masking, will disappear entirely.

Images of the Black in the White Mind

In the warm glow of postwar sentimentality, difference—between North and South, master and slave—could dissolve in images of a carefree, rural, ordered way of life, a plantation world that was preindustrial and preurban and happily removed from the corruption of the Grant era: in effect, another version of the pastoral, conjuring up the lost garden which R. W. B. Lewis, Leo Marx, and others have described. However effective these images of unity could be at the rather abstract national level, other images were employed at the level where people actually lived, since unity could not seriously characterize the interaction of white and black. To account for present reality and past experience, the black was imaged as either child or animal/beast. In effect, the whole middle ground of normal experience, at least in theory, had to be ignored, since how could there be normal experience with a slave?[21] Or, to phrase it differently, how could you enslave someone with whom you could conceivably engage in normal interaction? Only their difference could have permitted, and justified, enslavement in the first place. If they were children, and the metaphor of the family persisted into the twentieth century, they must be controlled. If they were not children, then they must be uncivil and, therefore, subject to control.

In George Fitzhugh's writings, slaves belonged to "the family circle."[22] As historian George M. Frederickson notes, for Fitzhugh "the master became a 'parent or guardian,' and the slave a child."[23] The childlike nature of the black is the quality stressed by even so strong a supporter as Thomas Wentworth Higginson. He describes the blacks under his command in the First South Carolina Volunteers: "It is a dark, mild, drizzling evening, and as the foggy air breeds sand-flies, so it calls out melodies and strange antics from this mysterious race of grown-up children. . . . They seem the world's perpetual children, docile, gay, and lovable. . . . Severe penalties would be wasted on these people, accustomed as they have been to the most violent passions on the part of white men; but a mild inexorableness tells on them, just as it does on any other children. . . . This delighted our men, who always took a childlike pleasure in being out of bed at any unreasonable hour."[24] Henry M.

Field, a northern Presbyterian minister, employed the metaphor of the family and at the same time revealed the range of invention in postwar nostalgia in his book *Bright Skies and Dark Shadows* (1890):

> [The Negroes] "'belonged to the family,' and were the objects of a degree of family affection." Field described the plantation as easygoing and indulgent, a mirthful place in which singing and dancing were the principal activities. Slaves responded to their kindly treatment with "gratitude and devotion." . . . On the subject of relations between the races, Field argued that the best hope lay in a revived paternalism, which would give the Negroes the kind of guidance from whites that they had received from good masters under slavery. ". . . in time," he predicted, "unfailing kindness will do its work."[25]

The image of the black as animal, or in its more clearly threatening formulation, "beast," is the potentially dark side of the image of the black as child.[26] According to both pre– and post–Civil War arguments, the black was by nature a savage brute. As Frederickson characterizes the earlier arguments: "Under slavery . . . he was 'domesticated' or, to a limited degree, 'civilized.' Hence docility was not so much a natural characteristic as an artificial creation of slavery. As long as the control of the master was firm and assured, the slave would be happy, loyal, and affectionate; but remove or weaken the authority of the master, and he would revert to type as a bloodthirsty savage. . . . As a slave he was lovable, but as a freedman he would be a monster."[27]

Black "savagery" is characterized as "bloodthirsty" in the pre–Civil War arguments, where revolt is the specter in the white psyche. Frederickson quotes from an 1836 study by a Charleston lawyer: "In the words of William Drayton, who drew on the example of Santo Domingo, 'the madness which a sudden freedom from restraint begets—the overpowering burst of a long buried passion, the wild frenzy of revenge, and the savage lust for blood, all unite to give the warfare of liberated slaves, traits of cruelty and crime which nothing earthly can equal.'"[28] But in the post–Civil War arguments, when de facto liberation has been secured, black "savagery" assumes a form in the white psyche which has had terrifying consequences for the black experience and important implications for black literature: the black as rapist. From the 1880s through the turn of the century, writers and speakers increasingly charge the black man with sexual assaults on white women. It is these assaults that are cited to explain, and often to justify, the increasing violence of lynching. Atticus G. Haygood, writing in *Forum* in 1893, denounced lynching as a barbarous "crime against society," but "he went on to ask the critics of the South to 'consider the provocation': 'Sane men who are righteous will remember not only the brutish man who dies by the slow fire of torture; they will also think of the ruined woman, worst tortured than he.' Such lynchings as had recently taken place were the result of 'the elemental forces that control human nature throughout all time and the world over' and must be understood as the reaction to a recent wave of sexual assaults committed by blacks against women. Lynching would not stop, he suggested, until black leaders and Northern liberals moderated their one-sided denunciation of the practice and prevailed upon Negroes to stop raping white women."[29] The "uncontrollable lust of black men for white women" was one of the consequences of the removal of the restraints imposed by slavery; the black-as-beast was expressing his animal nature, and lynching both avenged the immediate act and served to replace the former restraints with fear.

Not even the mulatto could escape the intricacies of racist argument. In fact, for some the mulatto was more dangerous for his admixture of white blood. As a southern woman, Mrs. L. H. Harris, writing to the editor of the *Independent*, declared in 1899, "the 'negro brute' who attacked some Southern women and struck fear and terror in the hearts of all others was 'nearly always a mulatto,' with 'enough white blood in him to replace native humility and cowardice with Caucasian audacity.' This monster had 'the savage nature and murderous instincts of the wild beast and the cunning and lust of a fiend.' "[30]

The image of the black as beast-rapist had a profound impact in the writings of best-selling novelist Thomas Dixon, who, in effect, returned to the prewar battle of the images. This is most clearly revealed in his remarks regarding his first novel, *The Leopard's Spots* (1902): "It may shock the prejudices of those who have idealized or worshiped the negro as canonized in 'Uncle Tom.' Is it not time they heard the whole truth? They have heard only one side for forty years."[31] This prominent Baptist minister, who spoke of his work as an evangelical effort to transform the stereotype of the Negro, had his greatest impact with his 1905 publication of *The Clansman*, which ten years later became D. W. Griffith's highly successful film *Birth of a Nation*. The novel includes the rape of a young white virgin: "A single tiger-spring, and the black claws of the beast sank into the soft white throat."[32] This act is followed by the suicide of both the girl and her mother and the lynching of the black "beast" by the righteous Ku Klux Klan. The language of the conclusion recalls the language of Thomas Nelson Page's 1898 novel *Red Rock*, in which a black Reconstruction political figure, appropriately named Moses, who is described variously as a "beast" and a "reptile," tries to assault a white woman—"He gave a snarl of rage and sprang at her like a wild beast"[33]—and is lynched several years later for a "terrible crime." Page had earlier, in his stories of the Old South, helped to popularize the image of the genial and lovable "old-time darky."

CHAPTER THREE

Differences in Perception:

Narrative of the Life of Frederick Douglass,

Walden, and *Invisible Man*

THE THREE ELEMENTS considered above—the vogue of sentimentalizing and idealizing, the celebratory mode and the insensitivity to
difference, and the image of blacks in the white mind—in conjunction with the early public role of black literature and the difference
in historical experience affected significantly the form and content
of black literary expression. Certain qualities emerged early and persisted, due in part to the retention, in "freedom," of the basic relationships and attitudes of slavery. In the absence of any fundamental
changes in land tenure and power, abolition, while often insuring
the ex-slave more control of his body and greater psychological well-
being, could not basically alter the pattern of black-white relations.
The peculiar relationship of white and black withstood the disappearance of the peculiar institution.

One of the important qualities that has persisted in the literature
is the tendency toward a collective perception. Black literature has
not been characterized by the romantic ego common to white literature; rather, black literature has tended to articulate a collective
consciousness that has strong roots in both the African village and
the daily experience of blacks under slavery and during the postwar
period.

Historian Nathan Irvin Huggins has stressed the importance of
the village in the experience of those West Africans who furnished
most of the slaves for the New World market:

> The village was the expression of the need to hold together for exis-
> tence. Isolation was unthinkable. Alone, awesome nature was a threat

rather than a blessing. . . . Alone, a person was nobody. . . . One was not
likely to wander far from one's village, but wherever one went within
the tribe, one was a person—the son or daughter of a person—related to
someone known. The web of relationships extended far and gave one a
sense of place and certainty. But it tied one to obligations and duties,
and made the concept of individual freedom the fantasy of a lunatic.[1]

So central has been the tendency for the individual West African to
think of his self in terms of the group that contemporary scholars
still cite this feature. Anthropologist P. C. Lloyd observes, "Loyalty
to, and identification with, the group is dominant; the conflict with
rival groups serves to reinforce the internal cohesion of each."[2] Elizabeth Colson has observed: "Probably it is safe to say that over
much of Africa, even today, life is conditioned by certain attitudes
toward property and persons which are characteristic of a non-
industrial stable society, in which opportunities and power depend
upon status within social groups rather than upon control of invest-
ments; where, indeed, the safest form of investment, and often the
only one, is still to be found in the building up of claims against
persons."[3]

In white America, by contrast, various elements converged in an
emphasis on the individual. For example, Perry Miller and Thomas
H. Johnson have noted that "there was a strong element of individualism in the Puritan creed; every man had to work out his own salvation, each soul had to face his maker alone. . . . they were maintaining a theology that brought every man to a direct experience of
the spirit and removed intermediaries between himself and the
deity."[4] This stress on the individual in turn helped to undermine
the theory of the divine right of kings. Harvey Wish has written:

[Sir Edward] Coke was the powerful champion of a revised common law
against the divine right principles of James I. . . . In Anglo-American ju-
risprudence, this came to mean a "rule of law" rather than of men, a
system binding upon all citizens and protecting the individual against
the state by elaborate technicalities of procedure and rule. Thus the
"natural-rights" philosophy of Puritanism, stressing the individual judgment and conscience, was substituted for the authority of the prince and
his judges.[5]

So in two of the traditional relationships—that between a person and his god and that between a person and his state—the emphasis in the early history of white America was on the individual.

Events and conditions exacerbated both tendencies: for blacks to think in terms of the group, for whites to stress the individual. Historians such as Winthrop D. Jordan and Kenneth Stampp have described how slavery quickly assumed the forms we traditionally associate with it.[6] By the 1660s laws passed in Virginia and Maryland, and later copied by the other states, had established (1) that a slave remained a slave for life; (2) that a slave inherited the status of his mother; and (3) that conversion to Christianity did not alter the status of a slave. Conditions under slavery readily bred a tendency for slaves to think in terms of "we" and "they," however divisive the differences in tribal backgrounds might have been or the differences which sometimes existed between field and house slaves. American slavery was not the slavery they had been accustomed to in Africa, and the differences were not lost upon them. American slavery, in its most extreme forms, required labor from dawn till dusk (from "day clean" to "first dark") or even later; determined who could or could not marry; disciplined slaves and their children; broke up families; abandoned elders to starvation; and provided inadequate food, housing, clothing, and medical care. Under African slavery, slaves were viewed more as members of the family. John Hope Franklin has written: "Slaves were predominantly persons captured in war and could not be sold or kept by the persons who captured them. Slaves were usually regarded as the property of the chief of the tribe or the head of the family. In law, slaves were chattel property, but in practice they often became trusted associates of their masters and enjoyed virtual freedom."[7] Under the conditions of American slavery, it was the group toward which the individual turned for his self-conception and his sense of self-worth. The original tendency on the part of the African to identify with family, clan, village, and tribe was reinforced by the Afro-American experience of slavery. The enemy from without tended to strengthen the bonds within. This group identification was also strengthened by the types of work engaged in: group work, which stressed mutual assistance and collective effort, such as cotton picking, cane cutting, lumbering and sawmill operating, turpentine production, and levee labor and stevedoring.

Events and conditions similarly reinforced the tendency of white Americans to view themselves as somehow separate. The earlier Puritan stress on diligence in one's "calling"—wherein success and the accumulation of wealth were viewed as assurance, and sign, of God's gifts and one's election—almost imperceptibly evolved into the secularism of Benjamin Franklin's "Advice to a Young Tradesman" and his *Autobiography*. By this point, competition was clearly at work. But there were plenty of other factors to undermine white American cohesion and cooperation and to emphasize the self and individualism. The very presence of the frontier, which under some conditions might have induced cooperation (for defense against the Indians, for example), also tended to separate the pioneers as well as to lure them westward, a process described in Frederick Jackson Turner's "Frontier Thesis." The presence of the frontier and the expansion westward similarly inflated wage rates in the cities and, for a time, made it difficult to secure labor, which often felt it could better its condition elsewhere. And both Daniel J. Boorstin and Russel Blaine Nye,[8] among others, have described the pervasive American belief in progress, growing out of the experience of "wresting a civilization out of the wilderness and building a nation." The combination of these factors, in conjunction with a burgeoning egalitarian ethos, was enough to make any hardy soul restive and to place him at odds with his condition, and perhaps with every man. From this perspective, the social Darwinism of the latter half of the nineteenth century is merely one of the more extreme manifestations of a potentially divisive spirit and ethic.

Blacks writing in the nineteenth century thought of their experience in terms of its representativeness rather than in terms of its uniqueness. Slave narratives, for example, described what it was like to be a slave; they did not dilate on the uniqueness of the self, either in the manner of the vaunting self of a Renaissance Cellini or the egoistic self of a Romantic Rousseau.[9] This difference can be illustrated by comparing Henry David Thoreau's *Walden* with Frederick Douglass's *Narrative of the Life of Frederick Douglass*. Thoreau's account is our grandest celebration of the separate, and separated, self; Douglass, throughout his narrative, stresses his ties to others. The opening lines from the two works effectively reflect this difference. *Walden* begins:

> When I wrote the following pages, or rather the bulk of them, I lived alone, in the woods, a mile from any neighbor, in a house which I had built myself, on the shore of Walden Pond, in Concord, Massachusetts, and earned my living by the labor of my hands only. I lived there two years and two months. At present I am a sojourner in civilized life again.[10]

The *Narrative* begins:

> I was born in Tuckahoe, near Hillsborough, and about twelve miles from Eaton, in Talbot county, Maryland. I have no accurate knowledge of my age, never having seen any authentic record containing it. By far the larger part of the slaves know as little of their ages as horses know of theirs, and it is the wish of most masters within my knowledge to keep their slaves thus ignorant. I do not remember to have ever met a slave who could tell of his birthday. They seldom come nearer to it than planting-time, harvest-time, cherry-time, spring-time, or fall-time.[11]

(The *Narrative* ends with a reference to his first speaking out at an antislavery conference in Nantucket in 1841, and concludes: "From that time until now, I have been engaged in pleading the case of my brethren—with what success, and with what devotion, I leave those acquainted with my labors to decide.")[12]

Thoreau's comments not only describe a separation and distance from others but reveal an attitude toward separateness that is borne out in his chapter on "Solitude": "I have never felt lonesome, or in the least oppressed by a sense of solitude, but once, and that was a few weeks after I came to the woods, when, for an hour, I doubted if the near neighborhood of man was not essential to a serene and healthy life." It is little wonder that "The Village" is *Walden's* briefest chapter. He goes to view its denizens as though he were an early naturalist or anthropologist:

> As I walked in the woods to see the birds and squirrels, so I walked in the village to see the men and boys; instead of the wind among the pines I heard the carts rattle. In one direction from my house there was a colony of muskrats in the river meadows; under the grove of elms and

buttonwoods in the other horizon was a village of busy men, as curious to me as if they had been prairie-dogs, each sitting at the mouth of its burrow, or running over to a neighbor's to gossip. I went there frequently to observe their habits.[13]

Thoreau's wit and metaphors act to deflate the pretensions and posturing of human activity, as when the big guns fired on gala days sound in his beanfield like popguns or puffballs. His stance is that of the outsider, viewing the quiddities of our beliefs, rituals, and social arrangements, and no one saw earlier, or more profoundly, their makeshift nature. But the viewing is distanced, even when he writes, "I wish, as you are brothers of mine, that you should have spent your time better than digging in this dirt";[14] the voice is less that of fellow sufferer, more that of the tradition initiated by the early Puritan biographies and reflected in Franklin's autobiography— life as exemplum. His pity—grand, rhetorical, sublime—seems the pity of the outsider. His "at present" return to "civilized life" as a "sojourner" suggests the tenuousness of a consciousness that has stepped through the looking glass and can never again step back, never again unknow that which it has known.

In contrast to Thoreau, Douglass's opening lines quickly move from his self to the experience of the group. He is not, as Thoreau, raising those grand and basic questions about the nature of the self and of our knowledge that make *Walden* so important and so timeless; he is, rather, describing the slave's condition and existence within the peculiar institution. His specialness is his likeness to others; he is others given voice, the bruted existence marvelously articulated. But not only is he their voice, he sees *his* existence in *their* existence. Thoreau had three chairs in his cabin, "one for solitude, two for friendship, three for society";[15] Douglass had over forty scholars in his illegal Sabbath school:

The work of instructing my dear fellow-slaves was the sweetest engagement with which I was ever blessed. We loved each other, and to leave them at the close of the Sabbath was a severe cross indeed. . . . For the ease with which I passed the year, I was, however, somewhat indebted to the society of my fellow-slaves. They were noble souls; they not only possessed loving hearts, but brave ones. We were linked and interlinked with each other. I loved them with a love stronger than any thing I have experienced since. It is sometimes said that we slaves do not love and confide in each other. In answer to this assertion, I can say, I never loved any or confided in any people more than my fellow-slaves, and especially those with whom I lived at Mr. Freeland's. I believe we would have died for each other. We never undertook to do any thing, of any importance, without a mutual consultation. We never moved separately. We were one; and as much so by our tempers and dispositions, as by the mutual hardships to which we were necessarily subjected by our condition as slaves.[16]

These differences in their views of the individual and the group reflect persistent differences in the black and white consciousness. One must be struck, for example, by the relative aloneness of so many of the protagonists in works by white writers that have been considered American classics: Hester Prynne in *A Scarlet Letter*, Captain Ahab in *Moby Dick*, Huck Finn in *Huckleberry Finn*, Henry Fleming in *The Red Badge of Courage*, Carrie Meeber in *Sister Carrie*, George Willard in *Winesburg, Ohio*, Nick Carroway in *The Great Gatsby*, Tod Hackett in *The Day of the Locust*, and Joe Christmas in *Light in August*; and, more recently, Hazel Motes in *Wise Blood*, Jack Burden in *All the King's Men*, Randall Patrick McMurphy in *One Flew over the Cuckoo's Nest*, Moses Herzog in *Herzog*, Yakov Bok in *The Fixer*, and Holden Caulfield in *The Catcher in the Rye*. The list could be considerably extended. While there have been exceptions to this pattern (protagonists in proletarian fiction, for example, and characters created by a number of southern and Jewish writers who have been bound more tightly in webs of kin, place, and ethnic relationships), the lonely figures have predominated.

It is possible, of course, to find solitary figures in black literature. In fact, the protagonist of Ralph Ellison's *Invisible Man* is one of the most solitary figures in modern literature. We never see him interacting with his family. He *recalls* some words his grandfather had spoken. He *mentions* his parents' concern over his grandfather's words and the excitement of everyone, including his neighbor, over his scholarship to the "state college for Negroes," but we never see them speaking together. When he is kicked out of the college by the president, Dr. Bledsoe, we do not see him speaking to any friend, classmate, or roommate, even though he had spent three years at the college. In his preparations for departure he is typically alone: "So while my roommate grinned and mumbled unaware in his sleep I packed my bags."[17] In Harlem, he takes a room at the Men's House; there is no suggestion that he might stay with a friend, relative, friend of the family, or acquaintance from his hometown, the kind of people who have historically eased the transition of blacks moving from rural to urban areas. This pattern of aloneness persists until the very end of *Invisible Man*, where we leave the protagonist sitting alone under the city, contemplating the possible end of his "hibernation."

This aloneness is uncommon in black literature, which has traditionally stressed the individual's communal, group ties. Black characters tend, more so than white characters, to be bound up by webs of relationship—group, peer, street, family, kin, and political—and both to define their selves through interaction with these larger groups and to project futures that include much more than a backward glance at such groups, groups that have traditionally held for them so much of their world's past and being. Jesse B. Simple, Langston Hughes's folk character, spoke for many of the nation's blacks when he replied to Boyd's question about why he liked Harlem with the remark, " 'It's so full of Negroes.' "[18]

And even the aloneness of the protagonist of *Invisible Man* seems about to end at the close of the novel. Ellison has posed this possibility by giving his character two kinds of awarenesses. More obvious is his existential sense of the malleability of essence, growing out of his being mistaken for Rinehart:

> His world was possibility and he knew it. He was years ahead of me and I was a fool. I must have been crazy and blind. The world in which we lived was without boundaries. A vast seething, hot world of fluidity. . . . How many days could you walk the streets of the big city without encountering anyone who knew you, and how many nights? You could actually make yourself anew. The notion was frightening, for now the world seemed to flow before my eyes. All boundaries down, freedom was not only the recognition of necessity, it was the recognition of possibility.[19]

But a contending awareness, and one that Ellison has developed over the course of the novel, is the protagonist's awareness of his communal, folk roots. The "plans man," for example, is a voice from the "old country" (from "down home") with whom the protagonist "found a certain comfort . . . as though we'd walked this way before through other mornings, in other places."[20] His store of folk responses "had me grinning despite myself. I liked his words though I didn't know the answer. I'd known the stuff from childhood, but had forgotten it; had learned it back of school."[21] In the surreal birth-from-the-machine scene the questions—"WHO WAS YOUR MOTHER?," "WHO WAS BUCKEYE THE RABBIT?," "BOY, WHO WAS BRER RABBIT?"—generate folk responses in the protagonist's consciousness (as, for example, "I looked at him, feeling a quick dislike and thinking, half in amusement, I don't play the dozens. And how's *your* old lady today?"), but they are unexpressed and thus, symbolically, repressed.[22] Mary Rambo, who takes him in off the street, is a representative of his folk past: "Nor did I think of Mary as a 'friend'; she was something more—a force, a stable, familiar force like something out of my past which kept me from whirling off into some unknown which I dared not face."[23] She embodies the folk yearning for leaders who might move the people to "higher ground" and an understanding, too, of the temptations to separateness in the city: "'It's you young folks what's going to make the changes. . . . Y'all's the ones. You got to lead and you got to fight and move us all up a little higher. And I tell you something else, it's the ones from the South that's got to do it, them what knows the fire and ain't forgot how it burns. Up here too many forgits. They finds a place for theyselves and forgits the ones on the bottom.' "[24]

In that centrally positioned chapter 13, the protagonist is exposed to the folk and folkloric through a series of encounters. The chapter opens with his walking past Harlem shop windows:

> I walked slowly on, blinking my eyes in the chill air, my mind a blur with the hot inner argument continuing. The whole of Harlem seemed to fall apart in the swirl of snow. I imagined I was lost and for a moment there was an eerie quiet. I imagined I heard the fall of snow upon snow. What did it mean? I walked, my eyes focused into the endless succession of barber shops, beauty parlors, confectioneries, luncheonettes, fish

houses, and hog maw joints, walking close to the windows, the snow-flakes lacing swift between, simultaneously forming a curtain, a veil, and stripping it aside. A flash of red and gold from a window filled with religious articles caught my eye. And behind the film of frost etching the glass I saw two brashly painted plaster images of Mary and Jesus sur-rounded by dream books, love powders, God-Is-Love signs, money-drawing oil and plastic dice. A black statue of a nude Nubian slave grinned out at me from beneath a turban of gold. I passed on to a win-dow decorated with switches of wiry false hair, ointments guaranteed to produce the miracle of whitening black skin.[25]

As though "through a glass darkly" vision seems both imminent and veiled. His reaction is to suppress "a savage urge to push my fist through the pane." This scene is immediately followed by the scene with the yam seller,[26] with all its implications for identity (ex-pressed seriocomically in his musing, "'I am what I am,'" and by his declaring, "'I yam what I am'"), and by the dispossession scene, in which, against his will, he finds himself emotionally racked while he sees and remembers more than he wishes: "*And why did I, standing in the crowd, see like a vision my mother hanging wash on a cold windy day, so cold that the warm clothes froze even be-fore the vapor thinned and hung stiff on the line, and her hands white and raw in the skirt-swirling wind and her gray head bare to the darkened sky—why were they causing me discomfort so far beyond their intrinsic meaning as objects? And why did I see them now as behind a veil that threatened to lift, stirred by the cold wind in the narrow street?*"[27]

After the chaos of the riot, after the "dream" beside the "river of black water," Ellison's protagonist is not unlike Eliot's speaker at the end of *The Waste Land*.[28] He too has shored up certain fragments against his ruins, and these fragments (though both Dante and Eliot, and even Melville, echo) are largely evocations of folk art and folk history. He says, "Call me Jack-the-Bear, for I am in a state of hiber-nation." Listening to Louie Armstrong records and under the spell of marijuana, he enters new dimensions of the music, descending into its depths, where he finds "an old woman singing a spiritual"; a beautiful girl standing before a "group of slaveowners who bid for her naked body"; a black preacher speaking on the "Blackness of

Blackness"; an old woman recalling her love for her white master who had given her sons.[29] But what recurs, like a thematic riff, is Louie Armstrong's question, which gathers in the many questions the protagonist poses to white society in the opening and closing chapters: "What did I do / To be so black / And blue?" (Though not included in the text, Louie Armstrong's lines, which precede those quoted, serve as an unexpressed counterpoint: "My only sin / Is the color of my skin.")

By the close of the novel the protagonist has asserted his collective, communal identity, both his blackness and his origins in the folk, and he has rejected the historical reality posited by the Brotherhood. In fact, it is in that central chapter 13, in which the protagonist first meets Brother Jack, where the Brotherhood's insensitivity to the meaning of race in history is first revealed:

> "But you were concerned with that old couple," he said with narrowed eyes. "Are they relatives of yours?"
> "Sure, we're both black," I said, beginning to laugh.
> He smiled, his eyes intense upon my face.
> "Seriously, are they your relatives?"
> "Sure, we were burned in the same oven," I said.
> The effect was electric. "Why do you fellows always talk in terms of race!" he snapped, his eyes blazing.
> "What other terms do you know?" I said, puzzled. "You think I would have been around there if they had been white?"[30]

After the shooting of Tod Clifton, the protagonist enters the subway and, in this symbolic subworld, becomes aware of the vast number of his people who are outside the "historical time" of the Brotherhood: "They were outside, in the dark with Sambo, the dancing paper doll; taking it on the lambo with my fallen brother, Tod Clifton."[31] He emerges from the subway, wrestling with the implications of his awareness:

> Now, moving through the crowds along 125th Street, I was painfully aware of other men dressed like the boys, and of girls in dark exotic-colored stockings, their costumes surreal variations of downtown styles. They'd been there all along, but somehow I'd missed them. I'd missed them even when my work had been most successful. They were outside

the groove of history, and it was my job to get them in, all of them. I looked into the design of their faces, hardly a one that was unlike someone I'd known down South. Forgotten names sang through my head like forgotten scenes in dreams. I moved with the crowd, the sweat pouring off me, listening to the grinding roar of traffic, the growing sound of a record shop loudspeaker blaring a languid blues. I stopped. Was this all that would be recorded? Was this the only true history of the times, a mood blared by trumpets, trombones, saxophones and drums, a song with turgid, inadequate words? My mind flowed. It was as though on this short block I was forced to walk past everyone I'd ever known and no one would smile or call my name. No one fixed me in his eyes. I walked in feverish isolation.[32]

At this point, the "blues" and "history" are struggling for mastery of his soul, and he is feeling his isolation. But also, at this moment, a couple of black boys dart out of the Five & Ten, "taking it on the lambo." As he suppresses the instinct to trip the pursuing white shopkeeper, the shopkeeper is tripped by an old black woman.

The struggle between opposing visions of reality is only finally resolved by his meeting with Brother Jack, his encounter with Rinehartism, and his meeting with Brother Hambro. He chooses, finally, to follow his grandfather's advice: "I'd overcome them [the Brotherhood] with yeses, undermine them with grins, I'd agree them to death and destruction." He would be a "spy in the enemy's country," a mask for their masking, a Sambo doll: "All they wanted of me was one belch of affirmation and I'd bellow it out loud. Yes! Yes! Yes! That was all anyone wanted of us, that optimistic chorus of yassuh, yassuh, yassuh!"[33]

The close of *Invisible Man*, while echoing *The Waste Land*, is more affirmative. While death and spring mix ("There's a stench in the air, which, from this distance underground, might be the smell either of death or of spring—I hope of spring. But don't let me trick you, there *is* a death in the smell of spring and in the smell of thee as in the smell of me"),[34] as in Eliot's "breeding lilacs out of dead ground," Ellison's "hope" suggests a difference. Different, too, is the protagonist's "possibility that even an invisible man has a socially responsible role to play" and his echoing of John Donne's sermon: "Who knows but that, on the lower frequencies, I speak for you?"[35]

The difference is in the stress on the social, the communal, a differ-ence in keeping with the protagonist's growing awareness over the course of the novel of his communal, folk roots. Which suggests that another way of viewing the difference between *Invisible Man* and *The Waste Land* is to view their difference as, ultimately, one of voice/voices: the protagonist's "emergent" voice will not be the separate, and separated, voices that characterize *The Waste Land*.[36]

CHAPTER FOUR

The "Probable and Ordinary Course

of Man's Experience": Antiromance Tendencies

in the Black Literary Tradition

HOWEVER MUCH one might question the precision of the terms *romance* and *novel* in identifying tendencies within the American narrative tradition, numerous writers and critics have found the distinction to be useful, and the categories suggest ways to view the differences between the black and white literary sensibilities. Quite simply, the distinction typically drawn between the American romance and the British novel can be applied to differences between white and black narrative strategies.[1]

Let us begin where others have begun: with Hawthorne's classic formulation of the distinction in his preface to *The House of the Seven Gables*:

When a writer calls his work a Romance, it need hardly be observed that he wishes to claim a certain latitude, both as to its fashion and material, which he would not have felt himself entitled to assume, had he professed to be writing a Novel. The latter form of composition is presumed to aim at a very minute fidelity, not merely to the possible, but to the probable and ordinary course of man's experience. The former—while, as a work of art, it must rigidly subject itself to laws, and while it sins unpardonably so far as it may swerve aside from the truth of the human heart—has fairly a right to present that truth under circumstances, to a great extent, of the writer's own choosing or creation. If he thinks fit, also, he may so manage his atmospherical medium as to bring out or mellow the lights, and deepen and enrich the shadows, of the picture. He will be wise, no doubt, to make a very moderate use of the privileges here stated, and especially, to mingle the Marvellous rather as a slight, delicate, and evanescent flavor, than as any portion of the actual substance of the dish offered to the Public. He can hardly be said, however, to commit a literary crime, even if he disregard this caution.[2]

Elements of the "marvellous" are already evident in Hawthorne's earlier *The Scarlet Letter*: the rosebush, Hester's "halo," the "letter" in the sky, the "letter" on Dimmesdale's chest. But even there the "latitude" Hawthorne claims is tainted by the "ordinary course of man's experience": the aspects of the marvelous are coupled with the mundane; that is, an event permits the reader both a marvelous and a mundane cause—the reader may choose. Even Pearl (elf? sprite? demon? spirit? small human?), whose insight recalls the earlier Natty Bumpo and later Ahab, presents the reader (as do Natty Bumpo and Ahab) dual possibilities: her insight is marvelous *or* it is a psychologically realistic portrayal of the acuity wrung from suffering. Hawthorne's "marvellous" is not Charles Brockden Brown's marvelous; the "ordinary course of man's experience" is, to borrow a term from Leo Marx, the huffing, puffing machine already in Hawthorne's marvelous garden.[3]

An event in Douglass's *Narrative* affords an interesting comparison with Hawthorne's mixing of the marvelous and the "ordinary course of man's experience." Before his fight with Covey, his fellow slave Sandy gives Douglass a root which is supposed to protect him from harm: "I must go with him into another part of the woods, where there was a certain *root*, which, if I would take some of it with me, carrying it *always on my right side*, would render it impossible for Mr. Covey, or any other white man, to whip me."[4] Douglass returns to the plantation, where Covey "spoke to me very kindly." But Douglass does not permit the reader to credit the marvelous in the ordinary course of a *slave's* experience: "Now, this singular conduct of Mr. Covey really made me begin to think that there was something in the *root* which Sandy had given me; and had it been on any other day than Sunday, I could have attributed the conduct to no other cause than the influence of that root; and as it was, I was half inclined to think the *root* to be something more than I at first had taken it to be. All went well till Monday morning. On this morning, the virtue of the *root* was fully tested."[5] The root fails the test. Covey attempts to tie up Douglass, and the epic struggle, which is the dramatic/moral/psychological turning point in the *Narrative*, begins. For Douglass, who stresses internal moral resources, outside agencies could have little efficacy. In words similar to those uttered in the twentieth century by Albert Camus in *The Rebel*, Douglass informs the reader that he gained his life only at the point at which he was prepared to lose it.

Hawthorne's preface asserts the right of the romancer to "present" the truth, to "manage" the atmospherical medium, drawing our attention to the role of the maker in the creation.[6] This claim for the writer is very different from the practice of the black writer, who draws our attention to the world his writing is meant to mirror (a world whose verifiability is attested, in the extreme case of the slave narratives, by affidavits and testimonials). So too Hawthorne's lonely Hester Prynne is very different from the slave Frederick Douglass; and Hawthorne's methods as a writer—winning fame in that "dark chamber" in his mother's house—are very different from those of a Douglass—telling his story many times on the stage before he ever considered writing it down.

More recently, Richard Poirier in *A World Elsewhere*, believing Chase's categories tend to "obscure the more challenging questions," has shifted the emphasis from genre to "states of consciousness," distinguishing between those works, regardless of genre, which stress freedom and those which stress constraint. He argues that those works which "constitute a distinctive American tradition within English literature" are

> bathed in the myths of American history; they carry the metaphoric burden of a great dream of freedom—of the expansion of national consciousness into the vast spaces of a continent and the absorption of those spaces into ourselves. Expansive characters in Cooper or Emerson, Melville, James, or Fitzgerald are thus convinced as if by history of the practical possibility of enclosing the world in their imaginations. . . .
> They resist within their pages the forces of environment that otherwise dominate the world. . . . Cooper, Emerson, Thoreau, Melville, Hawthorne, Mark Twain, James—they both resemble and serve their heroes by trying to create an environment of "freedom," and as if only language can create the liberated place. The classic American writers try through

style temporarily to free the hero (and the reader) from systems, to free them from the pressures of time, biology, economics, and from the social forces which are ultimately the undoing of American heroes and quite often of their creators.[7]

Poirier likens his approach to Henry James, Sr.'s view of the "artist as hero"; we might also identify his artists as "captains of the metaphorical," recognizing the aggrandizing impulse implicit in Poirier's description.[8]

Just as the demands of mimesis militate against the romance tradition, the social forces—which Poirier's representatives of a "distinctive American tradition" transcend—limit the black "dream of freedom." (It is significant that no black writer is cited in *A World Elsewhere*.) In fact, black freedom grows in opposition to those forces, not in consonance with white "myths of American history." The vaunting and the recognition of power, basic to Poirier's "tradition," was hardly available to the black writer in the nineteenth century, nor in the twentieth. Rather than impose his self (as viewed from either the romance tradition or as stylistic mappings of a national consciousness), the black writer was attempting to mirror his world, to present the mundane play of the material and the mannered that was the "ordinary course" of the slave's and, later, the black's experience; or else he was attempting to mask his presence, a topic considered later in my discussions of Dunbar, Chesnutt, Johnson, and Larsen. The private vision, the idiosyncratic style, the luxury, even, of the surreal—in the history of American literature, these have been largely the province of white writers.[9]

On those occasions when black fictional characters ignore the play of social forces, *we* know they are mistaken—that the writer is playing with them, with their terrible innocence. This can be seen, for example, in the black treatment of the "American dream," that debased version of Poirier's "dream," as in Ann Petry's characterization of Lutie Johnson in *The Street*. Lutie Johnson absorbs the belief of her white employers, the Chandlers, the "belief that anybody could be rich if he wanted to and worked hard enough and figured it out carefully enough. . . . These people had wanted only one thing— more and more money—and so they got it."[10] In order to save money she goes home to visit Jim, her husband, only once every two months, and their marriage breaks up. While walking down the streets of New York, she identifies with that archetype of the Protestant ethic, Benjamin Franklin: "She shifted the packages into a more comfortable position and feeling the hard roundness of the rolls through the paper bag, she thought immediately of Ben Franklin and his loaf of bread. And grinned thinking, You and Ben Franklin. You ought to take one out and start eating it as you walk along 116th Street. Only you ought to remember while you eat that you're in Harlem and he was in Philadelphia a pretty long number of years ago. Yet she couldn't get rid of the feeling of self-confidence and she went on thinking that if Ben Franklin could live on a little bit of money and could prosper, then so could she."[11] The novel is a progressive unraveling of this dream. For all her industry, frugality, thrift, and honesty she is forced to flee the city—a murderer, her son in a detention home. Lucius Brockway, who is in charge of making up the base for the Liberty Paints in *Invisible Man* and who describes himself as the machine inside the machine, has so absorbed his white employer's philosophy of work that he takes only fifteen minutes for lunch and fights the union. He tells the protagonist that he helped the old man write the company's ironic slogan: "If It's Optic White, It's the Right White."[12] As Fishbelly flees to Europe in Richard Wright's *The Long Dream*, he talks with an Italian returning to his native Italy on the same flight who speaks of "'my wonderful romance'" with America. Fishbelly ponders: "That man's father had come to America and found a dream: he had been born in America and had found a nightmare."[13]

A *thingy* world, the "ordinary course of man's experience," a particularized topography (both of landscape/street and dwelling interior) have characterized black literature from the slave narrative to the present. Slave narrative writers filled their accounts with geographical environments and places; concrete objects in the form of tools, buildings, articles of clothing, instruments of social control; the rituals of work *and* play in the cultures produced by the cultivation of cotton, rice, sugar, tobacco; details regarding such institutions as religion, law, economics. This information was provided a largely white audience so that a white reader might imagine the peculiar institution.

But two changes have occurred: the concept of audience has changed and a new use has evolved for the things and places cited by black writers. Quite simply, black writers have increasingly written for a black audience. Various signposts along the way—such as the writings of W. E. B. Du Bois, which both opposed the accommodationist approach of Booker T. Washington and celebrated the black self; the militant poetry of Claude McKay; the tender portrayal of the southern black experience in Jean Toomer's *Cane*; the opposition in Langston Hughes's essay "The Negro Artist and the Racial Mountain"[14]—point to the shift in the writer's conception of audience at the same time that increasing literacy and improving economic conditions have made that audience a more realistic possibility. This shift, in its most extreme form, finds expression in such work as the theater of Imamu Baraka: one of the most extreme expressions of committed theater, Baraka's work evolved during the 1960s and 1970s to express as morality play the moral and political struggle between blacks and whites, portrayed as the struggle between good and evil. Richard Wright had argued in *Black Boy* that words could be weapons;[15] Baraka's actors were esthetic soldiers aiming at the "honkey," whether in white or black skin. A gentler expression of this sense of a changing audience is expressed by the more political poetry of Gwendolyn Brooks, along with her more active community involvement with such Chicago organizations as Organization for Black-American Culture and the Blackstone Rangers. In a lecture at Clark College in Atlanta, Georgia, April 26, 1971, she stated that "she could not imagine herself today writing the kind of poem whose theme was a pleading of her humanity to a larger white society as she had done years earlier:

> Men of careful turns, haters of forks in the road,
> The strain at the eye, that puzzlement, that awe—
> Grant me that I am human, that I hurt,
> That I can cry.[16]

A new use for things and places has evolved in the twentieth century—what begins as documentary evidence becomes the loving evocation of a world. Things are cited to suggest qualities in the life of the person possessing such things. In the process of listing the things of this world, history tends to sacrament, as listing becomes rite. There is a rubbed, a touched, an epiphanic quality in the things the poor have managed to hold onto, as in the protagonist's listing of the things possessed by the old couple evicted from their apartment in *Invisible Man*:

> I turned aside and looked at the clutter of household objects which the two men continued to pile on the walk. And as the crowd pushed me I looked down to see looking out of an oval frame a portrait of the old couple when young, seeing the sad, stiff dignity of the faces there; feeling strange memories awakening that began an echoing in my head like that of a hysterical voice stuttering in a dark street. Seeing them look back at me as though even then in that nineteenth-century day they had expected little, and this with a grim, unillusioned pride that suddenly seemed to me both a reproach and a warning. My eyes fell upon a pair of crudely carved and polished bones, "knocking bones," used to accompany music at country dances, used in black-face minstrels; the flat ribs of a cow, a steer or sheep, flat bones that gave off a sound, when struck, like heavy castanets (had he been a minstrel?) or the wooden block of a set of drums. Pots and pots of green plants were lined in the dirty snow, certain to die of the cold; ivy, canna, a tomato plant. And in a basket I saw a straightening comb, switches of false hair, a curling iron, a card with silvery letters against a background of dark red velvet, reading "God Bless Our Home"; and scattered across the top of a chiffonier were nuggets of High John the Conqueror, the lucky stone; and as I watched the white men put down a basket in which I saw a whiskey bottle filled with rock candy and camphor, a small Ethiopian flag, a faded tintype of Abraham Lincoln, and the smiling image of a Hollywood star torn from a magazine. And on a pillow several badly cracked pieces of delicate china, a commemorative plate celebrating the St. Louis World Fair . . .

The listing of things continues: "a bent Masonic emblem, a set of tarnished cuff links, three brass rings, a dime pierced with a nail hole so as to be worn about the ankle on a string for luck, an ornate greeting card with the message 'Grandma, I love you' in childish scrawl: another card with a picture of what looked like a white man in black-face seated in the door of a cabin strumming a banjo beneath a bar of music and the lyric 'Going back to my old cabin home'; a useless inhalant, a string of bright glass beads with a tarnished clasp, a rabbit foot, a celluloid baseball scoring card shaped

like a catcher's mitt, registering a game won or lost years ago; an old
breast pump with rubber bulb yellowed with age, a worn baby shoe
and a dusty lock of infant hair tied with a faded and crumpled blue
ribbon." And finally, "three lapsed insurance policies with perforated
seals stamped 'Void'; a yellowing newspaper portrait of a huge black
man with the caption: MARCUS GARVEY DEPORTED" and "FREE PA-
PERS. *Be it known to all men that my negro, Primus Provo, has been
freed by me this sixth day of August, 1859, Signed: John Samuels.
Macon.*"[17] The protagonist, of course, lists and resists, since the
things force him to consider his own black identity and his roots in
a black, folk past.

The character Jim Kelly catalogs the possessions accumulated by
Miss Julie Rand, the old woman who had moved from the country
to South Baton Rouge in Ernest Gaines's *Of Love and Dust*, and the
effect, though more distanced, is not unlike that created by James
Agee in his portrayal of interiors in *Let Us Now Praise Famous Men*:

> Miss Julie had an old sofa chair against the wall and another little rocker
> by the bed. There was an old trunk by the window with a pile of quilts
> and blankets stacked on top of it. Against the other wall was an old ar-
> moire leaning to one side. There must have been a half dozen pasteboard
> boxes stacked on top of the armoire. In the corner by the armoire were
> several paper bags packed full of clothes. The mantelpiece was cluttered
> with all kinds of nick-nacks, and there was an old coal oil lamp there,
> too, just in case the electric lights went out. No matter what wall you
> faced, you saw pictures of Jesus Christ. These pictures were on old cal-
> endars that Miss Julie Rand had never thrown away. They dated from
> the late thirties up to this year—forty-eight. Above the mantelpiece,
> stuck inside an old black wooden frame, was a picture of a man and a
> woman. The man was sitting; the woman was standing beside him. I fig-
> ured that this was Miss Julie and her husband when she was much,
> much younger.[18]

Kelly will do her bidding, not only out of deference to her age, but
also out of tacit recognition of his position within the time, place,
and history her things evoke.

Like Adam naming the animals, the black writer names the things
of his world—an act that is magical, political, and historical. But
black things, in all their particularity, are located in places that are

also specific, so that the naming is often bound up with places that have figured historically and psychologically in the black experience. Two places have accumulated memories, sentiments, and characterizing "things": the South (or "down home") and Harlem. (A third "place," the "ghetto," which is wherever blacks have been pushed to live, whether the Chicago of Richard Wright and Gwendolyn Brooks, the Pittsburgh of John Edgar Wideman, or the Lorain, Ohio, of Tony Morrison, should, in the interests of thoroughness, also be cited. While I will not be discussing the generalized "ghetto," its "things," both material and nonmaterial, are similar to those of "down home" and Harlem.) In Richard Wright's *Lawd Today*, Jake Jackson and his three friends find relief from their boring, repetitive job of sorting mail by talking together. In one scene, continuing for thirty pages, Wright achieves a choric effect by removing identifying tags, which enables him to suggest the mythic pull of "down home" on these four migrants to Chicago:

> "Look like the South just makes a man feel like a millionaire!"
> "I use' to go swimming in the creek. . . ."
> "Fishing's what I love! Seems like I can smell them catfish frying right now!"
> "And in the summer when the magnolia trees is in blossom. . . ."
> ". . . you can smell 'em for half a mile!"
> "And them sunflowers. . . ."
> ". . . and honeysuckles."
> "You know, we use' to break them honeysuckles off the stem and suck the sweetness out of 'em."
> "And them plums. . . ."
> ". . . so ripe they was busting open!"
> "And sugarcane. . . ."
> ". . . and blackberries. . . ."
> ". . . juicy and sweet!"
> "And in the summer at night the sky's so full of stars you think they going to fall. . . ."
> ". . . and the air soft and warm. . . ."
> ". . . smelling like water."
> "And them long rains in the winter. . . ."
> ". . . rain sometimes for a week. . . ."
> ". . . and you set inside and roast corn and sweet potatoes!"[19]

In the great migration north many blacks settled in Harlem, long known as the "Negro capital of the world." Its preeminence is mirrored in the folk declaration "I'd rather be a lamppost in Harlem than the mayor of ———," whichever city the speaker was citing. The life of Harlem has been probed by innumerable writers, sociologists, psychologists, and historians. Max Reddick records some of its "things" as he walks with his girl, Lillian Patch, in John A. Williams's *The Man Who Cried I Am*:

> But now he was walking through upper Manhattan with Lillian. They came out of the subway at 116th Street, so different from Washington Square Park, the Village. They couldn't even see downtown Manhattan; it was hidden by the trees in Central Park. Up on 145th Street, Max knew, you could stand on a corner and see all the way downtown or, at least, that rigid, square spire, the Empire State Building. One and the same. Uptown where they were, life still flooded the streets. Horse-drawn junk wagons, their drivers asleep, clip-clopped past them. The new sounds drifted out of Minton's, new sounds that no one could dance to anymore. They called the music rebop and it was played by musicians with crazy names like Monk, Bird, Diz, Fats, Sweets, Little Jazz. These were the streets that belonged to Sugar Ray, the Cutie, The Unscarred, and to a fat, balding Joe Louis and a bullet-headed Jersey Joe Walcott. The streets belonged also to Wynonie Blues Harris whose voice was blasting into the street from a loudspeaker fastened to the front of a record shop. The double-deck buses, still vibrating the dust of Fifth Avenue, groaned up Seventh Avenue. Hipsters, their legs going loose, their shoulders held stiffly, passed from the shadows to the lights of chili joints, barbeque joints, and bars.[20]

For Max Reddick downtown is "that rigid, square spire, the Empire State Building"; it is uptown, Harlem, where "life still flooded the streets."

The thingy world of the black experience functions both as a black preserve within a white world and as the container of memory and the projection of self. It is communal, in part at least because of the black experience of otherness in white America. The novel, rather than the romance, is the form that has evolved to express this experience narratively.

CHAPTER FIVE

The Experience of Power and Powerlessness

and Its Expression in the Literature

THE RIGOR of the early Puritan period moderated in the eighteenth and nineteenth centuries. As early as the seventeenth century, the Half-way Covenant and the lamentations of true believers signaled change; sermons, essays, the lives of the "saints" all bemoaned the falling away from the true faith (Cotton Mather's "fall" from the heights of Pisgah). The Salem witch trials of 1694 were as much a reaction to change as a sign of Puritan rigor. Cotton Mather's celebrations of Puritanism were descriptions of a faith already on the wane. The Great Revival of the eighteenth century diluted theocratic control as it diffused religious excitement. By the time of such Enlightenment thinkers as Franklin and Jefferson, God is no longer the wrathful God, the ever-watchful God of secondary causation, making everything "to happen." Rather, he is the God of first and final causes, the great watchmaker, the geometrician of Newton. He comes less, as in the Old Testament, with fire and sword; he comes more often, as in the New Testament, eating and drinking. He is less the abstract ruler, more the human, and humane, father. Unitarians, such as Emerson, mount the former Puritan pulpits.

Man, too, was viewed differently. Calvinism had stressed an innate nature: man was either one of the elect or one of the damned. But the early boats contained more "strangers" than "saints." The hermetic nature of Puritan exclusiveness and judgment could not long withstand men's experience of others, the sheer number of others, and the expansive possibilities in this new country. Locke and Rousseau were the appropriate philosophers for a people questioning restrictions and hierarchies. Man's consciousness was a blank tablet, open to whatever might be written upon it, said Locke, or, in the words of Rousseau, man was born "free" but was everywhere in chains. These views shifted the emphasis from man's nature to man's nurturing—to the environment, which could be shaped by man himself. No longer could government, for example, be viewed in terms of the metaphor of the "body politic," with the king viewed as the head, workers the hands, etc.; rather, man entered into a social contract, reflected in such phrases as "the consent of the governed."

The concept of the gentle Christ, the growing emphasis on man's potential rather than on his damned nature, and the shifting emphasis on the shaping powers of the individual are reflected in the rise of reform movements in the eighteenth and nineteenth centuries. Central to many of these movements—prison reform, feminism, child welfare, Prohibition, pacifism, abolition—was a revulsion against force and violence. Corporal punishment—long accepted as a legitimate means of social control and inflicted on the imprisoned, the insane, the young, sailors, wives, and slaves—was increasingly censured. It is perhaps within this context that we can more fully appreciate an element that early appears in black literature: a recognition of the role of power in white/black relations.

An imbalance of power was implicit in the master-slave relationship. The slave was a possession, a chattel, liable to be sold (perhaps to be listed on the slave sale notice among the "slaves and other stock"), according to the needs of the master. However much affection might temper the economic nature of the relationship, the bottom line was profitability. The slave sale notices often reveal reasons for sale: to settle an estate, to acquire more land, to go North. Histories of the period and slave narratives list other reasons: falling cotton prices, gambling debts, internal discipline (as in the case of selling a troublesome slave or a runaway—"down the river," for example, to a Georgia trader), and the simple human responses of anger and lust (whether thwarted or fulfilled).

But the slave was not simply like "other stock." Because he had a consciousness and a will, conflict was latent, and sometimes conflict flared and became violent. Several factors served to curb violence against slaves: (1) *Economic self-interest*. Slaves were expensive possessions. A good slave might sell for thousands in the markets of Charleston, Louisville, St. Louis, or New Orleans. Some of the most thoughtful among the slave owners employed the most "modern" agricultural practices. They read agricultural journals, such as *De Bows Weekly,* and found, among the articles on fertilizers, crop yields, and rotation of crops, other articles on the care and regulation of slaves. (2) *Public opinion.* Public opinion could influence a master, though the sanction seems to have been more effective in the close quarters of cities than in the scattered habitations of the countryside. The cruel master gained some of the opprobrium typically reserved for the slave trader. At the same time, however, only rarely would whites testify against a cruel master, even in cases of murder. (3) *Affection.* The stereotype of the "faithful slave," historians agree, was largely the creation of nostalgia and insensitivity, and/or the defensive reaction to criticism. Still, the peculiar institution was complex and persisted for over two hundred years. Within its tangled webs of relationship—of deceit, hate, affection, and power—many emotions flowered. Even within more "normal" social systems it is not simply the lovable who are loved, and many a flower, as the poet reminds us, can grow in a crannied wall; so that affection—of slave for master, master for slave—can be found among the narratives, letters, journals, and other documents from the period. Leon F. Litwack furnishes two testimonials of the possibilities for affection even under extreme circumstances:

> On the plantation in Alabama where she labored under a tyrannical master and mistress, a young black woman who had been separated by sale from three of her own four children grieved over the death of the master's son. "Master Ben, deir son, were good, and it used to hurt him to see us 'bused. When de war came Master Ben went—no, der ole man didn't go—an' he were killed dere. When he died, I cried. . . . he were a kind chile. But de oders, oh, dear."

> . . . . .

> "Dere was good white folks, sah, as well as bad," an elderly freedman remarked, after being asked his opinion of *Uncle Tom's Cabin,* "but when they was bad, Lord-a-mercy, you never saw a book, sah, that come up to what slavery was."[1]

But all the factors acting to curb violence could not eliminate violence from a relationship which was inherently violent and latently unstable. Given the imbalance of power, the conflict of interest, and the slaves' separate consciousness and will, a willingness to use force was necessary to the preservation of the relationship. This force had the general sanction of law throughout the South, and even in those infrequent instances of court trial white violence could count on the legal sanctions that prohibited blacks from testifying against whites and on the informal pressures that kept whites from testifying against each other. It is only at the edges of this world, in the underground of folklore and in the democracy of Christian salvation, that the tables were absolutely turned, that the lowly were elevated. It is only there that Brer Rabbit triumphed, that John outwitted Master, that the slave strode about God's kingdom and walked with Jesus.

In the day-to-day world of the slaves "turning the tables," *triumph*, and *victory* are inappropriate terms to apply to a system where the daily maintenance of dignity and self-respect—as in the song's depiction of the "po' inch worm" that "jus' keeps a inchin' along"—is a victory, a triumph. Victory, in the scale of slave versus institution, had to be made of smaller stuff, and the smaller stuff was often the quiet, private preservation of the self. But the resistance that could act to preserve the self could also assume more public forms. Contrary to the "Sambo" image of the slave, white power was often responded to by black resistance, ranging from malingering (as in labor slowdowns) to physical resistance. Just as white violence included the possibility that a master might murder a slave, black resistance included the possibility of ultimate defiance, in which the slave understood that his self-assertion could lead to his death.[2]

The day-to-day relations of master and slave were not, of course, sustained at such an absolute pitch, but violence (physical/psychological/sexual) recurs in the slave narratives. Endemic as force was to the nature of slavery, excesses could be readily exploited for their propaganda value in the prewar reform atmosphere; and they could, further, furnish the reader with that thread needed to lead him to an awareness of the essential violence in a relationship of ownership. For Frederick Douglass, whose *Narrative* is the classic account of the impact of slavery upon the slave, violence was an element in two of the most significant events of his life. He dates his consciousness of slavery, metaphorically viewed as a "birth," from his witnessing the whipping of his Aunt Hester:

> The louder she screamed, the harder he whipped; and where the blood ran fastest, there he whipped longest. He would whip her to make her scream, and whip her to make her hush; and not until overcome by fatigue, would he cease to swing the blood-clotted cowskin. I remember the first time I ever witnessed this horrible exhibition. I was quite a child, but I well remember it. I never shall forget it whilst I remember any thing. It was the first of a long series of such outrages, of which I was doomed to be a witness and a participant. It struck me with awful force. It was the blood-stained gate, the entrance to the hell of slavery, through which I was about to pass.[3]

Later, the fight with Covey, which resulted from Douglass's refusal to be whipped, is depicted as a rebirth: "It was a glorious resurrection, from the tomb of slavery, to the heaven of freedom. My long-crushed spirit rose, cowardice departed, bold defiance took its place; and I now resolved that, however long I might remain a slave in form, the day had passed forever when I could be a slave in fact."[4]

These acts of violence, because they are physical and visible, are clearly violations of the person. But perhaps at least as common were the acts of psychological violence (both implicit and explicit) in a system that could view a person as property and that could frame moral, legal, and social justifications for such a view. Douglass, for example, observes in the first paragraph of his *Narrative* that he did not know his birthdate, though white children knew theirs, and that his master would have regarded inquiries on the part of a slave as "improper and impertinent." He later records the separation from his mother, the violence toward his aunt, the cruel treatment of his grandmother, the *fear* of violence from various overseers, and so on.

Douglass's *Narrative* alerts us, too, to the fact that slaveholding served more than instrumental ends; the slaveholder was not simply Adam Smith's economic man. The uses of force within the institution recall Lord Acton's observation about the corruption inherent in power. This corruption is reflected in Douglass's descriptive definition of a "good" overseer: Mr. Hopkins "whipped, but seemed to take no pleasure in it. He was called by the slaves a good overseer."[5] A different form of corruption is revealed in the beating of Aunt Hester, though Douglass discreetly only hints at it. After explaining that she was beaten for meeting a young man after her master had warned her against keeping company, Douglass comments, "Why master was so careful of her, may be safely left to conjecture. She was a woman of noble form, and of graceful proportions, having very few equals, and fewer superiors, in personal appearance, among the colored or white women of our neighborhood."[6] The South Carolina white woman Mary Chesnutt, writing later and leaving less to "conjecture," will characterize the plantations as "brothels."[7]

The imminence/threat/presence of white power in black lives has assured whites a significant place in both the consciousness and the literary expression of blacks from slavery to the present. In Richard Wright's classic autobiography *Black Boy*, his black remembrance of things past, the play of social power upon the naked, and sensitive, self is recurrent, arbitrary, and violent. The threat to his "uncle" in West Helena, the stories told about whites on the doorsteps of neighbors' houses, the fragility, bareness, and bleakness of his own environment—all contribute to a "dread of white people" that develops in Wright before the age of ten. White power, as in the psychological phenomenon of anxiety, seems, in his consciousness, to overflow any act that might contain or express it: "It was as though I was continuously reacting to the threat of some natural force whose hostile behavior could not be predicted." The threat of this power to his self is summed up in his reaction to the tale told of the black mother who avenged the death of her son: "I did not know if the story was factually true or not, but it was emotionally true because I had already grown to feel that there existed men against whom I was powerless, men who could violate my life at will."[8]

Wright's statement, with all the directness of the child's vision, exposes an important dimension in black-white interaction, one that black writers will frequently explore in the twentieth century. Black writers will probe white power, laying bare both its violence and its complexity and subtlety. It will be seen to affect plot, scene, character, language, image, and symbol because it will be seen to violate necessarily inviolable territories of the black self.

CHAPTER SIX

"The Day Had Passed Forever When I Could Be a Slave in Fact": The Gathering of a Self

THE "freedom" for which the slave narrative writer struggled was, most obviously, the freedom from physical bondage. But this freedom clearly becomes more complex once "freedom" is achieved. Increasingly, freedom has meant many things; civil freedom, for example, which includes voting rights, access to public accommodations, etc. Increasingly, too, it has meant freedom from the definitions of others. In this form it merges with the struggle for identity/self, from which it has never, in any of its forms, been wholly free. The merging of these facets can be illustrated in Douglass's *Narrative*, which shares the general preoccupation of all narratives with questions of freedom and self. Such preoccupation was a precondition to imagining difference: freedom rather than bondage, self-realization rather than property. Douglass attributes to a "special interposition of divine Providence" an early conviction that he would not remain a slave: "From my earliest recollection, I date the entertainment of a deep conviction that slavery would not always be able to hold me within its foul embrace."[1] His being sent to Baltimore permits him to master those skills which he will ultimately employ to gain his freedom. When Mr. Auld inveighs against teaching a slave to read, Douglass notes, "From that moment, I understood the pathway from slavery to freedom."[2] In a collection of speeches he encounters one of Sheridan's on behalf of Catholic liberties as well as antislavery documents: "The more I read and contemplated the subject, the more I was led to abhor and detest my enslavers. I could regard them in no other light than a band of successful robbers. . . . Freedom now appeared, to disappear no more forever. It was heard in every sound, and seen in every thing. It was ever present to torment me with a sense of my wretched condition. I was nothing without seeing it, I heard nothing without hearing it, and felt nothing without feeling it. It looked from every star, it smiled in every calm, breathed in every wind, and moved in every storm."[3] After recounting his curiosity regarding the word *abolition*, he describes his discussion with the two Irish dockworkers, who, sympathetic, urge him to run away to the North. Fearing treachery ("White men have been known to encourage slaves to escape, and then, to get the reward, catch them and return them to their masters"), he feigned uninterest and ignorance, "but I nevertheless remembered their advice, and from that time I resolved to run away."[4]

The resolution to run away is a critical decision in a slave narrative. Up to this point, the narrative describes its author's degradation, humiliation, and pain (sometimes in excessive detail, according to the criticism of Charles Ball's narrative)—all of which help to explain the decision to run. Once this decision is reached, suspense—which earlier may have been generated by the simple everyday dangers attendant on being a slave at the mercy of a possibly cruel and unpredictable master—surrounds the slave's preparations to escape, his agonized speculations, and his flight. But once that flight is concluded, the narrative ends.

The slave narrative structure reflected elements of two earlier forms—the Puritan conversion narrative and the narrative of escape from captivity, both Indian and British—and these similarities help to explain some of the popular acceptance of the form.[5] Another quality in the narratives that must have appealed to an audience increasingly influenced by what we have come to call the romantic movement is the heroic struggle of the writer to define a self, a self different from that imagined by his owner/master and by the environing social order. But this self-defining was no easy task, since our selves are so much the result of the way others look at us, and look *to* us. One social scientist has described the process of socialization by use of the term "looking-glass self" (in the process of becoming socialized we incorporate the values and judgment of others in the mirroring manner of the looking glass); another has stated that man is society writ small, that society is man writ large. Both formulations, while descriptive, oversimplify a complex process. As sociologist Robert K. Merton stresses in his discussion of "reference groups," all judgments and valuings are not equally regarded; that is, we tend to rank-order others—some become the "significant others" whose valuing and judgments influence both our actions and our self-evaluations.[6]

That the process of gathering a self that is worthy and worth struggling to sustain is difficult is well illustrated in Douglass's *Narrative*. Douglass early indicates that slaves were lumped in the owner's consciousness with other animals: "By far the larger part of the slaves know as little of their ages as horses know of theirs."[7] The comparison of slaves with animals is recurrent:

> The children were then called, like so many pigs, and like so many pigs they would come and devour the mush [which had been placed on a wooden tray or trough on the ground]. . . .
>
> We were all ranked together at the valuation. Men and women, old and young, married and single, were ranked with horses, sheep, and swine. There were horses and men, cattle and women, pigs and children, all holding the same rank in the scale of being. . . .
>
> She saw her children, her grandchildren, and her great-grandchildren, divided, like so many sheep. . . .
>
> He bought her, as he said, for *a breeder*.[8]

Slaves were not permitted to assume that their self-evaluations counted in the eyes of the master. Nor could they assume that their selves had limits which the other was obliged to respect; that is, that territoriality which we implicitly acknowledge as a quality of the self must be tenuously claimed in the presence of persons who have the right to breach its supposed boundaries. In fact, if we pause to consider the interrelation of territoriality and self (which is to consider self from only one of several possible perspectives), we can more readily appreciate the vulnerability of the slave's self. Ethologists such as Edward Hall define territory as the area or space an organism lays claim to and defends. Citing the work of H. Hediger, Hall describes the importance of territory:

Territoriality, he says, insures the propagation of the species by regulating density. It provides a frame in which things are done—places to learn, places to play, safe places to hide. Thus it coordinates the activities of the group and holds the group together. It keeps animals within communicating distance of each other, so that the presence of food or an enemy can be signaled. An animal with a territory of its own can develop an inventory of reflex responses to terrain features. When danger strikes, the animal on its home ground can take advantage of automatic responses rather than having to take time to think about where to hide.[9]

Similarly, humans develop territorial responses, even when their territories are termed neighborhoods or turfs.

A history of the violation of black space could begin with the initial enslavement: with the violation of the body (since the body can be viewed as space, a point which I will elaborate on shortly), the crowding during the "middle passage," and so on. For the sake of brevity, however, I shall focus on only two types of spatial violation: the violation of the slave's cabin and the violation of the slave's body. Ethologists have focused on the territorial imperative as it operates in nonhuman organisms; I shall designate this response, when expressed by humans, as the need for "psychic space," which is the space which people have grown to feel is significant for their well-being, either because that space is felt to belong to them, because they feel comfortable or safe within it, or for whatever other reason. Ethologists tend to view territory as fixed in space; however, people move out from their specific space-fixed territories and yet carry with them beliefs and attitudes regarding their own violability. These beliefs and attitudes can be said to center in the body, and the body itself can be viewed as territory, with more or less space surrounding it. The amount of territory or space one can control is often a function of power, as when Louis XIV declared, "La France, c'est moi"; more modestly, perhaps, other kings have asserted an identity between the seat of power and their presence as they made their progresses through their kingdoms. Space-as-body can be breached by a look, and the history of manners carefully delineates the ways in which slaves, and later freed blacks, may look at whites; Bertram Doyle, for example, describing the "etiquette" of antebellum interrelations, observes that a slave, when conversing with whites, "kept his eye on the ground during the conversation."[10]

The space enclosed by the slave's cabin could be violated at any time at the wish of master or overseer. This might occur, for example, if the slave is suspected of concealing something. It is typical for the slave narratives to cite the presence of the overseer in the cabin door, driving the slaves out to work. In addition, the cabin was no security against the lust of overseer or master. Ex-slave Henry Bibb declared that "licentious white men, can and do, enter at night or day the lodging places of slaves; break up the bonds of affection in families; destroy all their domestic and social union for life; and the laws of the country afford them no protection."[11] Even the patrollers (the night riders empowered to patrol the plantations to check slaves for passes and to generally govern the night world of the plantations) were permitted unimpeded entry into the quarters. Article 40 of the Louisiana slave code of 1852, described by Gilbert Osofsky as typical for the period, states in part: "The patrols ordered by the police juries shall have the right to enter on all plantations to visit the negro huts."[12] These huts or cabins are surely a far cry from the "house" imagined by Gaston Bachelard in *The Poetics of Space*: "If I were asked to name the chief benefit of the house, I should say: the house shelters daydreaming, the house protects the dreamer, the house allows one to dream in peace. . . . In the life of a man, the house thrusts aside contingencies, its councils of continuity are unceasing. Without it, man would be a dispersed being."[13]

The ultimate territory is perhaps the body surface itself. Under slavery, the slave's body could be stripped of the rights we customarily identify with the person. The slave could be beaten, and few (during their lives as slaves) escaped the lash, the paddle, the irons. Nor was there any way to shield the body from the look of others, since an element in the efficacy, and sometimes sadism, of beating was its function as example. Henry Bibb describes the beating of a mulatto house slave: "this flogging was carried on in the most inhuman manner until she had received two hundred stripes on her naked quivering flesh, tied up and exposed to the public gaze of all."[14] The body was not the person's property but the master's. As such, it was liable to being viewed as object, as thing. It was vulnerable to probing, handling, casual violence. Rape, or less violent violation, was practiced by some, though not all, of the overseers, masters, slave traders. Less spectacular, though perhaps as significant psychologically, were the instances of casual handling. Slave narrative writer Gustavas Vassa records how after he was carried on board the slave ship "I was immediately handled, and tossed up to see if I were sound, by some of the crew."[15] Another narrative writer, Solomon Northup, describes how his master, Epps, displayed him to another man: "'Yes,' replied Epps, taking hold of my arm and feeling it, 'there isn't a bad joint in him.'"[16]

The slave auctions provide numerous examples of the violability of the body. The body, like some mule of the southern trader tales, could be "improved upon." William Wells Brown describes the preparing of old slaves for the market: "I was ordered to have the old men's whiskers shaved off, and the gray hairs plucked out where they were not too numerous, in which case he had a preparation of blacking to color it, and with a blacking brush he would put it on."[17] Henry Bibb, speaking of his own auction, recalls that "those who were inclined to look dark and rough, were compelled to wash in greasy dish water, in order to make them look slick and lively."[18]

At every stage in the life cycle the body could be treated casually. Its coming into the world was generally not recorded. Frederick Douglass states, "I do not remember to have ever met a slave who could tell of his birthday."[19] During its lifetime it could be moved from place to place, job to job, homeplace to homeplace, at the will of the owner; employed as a stud, employed as a breeder; separated from family, friends, associates, sometimes with absolutely no prior notice. Its death could result from some act of casual violence, however valuable it might be. The casualness could not help but impress other slaves with their slave body's dispensability. Its disposal after death was often perfunctory, a far cry from the elaborateness of African burial procedures.

Frederick Douglass's physical extension of his self, his body, could be beaten; further extensions of his self—in the persons of his mother, his Aunt Hester, his grandmother—could be taken from him, beaten, abandoned. Nevertheless, Douglass struggled for and achieved a sense of self, and in the process he redefined the animal-human distinction, which had been blurred in the owner's casual rankings. At times, he states, his consciousness and his discontent were too painful: "I have often wished myself a beast. I preferred the condition of the meanest reptile to my own. Any thing, no matter what, to get rid of thinking!" Master Thomas Auld finds him less tractable after his exposure to Baltimore: "My city life, he said, had had a very pernicious effect on me." He is sent to the slave breaker Covey. Covey does break him, a condition likened to that of a brute: "A few months of this discipline tamed me. I was broken in body, soul, and spirit. My natural elasticity was crushed, my intellect languished, the disposition to read departed, the cheerful spark that lingered about my eye died; the dark night of slavery closed in about me; and behold a man transformed into a brute!"[20]

Imbrutement is, for Douglass, essential to enslavement; it is this quality of the consciousness that distinguishes between formal and actual slavery. His fight with Covey illustrates this distinction: "You have seen how a man was made a slave; you shall see how a slave was made a man." A slave is a brute; a man is free (in terms similar to those employed by the Stoic philosophers) regardless of his formal state. These distinctions coalesce in his summary statement: "I felt as I never felt before. It was a glorious resurrection, from the tomb of slavery, to the heaven of freedom. My long-crushed spirit rose, cowardice departed, bold defiance took its place; and I now resolved that, however long I might remain a slave in form, the day had passed forever when I could be a slave in fact. I did not hesitate to let it be known of me, that the white man who expected to succeed in whipping, must also succeed in killing me."[21]

The struggle for a self, free from the definitions of others, is the psychological dimension of the black-white struggle. However, the clarity that Douglass had achieved in the perception of its nature will be blunted in the later decades of the nineteenth century and in the early years of the twentieth. The rise to prominence of Booker T. Washington with his Atlanta Exposition speech—in 1895, the same year in which Douglass died—reflects what we would contemporaneously refer to as the backlash following Reconstruction. Louis R. Harlan assesses the timeliness of Washington's Atlanta address: "It was not as original or wise as it was said to be, but it was timely. Washington was indeed the Negro the nation awaited. Not only had Frederick Douglass died earlier in the year; his whole era of black pride and hope had died. Booker Washington's incorrigible humility made him the kind of symbolic black figure that whites accepted."[22] The blurring of Douglass's clear, and militant, vision of the self—represented by Washington's 1895 address and by his public career—will be further reflected in the writings of many of the black writers who have been identified with the emergence of modern black literature in America, a theme which will be explored in the second half of this study.

CHAPTER SEVEN

"Who Gave You a Master and a Mistress?—

God Gave Them to Me":

The Role of Morality in Black Literature

MORALISM runs like a taproot through the American public posture over the centuries.[1] Americans may have sought a republican form of government, but it and they have seemed to require divine sanction. John Winthrop's sermon aboard the *Arbella* in 1630 will be invoked by a Republican president more than three hundred years later—Winthrop's cautionary words mix, in our public memory, with words beamed from a satellite.

This predilection for moralizing suggests other implications for Trollope's remark about "beef and ale"—the blandness of a Macauley was never the American mode: "Our rulers will best promote the improvement of the nation by strictly confining themselves to their own legitimate duties, by leaving capital to find its most lucrative course, commodities their fair price, industry and intelligence their material reward, idleness and folly their natural punishment, by maintaining peace, by defending property... and by observing strict economy.... let the Government do this: the People will assuredly do the rest."[2] Missing from Macauley's formulation for Britain is the American penchant for thinking in terms of the Government, the People, and *God*. Daniel J. Boorstin sums up his discussion of the American search for national heroes and national symbols: "The American vagueness made Americans, more than others, feel a need to assert their nationality and their purpose with hyperbolic clarity."[3] Similarly, it would seem, religion must be invoked—in the absence of precedents and in response to both metaphysical vagueness and the multiplicity of metaphysical claimants—to justify American actions.

This justifying did not stop at the plantation gate. Rather, religion in the South, just as the institution of the law, justified and rationalized the peculiar institution. The Bible was quoted in its defense; ministers both owned slaves and preached in support of the system, and sermons and catechisms were written to justify God's ways to slaves. In view of the use of religion to justify slavery, just as religion has been used until quite recently to justify racism, it would be surprising if black literature had not included, along with its report on conditions, a counterstatement regarding what ought to be. The moral injunction, implicit in the very statement of conditions, has been an important element in the literature in both the nineteenth and twentieth centuries.

The general position of the slaveholder regarding the soul of his slave was, in its articulated form, some variation of the following. God had created blacks to be servants to whites, and the slaves had benefited morally from this role in which God had placed them. They had been removed from Africa, which was a moral sink: uncivilized, savage, brutish, licentious. They had been placed within a paternalistic institution, not unlike the family, where their physical wants were secure, their uncivil nature was civilized (or at least held in check), and they were exposed to the blessings of religion. Since individualism of the romantic sort never found particular favor in the South, and since the South was predisposed to images of hierarchical orderliness derived from the medieval period, and since there were always questions regarding whether blacks actually belonged to the same species as whites—in view of these attitudes, the social control and discipline of slavery were deemed necessary, and its overturning implied chaos, anarchy, race war.

This view of the world was incorporated into sermons and catechisms, where grand moralizing gave way to immediate practical ends: the language of religion became the language of social control. "God's design" became lectures against stealing, lying, laziness, disobedience. From a sermon to a Maryland slave congregation:

> I now come to lay before you the duties you owe to your *masters* and *mistresses* here upon earth. And for this, you have one general rule that you ought always to carry in your minds;—and that is,—*to do all service for them, as if you did it for* GOD *himself.*—Poor creatures! you

little consider, when you are idle or neglectful of your master's business,—when you *steal* and *waste*, and *hurt* any of their substance,—
when you are *saucy* and *impudent*,—when you are telling them *lies*,
and deceiving them, or when you prove *stubborn* or *sullen*, and will not
do the work you are set about without stripes and vexation;—you do
not consider, I say, that what faults you are guilty of towards your masters and mistresses are faults done against GOD himself, who hath set
your masters and mistresses over you, in his own stead, and expects that
you will do for them, just as you would do for him.[4]

From a South Carolina slave catechism:

Who gave you a master and a mistress?—*God gave them to me.*
Who says that you must obey them?—*God says that I must.*
What book tells you these things?—*The Bible.*
How does God do all His work?—*He always does it right.*
Does God love to work?—*Yes, God is always at work.*

From a Mississippi slave catechism:

Q. If the master be unreasonable, may the servant disobey?
A. No. The Bible says, "Servants, be subject to your masters with all
fear, not only to the good and gentle, but also to the forward."
Q. What does the Bible say to servants on this subject?
A. They are to obey, not with eye-service as men-pleasers, but as the
servants of Christ.[5]

Slaves were generally sensitive to the manipulative, instrumental
intent of this language. After listening to a sermon on obedience, ex-
slave Harriet Jacobs said, "We went home highly amused at brother
Pike's gospel teaching, we determined to hear him again."[6] Lawrence Levine observes that slaves "generally suffered these sermons
in silence but there were exceptions. Victoria McMullen reported
that her grandmother in Arkansas was punished for not going to
church on the Sabbath but still she refused, insisting: 'No, I don't
want to hear the same old sermon: "Stay out of your missus' and
master's henhouse. Don't steal your missus' and master's chickens.
Stay out of your missus' and master's smokehouse. Don't steal your
missus' and master's hams." I don't steal nothing. Don't need to tell
me not to!' "[7]

Many of the slave narrative writers recorded these slave sermons in order to mock them; and many, too, noted the extremes of exquisite cruelty of the "men of God," whom narrative writer John Thompson characterized as "God in the face, and the devil in the heart."[8] The most damning portrayal of the unchristian uses of Christianity is Douglass's caustic summing up:

> I love the pure, peaceable, and impartial Christianity of Christ; I therefore hate the corrupt, slaveholding, women-whipping, cradle-plundering, partial and hypocritical Christianity of this land. Indeed, I can see no reason, but the most deceitful one, for calling the religion of this land Christianity. . . . We have men-stealers for ministers, women-whippers for missionaries, and cradle-plunderers for church members. The man who wields the blood-clotted cowskin during the week fills the pulpit on Sunday, and claims to be a minister of the meek and lowly Jesus. The man who robs me of my earnings at the end of each week meets me as a class-leader on Sunday morning, to show me the way of life, and the path of salvation. He who sells my sister, for purposes of prostitution, stands forth as the pious advocate of purity. He who proclaims it a religious duty to read the Bible denies me the right of learning to read the name of the god who made me. He who is the religious advocate of marriage robs whole millions of its sacred influence, and leaves them to the ravages of wholesale pollution. The warm defender of the sacredness of the family relation is the same that scatters whole families,—sundering husbands and wives, parents and children, sisters and brothers,—leaving the hut vacant, and the hearth desolate. We see the thief preaching against theft, and the adulterer against adultery. We have men sold to build churches, women sold to support the gospel, and babes sold to purchase Bibles for the *poor heathen! all for the glory of God and the good of souls!* The slave auctioneer's bell and the church-going bell chime in with each other, and the bitter cries of the heart-broken slave are drowned in the religious shouts of his pious master.[9]

In response to the religion proferred by the slaveholders, the slaves tended to conform outwardly, to live inwardly—at least, so long as whites were present. Alone with their own black preachers, the response changed. Ex-slave Anthony Dawson reported, "Mostly we had white preachers, but when we had a black preacher, that was heaven!"[10] Nancy Williams observed, "Ole white preachers use to talk wid dey tongues widdout sayin' nothin' but Jesus told us slaves to talk wid our hearts," and Henrietta Perry declared, "White folks cant pray right to de black man's God!"[11] Even when black preachers were forced by the presence of whites to sound like white preachers, they often changed their sounds in the absence of whites: "Litt Young, a former slave from Mississippi, reported that her mistress had built the slaves a fine and well-appointed church and had provided a mulatto preacher. Under orders from his mistress and in her presence, he would stay close to the 'Obey your master' theme. When she was not present, 'He come out with straight preachin'' from the Bible.'"[12]

And what was the message in this "straight preachin'"? Levine, Genovese, and others identify certain qualities stressed in the spirituals, sermons, recollections: a concreteness and an application to the day-to-day life of the slaves; a valuing of the individual, however poor, distressed, or violated; a promise of this-worldly surcease from pain and the gaining of justice and glory; a personalized relationship with Old Testament figures, including Jehovah, reminiscent of the more intimate, human relationship of African religions. Levine has summarized the implications of the Old Testament for understanding slave religion:

> The essence of slave religion cannot be fully grasped without understanding this Old Testament bias. It is important that Daniel and David and Joshua and Jonah and Moses and Noah, all of whom fill the lines of the spirituals, were delivered in *this* world and delivered in ways which struck the imagination of the slaves. Over and over their songs dwelt upon the spectacle of the Red Sea opening to allow the Hebrew slaves past before inundating the mighty armies of the Pharaoh. They lingered delightedly upon the image of little David humbling the great Goliath with a stone—a pretechnological victory which postbellum Negroes were to expand upon in their songs of John Henry. They retold in endless variation the stories of the blind and humbled Samson bringing down the mansions of his conquerors; of the ridiculed Noah patiently building the ark which would deliver him from the doom of a mocking world; of the timid Jonah attaining freedom from his confinement through faith. The similarity of these tales to the situation of the slaves was too clear for them not to see it; too clear for us to believe that the songs had no worldly content for blacks in bondage.[13]

It would be a mistake, of course, to view these qualities of the black religious experience as limited to the period of slavery. The qualities noted above persist into the twentieth century, because the conditions to which they were a response have persisted. As Genovese notes: "The evidence suggests far greater continuity than discontinuity, and much can be learned about the antebellum preachers by following the accounts of today's black 'folk preachers' in the studies of Bruce A. Rosenberg and the Reverend Henry H. Mitchell."[14]

The message in, ostensibly, nonreligious forms of black literature has been a variation of the message from the more overtly religious forms of expression:[15] the dignity and valuing of the self; the achieving of freedom, which includes freedom from the definitions of others, and freedom of access, along with the achieving of justice; and the sensitive and loving portrayal of a concrete world (stressed early out of the emphasis on mimesis, but increasingly reflecting a loving dwelling on black culture). The message both implied and expressed in the "noble and thrilling" reflections of a Douglass continues in Wright's portrayal of the experiences of a sensitive black boy growing up in the South. The audience, of course, changes, as does the artist's relationship to it.

The moral thrust in black literature has had its clear roots in Judeo-Christian teachings, but it also develops out of the consciousness of the gap between the national promise and the national reality. Although stressed during the civil rights movement of the sixties and seventies, this secular dimension emerged as early as the eighteenth century: in the ambience of the Revolutionary War and through the language of the Declaration of Independence.

The ambience included both deeds and ideals. The central deed of the period was of course the war itself. The slave was courted by the British during the hostilities; at the same time, he was often promised freedom by a hard-pressed Colonial government if he would but take up arms. Free blacks, on the other hand, were made to feel that their support would open up more opportunities; these "promises" served as the basis for later petitions.[16] The ideals were expressed in such phrases as "No taxation without representation" and "Give me liberty or give me death." Freedom was continually stressed, both freedom from and freedom to: freedom from taxation (as, for example, the stamp tax), from quartering of troops, from search and seizure; and freedom to pass laws for the public good, to develop native industries, to administer justice. These expressions of ideals were not lost upon blacks, who, through committees and petitions, sought redress of their grievances, often in the very language of the colonists/Revolutionaries.[17]

Perhaps the most inspiriting language of all has been that of the Declaration of Independence, that document long dear to the hearts of liberals, though often suspect by conservatives. It was the Declaration of Independence that largely spoke for liberty and equality, the Constitution that spoke for property. It was the Declaration of Independence that declared that "all men are created equal, that they are endowed by their Creator with certain unalienable Rights"; but it was the Constitution that transformed the blacks' otherness into a kind of neitherness, as it officially spoke of blacks without speaking of them. While even Indians were considered under a categorical term, blacks—for purposes of enumeration, to determine numbers of representatives and amount of taxation—were subsumed under the term "three fifths of all other Persons."[18] The subversive content of the Declaration of Independence was not lost on the South, nor on those seeking the southern vote: in 1831, the Democratic national convention refused, for the first time, to embody its language in their platform.

Thus blacks, over the centuries, have been in the ironic position of hearing about the "city of God" but living in the city of man, of being exposed to national ideals but subjected to national reality. They worked in the nation's drawing room but lived in the country's kitchen. Little wonder their view from backstage has portrayed a different America.[19] Their silence in the face of the manipulative uses of the language of moralism (whether of religion or of nation) has tended, however, to conceal a considerable linguistic sophistication—a sophistication generally unbeknown to whites, who were too often bemused by a perceived "broken" tongue to perceive their perceiver. Regardless, slaves, and blacks generally, restricted in their power in the material world, have had underground possession of a verbal world. Blacks have been formally sophisticated and have had to distance themselves on both the reported and the reporter. Thus, though often not owning/possessing things, they have possessed the language to talk about the things. Throughout black history, from the African *griot*, whose store of words from the past furnished maps into the present so that the new could be framed within the old, to the rapper of the street, the pulpit, the election circuit, the "man of words" has been a vital force, as reflected in the careers of such diverse twentieth-century figures as Martin Luther King, Jr., Malcolm X, James Baldwin, Jesse Jackson, Barbara Jordan, Stokely Carmichael, and Muhammed Ali. James Baldwin's development— from child preacher to adult writer, from preacher of the Word to writer of words—is a metaphor for the continuing importance of language in providing a black structuring for experiences which are too often at variance with white descriptions of the world.

One of the linguistic responses to the awry perspective blacks have had to cast upon language and its often fanciful expression in myths has been to respond ironically. Irony is the ideal linguistic form for a world where ideal and practice are so separate; the doubleness of the world is caught in the doubleness of language.[20] In irony, that "twoness" spoken of by W. E. B. Du Bois is expressed verbally.[21]

The irony employed ranges along a scale of overtness. In its most public form, it is sarcastic, vividly satirical, exposing posturing through wit, as in the long passage from Frederick Douglass's *Narrative* quoted earlier. It is the "J'ai accusé!" of literature, as in the ringing denunciation of Moses Grandy's narrative: "But when I thought of slavery with its Democratic whips—its Republican chains—its evangelical bloodhounds, and its religious slaveholders—when I thought of all this paraphernalia of American Democracy and Religion behind me—I was encouraged to press forward."[22] Physical escape for Grandy was an escape not only from The Man but an escape, too, from the nets and snares of The Man's language.

In its most private form, irony can only be perceived by its user and has no public. But between these two extremes, irony occurs in rich profusion. One of its more obvious uses results from the filling of old forms with a black content, as in parody or mythic subversion. Parody simply takes an existent, and well-known, vehicle and fills it with what Gates terms a "ludicrous or incongruent content."[23] Osofsky cites an example when he instances Douglass's mimicking of a white sermon: "In his earliest years as an antislavery lecturer Frederick Douglass convulsed Northern audiences by derisively mimicking sermons he had listened to: 'Oh, consider the wonderful goodness of God! Look at your hard, horny hands, your strong muscular frames, and see how mercifully he has adapted you to the duties you are to fulfill! . . . while to your masters who have slender frames and long delicate fingers, he has given brilliant intellects, that they may do the thinking while you do the working.'"[24] Mythic subversion might be described as a more subtle, or indirect, form of parody, since it involves pouring black content into a mythic form derived originally from white experience, as in the earlier example (from Ann Petry's *The Street*) of Lutie Johnson's imagining herself as Ben Franklin. I term it mythic *subversion* in order to focus on the manner in which this form exposes the white, particularistic content under the appearance of universalism. The black perspective reminds us that the world is not so simple as it seems while stripping from myth some of its seemingly timeless, universal aura.[25]

Irony is, in its essence, moral/political. In most of its forms it is language masking, language engaged in guerrilla warfare, Emily Dickinson's "tell the truth / but tell it slant." Gates notes that "black people have always been masters of the figurative: saying one thing to mean something quite other has been basic to black survival in oppressive Western cultures."[26] The skills are learned early: on the street, through folklore, in which literal and figurative meanings are often played off against each other, as in that game of verbal insult, the dozens, where the "cool" player is played off against the emotional content. There will be many instances, in the black experience and in black literature, where irony will be employed as secret weapon, where the white audience will assume that the appearances in a scene express the content, not knowing that the blacks are privy to irony, which functions at that moment as covert language—as in Wright's *Black Boy*, where the elevator operator, Shorty, plays the fool to get a quarter from a racist white man.[27] In those examples where the irony is clear to the black actors but not obvious to the whites (who assume literalness, an identity between appearance and reality), irony mixes the private and public ranges on the scale of overtness and most clearly acts as the verbal equivalent of masking.

CHAPTER EIGHT

"A Spy in the Enemy's Country":

"Masking" in Black Literature

IN *The Second Sex* Simone de Beauvoir illustrates the existence and nature of the two universes created by sexual politics:

> The female friendships that she succeeds in keeping or forming are precious to a woman, but they are very different in kind from relations between men. The latter communicate as individuals through ideas and projects of personal interest, while women are confined within their general feminine lot and bound together by a kind of immanent complicity. And what they look for first of all among themselves is the affirmation of the universe they have in common. They do not discuss opinions and general ideas, but exchange confidences and recipes; they are in league to create a kind of counter-universe, the values of which will outweigh masculine values. Collectively they find strength to shake off their chains; they negate the sexual domination of the males by admitting their frigidity to one another, while deriding the men's desires or their clumsiness; and they question ironically the moral and intellectual superiority of their husbands, and of men in general.[1]

The female friendships she describes occur in the region Erving Goffman has characterized in *The Presentation of Self in Everyday Life* as the "backstage." It is there that women can "let their hair down," be themselves with other women, away from the on-stage politics of intersexual tactics and its often attendant intrasexual competitiveness.

The world of white power has similarly fashioned universes: one black, one white, and a third—the world of interethnic relations, where blacks and whites share (in the dramaturgical metaphors of

69

Goffman) the same stage. When this occurs (in reality and in literature), blacks often engage in elaborate acts: of being black. As Jean-Paul Sartre's waiter plays at "being a waiter in a cafe,"[2] blacks, in the presence of whites, often play at being blacks in the expressive ways expected of them. This is true of Lutie Johnson while working at the Chandlers' in Ann Petry's *The Street*; of Bob Jones interacting with the union representative in Chester Himes's *If He Hollers Let Him Go*; of Fishbelly's father talking with the sheriff in Richard Wright's *The Long Dream*; of Max Reddick interacting with various "liberals" in John A. Williams's *The Man Who Cried I Am*—the list could go on and on.

But there are times when the expected role playing does not take place, when black actors fail to act their parts, almost as though they didn't know their lines. In the world of the theater, we might attribute this to poor directing, in "real life" to inadequate socialization. But it is at such moments that we can often catch the clearest view of the taken-for-granted. For there is an implicit grammar of conduct for black, and white, responses. As sentences slide securely into tenses, clauses, modifiers, number, and order without a jar, without an error, so conduct occurs in its eternal dance, with difference, like grammatical error, jarring, drawing attention to itself, disrupting the patterns of interchange. Such jarring disturbs the gestalt, draws attention to the machinery of staging. Such a situation was faced by James Baldwin on his first visit "home" ("down home," to Montgomery, Alabama) when he, by mistake, walked into a white restaurant and stood, frozen, bereft of lines and cues, upon the white stage. So too in *Black Boy* Richard Wright reports being smashed in the face by an empty whiskey bottle as he is riding on the running board of a speeding automobile because he forgot to answer a white man's question with "sir." Later his friend Griggs lectured him for his insensitivity to the "system": "'You act around white people as if you didn't know that they were white. And they *see* it. . . . When you're in front of white people, *think* before you act, *think* before you speak. Your way of doing things is all right among *our* people, but not for *white* people. They won't stand for it.'" Wright analyzed his problem: "In my dealing with whites I was conscious of the entirety of my relations with them, and they were conscious only of what was happening at a given moment. I had to keep remembering what others took for granted; I had to think out what others felt. I had begun coping with the white world too late. I could not make subservience an automatic part of my behavior."[3] It is the innocence of the protagonist in *Invisible Man*, regarding power and masking in his relations with whites, that Bledsoe stresses and finds so dangerous; on the bus traveling to New York, the black vet advises him, "'Play the game, but don't believe in it—that much you owe yourself.'" It is this game playing that the protagonist's grandfather had alluded to:

> "Son, after I'm gone I want you to keep up the good fight. I never told you, but our life is a war and I have been a traitor all my born days, a spy in the enemy's country ever since I give up my gun back in the Reconstruction. Live with your head in the lion's mouth. I want you to overcome 'em with yeses, undermine 'em with grins, agree 'em to death and destruction, let 'em swoller you till they vomit or bust wide open."[4]

Most actors play the game. The "taken-for-granted" occurs so naturally that the machinery doesn't obtrude. But it is the rattles in the smooth hum, the potential for breakdown that are often the stuff of fiction. One result of the disparity between the two universes of black and white (their historical, and continuing, separation), of the ignorance of the other (particularly of the ignorance of the nature of black lives), of white power and racism is the tension often present in the interaction of black and white, a tension that freights the commonplace with significance, that overlays the casual with emotions often too heavy to bear. This tension appears, in one form or another, in scene after scene. When whites enter a scene they bring more than their bodies. There may be nothing more than a heightened awareness of presence, a greater alertness. But there may also be a sense of the increased potential for conflict, even violence, or the suggestion of erotic possibilities. Bigger Thomas is acutely self-conscious before Mr. Dalton: "The man was gazing at him with an amused smile that made him conscious of every square inch of skin on his black body," and later he is terribly conscious of Mary Dalton's sexuality: "He smelt the odor of her hair and felt the soft pressure of her thigh against his own."[5] Tension, which later becomes violence, is present in the scene from William Attaway's *Blood on the Forge* in which Big Mat is killing hogs for Mr. Johnston, the plantation owner. Big Mat has just asked Mr. Johnston for the loan of a mule to plant his crops:

> "Us'll have a hard time makin' it on our share, mule or no—a hard time. . . ."
>
> Mr. Johnston caught Big Mat with his eyes. He came forward. Big Mat looked doggedly into the hard eyes. For a long second they hung on the edge of violence.
>
> Mr. Johnston said, "You ain't kickin', are you, Mat?"
>
> Big Mat's eyes dropped to the bloody entrails. He presented a dull, stupid exterior.
>
> "Nosuh, I ain't kickin'."[6]

Whites have been both aware and unaware of the game, of the stage where the players walk. (The powerful often walk about less self-consciously than the powerless, who must often be more sensitive—as must women, wives, children, the poor—to the guerrilla warfare of daily life.) So blacks, as Beauvoir's women, have often masked their deepest sensibilities. At times, in literature, the mask is stripped away, as in Baraka's *The Dutchman*. But rarely has either literature or "real life" provided such revealing instances of the phenomenon of masking as those witnessed in the South in the transition from slavery to "freedom." It was the approach of the Union army that often made the difference. Almost as though they were members of a large cast of a costume drama whose acting had been interrupted by the director, the slaves milled about on the plantation-stage, stepping out of the roles customarily played for the whites: "Mary Brodie, a thirteen-year-old slave in Wake County, North Carolina, could easily sense the change that had come over the plantation on which she resided. 'Missus and marster began to walk around and act queer. The grown slaves were whisperin' to each other. Sometimes they gathered in little gangs in the grove.' In the next several days, the noise of distant gunfire grew louder, everybody 'seemed to be disturbed,' the slaves walked about aimlessly, nobody was working, 'and marster and missus were crying!'"[7] Almost as revealing, and disturbing to the whites, was the apparent absence of affect:

> The mood of the slaves often defied the analysis of the master. On certain plantations, the slaves continued to act with an apparent indifference toward the war and the approaching Union troops, leaving their owners to speculate about what lay behind those bland countenances. In early 1865, as General Sherman's troops moved into South Carolina, a prominent rice planter observed little excitement among his slaves; in fact, they seemed "as silent as they had been in April, 1861, when they heard from a distance the opening guns of the war." Each evening the slave foreman dutifully obtained his instructions for the next day, and the work proceeded smoothly and silently. "Did those Negroes know that their freedom was so near? I cannot say, but, if they did, they said nothing, only patiently waited to see what would come." ... Until the Union Army made its presence felt, plantation life tended to remain relatively stable, crops were made, and most slaves went about their daily tasks. ... But news that Yankee soldiers were somewhere within reach precipitated the rapid depopulation of the slave quarters, often without the slightest warning. "They have shown no signs of insubordination," one observer noted. "Down to the last moment they cut their maize and eat their corn-cake with their old docility—then they suddenly disappear."[8]

A slave owner's daughter reflects in her journal her dismay as her reality changes and she begins to distrust the lines her father's slaves are uttering:

> Preparing to abandon the family plantation, as the Yankees approached, Eliza Andrews took time to note in her journal: "There is no telling what may happen before we come back; the Yankees may have put an end to our glorious old plantation life forever." That night, she paid a final visit to the slave quarters to bid her blacks farewell. "Poor things, I may never see any of them again, and even if I do, everything will be different. We all went to bed crying ..." [Ellipses in Litwack's text.] Four months later, returning to her home, she confided to her journal: "It is necessary to have some nickname to use when we talk before the servants, and to speak very carefully, even then, for every black man is a possible spy. Father says we must not even trust mammy too far."[9]

Planter Louis Manigault's account reflects the psychological disorientation that many whites must have experienced when faced with the unmasking central to the new social relations: "Conversing now with his former slaves, Manigault was suddenly overcome by a strange feeling. 'I almost imagined myself with Chinese, Malays or even Indians in the interior of the Philippine Islands.' It was as though he were on alien turf and had never really known these people who had once been his slaves."[10]

The conduct of slaves undermined white assumptions. Masters who had boasted they "knew their niggers" were faced with inexplicable conduct, often from those nearest and dearest:

> No more plaintive cry resounded through slave-holding society than that the slaves in whom they had placed the greatest trust and confidence were the very first to "betray" them. If this complaint recurred most frequently, perhaps that was because it seemed least comprehensible. "Those we loved best, and who loved us best—as we thought— were the first to leave us," a Virginian lamented, voicing an experience that would leave so many families incredulous. To Robert P. Howell, a North Carolina planter who had lost a number of slaves, the behavior of Lovet "disappointed" him the most: "He was about my age and I had always trusted him more as a companion than a slave."[11]

What the approach of the Union Army revealed, more clearly than ever before, was the phenomenon of masking: the composing of one's features for the benefit of the other when that other has the power to require only those appearances he desires. Whites had required of blacks a certain role; some few whites had had the wit to know they didn't know, but they had also had the power that, ultimately, vindicates, and assuages, ignorance. Blacks, who could possess so little, possessed a secret life: "When asked if the masters knew anything of 'the secret life of the colored people,' Robert Smalls, a former South Carolina slave, would later testify: 'No sir; one life they show their masters and another life they don't show!'"[12]

Frederick Douglass reveals the rewards of imprudent honesty in his account of the slave on Colonel Lloyd's plantation who, not knowing he was responding to his master, since he lived on one of the "out-plantations," said, "No sir," in reply to the question "Does the colonel treat you well?" The consequence of this brief exchange upon the road was that the slave was sold to a "Georgia trader":

> He was immediately chained and handcuffed; and thus, without a moment's warning, he was snatched away, and forever sundered, from his family and friends, by a hand more unrelenting than death. This is the penalty of telling the truth, of telling the simple truth, in answer to a series of plain questions. It is partly in consequence of such facts, that slaves, when inquired of as to their condition and the character of their masters, almost invariably say they are contented, and that their masters are kind. . . . a still tongue makes a wise head.[13]

The slave narratives reveal a sophisticated understanding of the distinction between public faces and private lives. Henry Bibb wrote: "The only weapon of self-defence that I could use successfully, was that of deception. It is useless for a poor slave, to resist the white man in a slaveholding state."[14] Gilbert Osofsky, in his discussion of slave narratives, has noted the need for slaves who were planning their escape to appear "most satisfied at the moment they were most discontented,"[15] and narrative writer Lunsford Lane has focused on the dissimulation required of the imminent fugitive: "The two points necessary in such a case I had kept constantly in mind. First, I had made no display of the little property or money I possessed, but in every way I wore as much as possible the aspect of slavery. Second, I had never appeared to be even so intelligent as I really was. This all colored people at the south, free and slaves, find it peculiarly necessary for their own comfort and safety to observe."[16]

Historically, the statement "He's a smart nigger" uttered in that special way by a certain cold-eyed Southerner was enough to chill the loins, revealing as it did a perception and a valuation and a singling out that could mark one for terrifying consequences. The same statement, of course, uttered in amusement and proprietarily by a slave owner, or even quite recently, carried quite different suggestions and was not unlike the way one spoke appreciatively of a particularly smart animal. Ralph Ellison has observed that the black man who invokes the "darky act" is not so much "a 'smart-man-playing-dumb' as a weak man who knows the nature of his oppressors' weakness. . . . His mask of meekness conceals the wisdom of one who has learned the secret of saying the 'yes' which accomplishes the expressive 'no.'"[17]

The look of the white other—a look which can express hatred, unawareness, even inability to "see"—has profoundly affected the black psyche and the black literature that emerged in the closing years of the nineteenth century and the early decades of the twentieth. In the second half of this study I shall be considering that literature in the writings of Charles Chesnutt, Paul Lawrence Dunbar, James Weldon Johnson, Wallace Thurman, Nella Larsen, and Jean Toomer. The literature of the period will often be characterized by confusion and ambivalence, even self-hatred, with regard to identity. Masking, that defensive response which permits the black to be absent while present, will be employed as a complex literary strategy. And even passing, that ultimate form of masking in which black is transformed into white, will appear frequently in the literature.

PART TWO

CHAPTER NINE

Introduction

THE UNMASKING that had so disturbed some Southerners was, at best, a brief glimpse "behind the veil."[1] The independence and other qualities exposed were too foreign to the plantation stereotype, and it was this view of the nature of slaves that white Southerners felt comfortable with, and it was this view that had helped them rationalize and justify slavery. In addition, those qualities revealed behind the mask were viewed as barriers to the revival of the southern economy, which was conceived very much in pre–Civil War terms, so that very quickly northern Reconstructionist joined with southern planter to end the migrations of the former slaves and enforce contractual relations between workers and planters in order to ensure stability in the work force. And very quickly, too, it became apparent to former slaves that there was little place for them in the cities, where whites monopolized the crafts, and that there were no forty acres and a mule for them in the country. It was, largely, the old plantations for them under contracts; or, later, the old plantations under sharecropping arrangements.

But while order might be restored in the economy, with the assistance of convict-leasing schemes and the extralegal threat of the night riders, much had to be done to restore the public mask. Social history from the Civil War into the modern period will be preoccupied with first restoring, then retaining, the old relations under the new "freedom." Central to this restoration will be the assertion of difference between whites and blacks, a difference earlier presumed under slavery but now formulated into laws and given vivid form through the arts. At the same time that physical separation was enforced by Jim Crow laws, images of blacks—in plantation literature, in the various media of graphic representation, and on the minstrel stage—continually reinforced the view that blacks were not like whites; that they were, in fact, large children untimely, and unfortunately, wrenched from the dependency relationship which was their natural condition and which had benefited both them and their masters.

In this chapter I will first explore the confused status of the black self in the postwar period. Jim Crow laws will be seen to evolve as one of the major ways to reassert difference: through physical separation. But that which is separated must also be viewed as different. Images of blacks—those "pictures in the head," as Walter Lippmann terms them—will shape the peopled landscape; what is seen will first be believed.[2] In addition to the plantation literature, the various graphic media, as well as the minstrel performance, will be seen to have crafted a burlesque image of the black that has persisted well into the twentieth century. I will explore the lineaments of this image as it was expressed by toys, dolls, postcards, lithographs, and the minstrel stage. I will then consider the reception of Paul Lawrence Dunbar's poetry by an age accustomed to the tradition and the image. I will conclude by briefly considering the role of two institutions—the black family and black religion—and one expressive form—the spirituals—in nurturing an alternative, positive image for the black self.

The Black Self after the War

The protagonist in Ellison's *Invisible Man* recalls his teacher telling him that his problem was one of "creating the *uncreated features of his face*,"[3] but it is only in the epilogue that his problem is tentatively resolved. Until that point in the novel, he wanders nameless (Jack gives him a name but we are never privy to it) and faceless, his face changing with his role, his role becoming his identity. Rinehart, the man with the paradoxical name, surfaces to suggest not only the nature of others but also the nature of the protagonist's self. The search for the uncreated features of his face, for "what lies behind the face of things," drives him underground.[4] And it is only in the closing pages that his scattered self coheres into the relative solidity he is finally able to perceive in his grandfather:

> Perhaps that makes me a little bit as human as my grandfather. Once I thought my grandfather incapable of thoughts about humanity, but I was wrong. Why should an old slave use such a phrase as, "This and this or this has made me more human," as I did in my arena speech? Hell, he never had any doubts about his humanity—that was left to his "free" offspring. He accepted his humanity just as he accepted the principle. It was his, and the principle lives on in all its human and absurd diversity.[5]

It is this self-understanding that permits him to anticipate coming up from underground (in that western pattern of emergence, which is so often a rebirth of the self), regardless of how invisible he might still remain to others or how much those others might lose by failing to see.

The protagonist's problem was, to some degree, every black's problem in the postwar period. For part of the implication of "freedom" was the casting off of the slave role and the slave identity. But if you weren't Massa Henry's Bob, who were you? This was a question more easily answered by blacks than by whites, because blacks had always performed a wider range of roles and expressed a more complex range of emotions than the stereotypes had credited. These relatively successful performances, under extreme hardship, had helped to foster personal and social strengths, so that they were always more than the dependent children of the stereotype of the plantation family.

Stressed in the plantation stereotype is the slave's dependency. Often that dependency cast the black in the role of child, the master in the role of kindly, indulgent, but also responsible and stern parent. The qualities of the one called out, and required, the qualities of the other. But the child sometimes misbehaves, and the black child misbehaved more commonly in the postwar period. As Maurice Oakley observed to his brother in Paul Lawrence Dunbar's novel *The Sport of the Gods* (1902): "'We must remember we are not in the old days now. The negroes are becoming less faithful and less contented.'"[6] However, the stereotype was sufficiently flexible to accommodate misbehavin'. Ruth McEnery Stuart's volumes of local color short stories, for example, pictured a postwar world of the slave quarters whose blacks were "improvident, emotional, gossipy, kind-hearted, high-tempered, vain, dishonest, idle, working two or three days in each week and 'res'n' up' the remainder, with always a healthy appetite and a 'mizry in de bre's'.'"[7] Her blacks were, for the most part, large children. Their traits, while expressive, were not serious, sober traits. They were not, for example, the traits associated with the Protestant ethic of the Puritans or with the spirit of enterprise of a Benjamin Franklin; nor were they those traits considered necessary for survival in a Darwinian world. In a world increasingly peopled by the go-getters that Sinclair Lewis will later immortalize, theirs were the traits that called forth indulgence and discipline. Paradoxically, they were also traits that revealed imitativeness, a debased version of aristocratic virtues, a proclivity to ape your betters that both amused and exasperated but that was ultimately indulged in that flexible economy of emotions where flattery finds its place. In exaggerated form, the perceived tendency to imitate whites will be burlesqued on the minstrel stage, where the comic attempts of "blacks" to speak and dress like whites will reinforce black stereotypes for more than a hundred years.

When the black left the plantation (or, more abstractly, with emancipation generally) he left the restraining influence of his "white man." Several of Charles Chesnutt's white Southerners have reflected on these changes. In *The Marrow of Tradition*, Major Carteret comments on the changing times to Mammy Jane, an old black woman, formerly a slave in his household who has returned to the big house to nurse the major's baby:

> "Well, Jane," returned the major, . . . "the old times have vanished, the old ties have been ruptured. The old relations of dependence and loyal obedience on the part of the colored people, the responsibility of protection and kindness upon that of the whites, have passed away forever. The young negroes are too self-assertive. Education is spoiling them, Jane; they have been badly taught. They are not content with their station in life. . . .
>
> "If all the colored people were like you and Jerry, Jane, . . . there would never be any trouble. You have friends upon whom, in time of need, you can rely implicitly for protection and succor. You served your mistress

faithfully before the war; you remained by her when the other negroes were running hither and thither like sheep without a shepherd; and you have transferred your allegiance to my wife and her child. We think a great deal of you, Jane."[8]

In *The Colonel's Dream* (1905), Major McLean informs the recently arrived Colonel French about the essential nature of the black worker: "'You'll have trouble if you hire niggers. . . . You'll find that they won't work when you want 'em to. They're not reliable, they have no sense of responsibility. As soon as they get a dollar they'll lay off to spend it, and leave yo' work at the mos' critical point.'"[9]

The southern view of black dependency ruled out such virtues as independence, industry, manhood, dignity, and self-respect. This is clearly revealed in the testimony in 1880 of witnesses before the Senate committee investigating the mass migrations of the Exodusters to Kansas in the 1870s. The committee had apparently believed that the migration of these southern blacks "was a Republican plot to discredit Southern Democrats and lessen Southern representation in Congress." Benjamin ("Pap") Singleton assured the committee it was no Republican plot: "'*I* was the whole cause of the migration. Nobody but me. . . . *I* am the Moses of the colored exodus.'"[10] The testimony to the committee revealed, however, that if Pap Singleton was the Moses, postwar blacks were the Hebrews ready for a leader to call them to Kansas to establish all-black towns. The seventeen hundred pages of testimony did document violence against Republican organizers and voters; but more important, for my purposes, is the recurring pattern of violence directed toward black expressions of independence, industry, manhood, dignity, and self-respect. Herbert G. Gutman, exploring the motivations of the migrants in the Senate testimony, details a background of violence and violation: toward the man who was organizing tenant farmers to pressure for a rent reduction and who fled because he feared being killed; toward the son who was "shot all to pieces and was dead" and who "was a smart boy and read the papers, and the white people there won't allow that"; toward a brother who died in a dispute over a debt; toward the black men who attempted to protect their wives and daughters from the lust of white men ("'a great many of these women rose up and said that if their husbands did not leave they would' "); toward the men who took their landlord to court to seek redress from his exorbitant charges of debts levied against their year's industry.[11] Industry, which is a virtue in abstraction, when practiced by a black farmer could earn him the envy and/or covetousness of his white neighbors; the loss by blacks of thriving farms due to land title dispute is a recurring theme in black history and literature. In general, the good old American virtue of success, whether Puritan or secular, whether preached from pulpit or blue-backed speller, became objectionable when evidenced by blacks. For blacks, as for women, were reserved the less aggressive virtues of fidelity, obedience, dependency, loyalty, and love. The "bad nigger" was often the black who perceived this too clearly and who, ultimately, refused to mask his opposition, as Josh in Chesnutt's *The Marrow of Tradition*:

> "De niggers is be'n train' ter fergiveniss; an' fer fear dey might fergit how ter fergive, de w'ite folks gives 'em somethin' new ev'y now an' den, ter preactice on. A w'ite man kin do w'at he wants ter a nigger, but de minute de nigger gits back at 'im, up goes de nigger, an' don' come down tell somebody cuts 'im down. If a nigger gits a' office, er de race 'pears ter be prosperin' too much, de w'ite folks up an' kills a few, so dat de res' kin keep on fergivin' an' bein' thankful dat dey're lef' alive. Don't talk ter me 'bout dese w'ite folks,—I knows 'em, I does! Ef a nigger wants ter git down on his marrow-bones, an' et dirt, an' call 'em 'marster,' *he's* good nigger, dere's room for *him*. But I ain' no w'ite folks' nigger, I ain'. I don' call no man 'marster.' I don' wan' nothin' but w'at I wo'k fer, but I wants all er dat. I never moles's no w'ite man, 'less'n he moles's me fus'."[12]

The demonstration by blacks of "white-only" virtues threatened fragile webs of interrelations, and it was these interrelations the Redeemers sought to restore. (Even the responsibility for their former slaves, which many believed they no longer felt, was to a degree restored as an element in various relationships of interdependence.) While they might emphasize restricting the ballot in state after state during the postwar period, the vote was principally one of the more formal, and of course imposed, features of that threatening complex identified as "social equality." The ballot, with its leveling implications in the notion of one man—one vote, involved more than simply political equality—it was, for the southern psyche, tantamount to social equality. "'It's a social matter down here, rather than a political one,'" General Thornton explains to Colonel Carteret, who has returned in *The Colonel's Dream* from the North to his southern hometown after an absence of thirty years:

> "For instance, I had fully made up my mind to vote the other ticket [the Republican ticket] in the last election. I didn't like our candidate nor our platform. There was a clean-cut issue between sound money and financial repudiation, and I was tired of the domination of populists and demagogues. All my better instincts led me toward a change of attitude, and I boldly proclaimed the fact. I declared my political and intellectual independence, at the cost of many friends; even my own son-in-law scarcely spoke to me for a month. When I went to the polls, ole Sam Brown, the triflingest nigger in town, whom I had seen sentenced to jail more than once for stealing—ole Sam Brown was next to me in the line.
>
> "'Well, Gin'l,' he said, 'I'm glad you is got on de right side at las', an' is gwine to vote *our* ticket.'
>
> "This was too much! I could stand the other party in the abstract, but not in the concrete. I voted the ticket of my neighbours and my friends. We had to preserve our institutions, even if our finances went to smash. Call it prejudice—call it what you like—it's human nature, and you'll come to it, colonel, you'll come to it—and then we'll send you to Congress."[13]

Ultimately it was fear of social equality that bound redneck to patrician and doomed the Populist movement in the South.

It was the inevitability of social equality that Booker T. Washington was denying in the 1895 Atlanta Exposition address when he declared, "In all things that are purely social we can be as separate as the fingers."[14] His assurance—his "stay against confusion"—brought him honor, power, and white patronage; in white eyes, he was the new black Moses. It was the confusion of social equality, the disorientation, the leveling, the threat at every level that were feared. And, ultimately, whether in a series of events or within a single conversation, the fear would fix on miscegenation, on the threshold, the door, the bedchamber, the daughter—the black hole of every argument, the chaos that yawned beneath the surface of decorum. A candidate for governor in Chesnutt's *The Colonel's Dream* illustrates the dynamics of the process of argumentation:

> "So long as one Negro votes in the State, so long are we face to face with the nightmare of Negro domination. For example, suppose a difference of opinion among white men so radical as to divide their vote equally, the ballot of one Negro would determine the issue. Can such a possibility be contemplated without a shudder? Our duty to ourselves, to our children, and their unborn descendants, and to our great and favoured race, impels us to protest, by word, by vote, by arms if need be, against the enforced equality of an inferior race. Equality anywhere, means ultimately, equality everywhere. Equality at the polls means social equality; social equality means intermarriage and corruption of blood, and degeneration and decay. What gentleman here would want his daughter to marry a blubber-lipped, cocoanut-headed, kidney-footed, etc., etc., nigger?"[15]

The "etc.," while tipping Chesnutt's hand, also indicates how commonplace was the argument.

The exercise of "white" virtues, the presumption of social equality, threatened to blur differences essential to the southern way of life. In the prewar period, difference was fixed by the categories of slave and nonslave. (Even then, however, the existence of free blacks in slaveholding states created a group, small relative to those enslaved, whose rights and privileges were often ambiguously defined and subject to change.) But in the postwar period the often informal understandings that had governed slaves' actions no longer assured compliance,[16] just as attitudes of responsibility for the slaves, which had developed within the paternalism of slavery, could no longer be relied on. Segregation, Jim Crow, evolved to reassert the difference threatened by the overthrow of slavery.[17] Slowly—though sometimes more quickly, often in a piecemeal fashion, with here a separated waiting room, there a separated streetcar—but ineluctably, the former Confederate states moved toward separation, "from cradle to grave." Chesnutt will declare in 1903 that "the rights of the Negroes are at a lower ebb than at any time during the thirty-five years of their freedom, and the race prejudice more intense and uncompromising."[18]

To appreciate the degree of change that full-blown, turn-of-the-century segregation represented it is necessary to consider the intimacy that often characterized slavery and the "confusion" that marked the interregnum period between the abolition of slavery and the full institutionalization of segregation. Joel Williamson in *After Slavery* has stressed that "slavery necessitated a constant, physical intimacy"; and Richard C. Wade in *Slavery in the Cities* has pointed out that "in every city in Dixie . . . blacks and whites lived side by side, sharing the same premises if not equal facilities and living constantly in each other's presence."[19] But "intimacy" and "living constantly in each other's presence" do not denote social equality. It was social equality that was suggested by the actions of some blacks in the period between abolition and the "triumph of white supremacy." C. Vann Woodward has portrayed the unsettled, and unusual, quality of this period:

Black faces continued to appear at the back door, but they also began to appear in wholly unprecedented and unexpected places—in the jury box and on the judge's bench, in council chamber and legislative hall, at the polls and the market place. Neither of these contrasting types of contact, the old or the new, was stable or destined to endure for very long, but for a time old and new rubbed shoulders—and so did black and white—in a manner that differed significantly from Jim Crow of the future or slavery of the past.

What happened in North Carolina was a revelation to conservative whites. "It is amazing," wrote Kemp Battle of Raleigh, "how quietly our people take negro juries, or rather negroes on juries." Randolph Shotwell of Rutherfordton was dismayed on seeing "long processions of countrymen entering the village by the various roads mounted and afoot, whites and blacks marching together, and in frequent instances arm-in-arm, a sight to disgust even a decent negro." It was disturbing even to native white radicals, as one of them admitted in the Raleigh *Standard*, to find at times "the two races now eat together at the same table, sit together in the same room, work together, visit and hold debating societies together." It is not that such occurrences were typical or very common, but that they could happen at all what was important. . . .

Their impact [the impact of comprehensive antidiscrimination statutes] was noted in South Carolina in 1868 by Elizabeth H. Botume,

a Northern teacher, on a previously segregated river steamer from
Charleston to Beaufort. She witnessed "a decided change" among Negro
passengers, previously excluded from the upper deck. "They were everywhere," she wrote, "choosing the best staterooms and best seats at the
table. Two prominent colored members of the State Legislature were on
board with their families. There were also several well-known Southerners, still uncompromising rebels. It was a curious scene and full of
significance."[20]

It is ironic that the minstrels—a form of entertainment in which
whites imitated blacks—were the most popular form of theater in
the nineteenth century, but that blacks, walking upon the new
social stage, would arouse both dismay and outrage when they performed actions that cast them in the role of simply darker whites.

The role of white women—often an ambiguous role in view of the
sexual threat from comely black slave women and the contradictory
pressures to be both a woman-on-a-pedestal and a practical plantation manageress—seems to have been perceived as particularly
threatened. For some, it was apparently the assumption by blacks of
"white" clothing styles that symbolized the unraveling of social order: "In the fall of 1865 a Freedmen's Bureau officer stationed in
Wilmington, North Carolina, remarked to a northern journalist that
'the wearing of black veils by the young negro women had given
great offense to the young white women,' who consequently gave up
this form of apparel altogether."[21] It is the assertiveness of black
women's dress that particularly stands out in a postwar description
from South Carolina:

> White city dwellers in particular often associated "insolent" behavior
> with modes of freedwomen's dress that defied the traditional code of
> southern race relations. In his description of a Charleston street scene in
> the mid-1860s—"so unlike anything we could imagine"—Henry W.
> Ravenel implied that there was more than a casual connection between
> the two: "Negroes shoving white persons off the walk—Negro women
> drest in the most outre style, all with veils and parasols for which they
> have an especial fancy—riding on horseback with negro soldiers and in
> carriages."[22]

For others, it was the black male's desire that his wife not work in
the white man's fields that elicited scorn: "Employers made little

effort to hide their contempt for freedwomen who 'played the lady' and refused to join workers in the fields. To apply the term 'ladylike' to a black woman was apparently the height of sarcasm."[23]

But dismay and outrage were not limited to the woman's role. Litwack has summarized the kinds of actions often viewed as affronts:

> When freedmen declined to remove or touch their hats upon meeting a white person, or if they failed to stand while they spoke with whites, they were "growing too saucy for human endurance." When freedmen took to promenading about the streets or public places, refusing to give up the sidewalks to every white who approached, that was "impudence" of the rankest sort. . . . When black women attired themselves in fancy garments, carried parasols, and insisted upon being addressed as "ladies" (or "my lady" rather than "my ole woman"), that was "putting on airs"; and when black men dressed themselves conspicuously, that was a sufficient provocation to cut the clothes from their backs. When white "gentlemen" engaged in hunting encountered freedmen "enjoying themselves in the same way" (with shotguns and a pack of dogs), that was called still another instance of "insubordination and insolence." When freedmen staged parades, dances, and barbecues, like those scheduled to commemorate the Emancipation Proclamation, whites invariably characterized them as "orgies" or "outrageous spectacles." When freedmen roamed about at night, disregarding the old curfew and refusing orders to return to their quarters, that was "a terrible state of insubordination" bordering on insurrection. And when freedmen attended meetings in which they openly talked about "perfect equality with the whites," acquiring land, and even voting, that was an incitement to race war. "Such incendiary and revolutionary language," a white Louisianan wrote of one such meeting in New Orleans, "was enough to freeze the blood. I fear they will have trouble there soon."[24]

The assertion that "the bottom rail is on the top" would have been sufficient challenge if that rail had been a po'white. But when that bottom rail was black, the impudence was intolerable, the disorder to the white psyche often unbearable, which helps to explain the violence Litwack has commented on: "The violence inflicted upon freedmen seldom bore any relationship to the gravity of the alleged provocation. Of the countless cases of postwar violence, in fact the largest proportion related in some way to that broad and vaguely defined charge of conduct unbecoming black

people—that is, 'putting on airs,' 'sassiness,' 'impudence,' 'inso-
lence,' 'disrespect,' 'insubordination,' contradicting whites, and vio-
lating racial customs.''[25]

Neither the economic nor the political order would long permit
such assumptions of equality. "By the mid-1870s no more than 4
to 8 percent of all freed families in the South owned their own
farms";[26] and by the turn of the century virtually all blacks would
be disfranchised. Manners, too, would be controlled: the old, prewar,
seeming willingness to engage in the rituals of deference would
never be restored in the postwar period in all their earlier richness
of pretense and innuendo; but Jim Crow laws would evolve to man-
date at least the semblance of the conduct that had once been assumed. Segregation laws would separate blacks from whites in every
conceivable social situation: from "cradle to grave," from birth reg-
istry to segregated graveyard. "The ludicrous extent to which legis-
latures segregated the races later in the century was clearly anticipated in the instructions given black people in Natchez in 1866 that
henceforth the promenades along the river and the bluff to the right
of Main Street would be reserved 'for the use of the whites, for ladies
and children and nurses—the central Bluff between Main Street and
State for bachelors and the colored population, and the lower prome-
nade for the whites.' ''[27]

The Black Image in the White Eye

The image that has haunted black iconography is that of the grinning face. The grin—exaggerated to the grotesque by disproportion-
ate lips, by reddened lips,[28] by the minstrel's practice when making
up of leaving a white space around the mouth, and by the contrast
of white teeth with the unnaturally, evenly blackened face—was
generally accompanied by other exaggerated features: by a face uni-
formly black, without natural highlights; by white, usually over-
sized eyeballs seeming unnaturally large and white in contrast to
the black skin; and by hair done up in exaggerated fashion, as, for
example, in the style of the minstrel's "fright wig." But it is the grin
that dominates, seems almost to swallow up all other features, the
grin that floats, almost balloonlike, among the "pictures in our

heads," an icon for endless childhood, for the simple souls of "happy darkies." It was the nineteenth century's unfolding of the artlessly enfolded; not until the twentieth century will the grin become ambiguous.

The grin stares back at us from the nineteenth century: from toys and dolls, lithographs, picture postcards, sheet music, billposters, and the minstrel stage. It is in fact perhaps the minstrel stage that most firmly fixed the grin in the psyches of the nineteenth century. Carl Wittke, in *Tambo and Bones: A History of the American Minstrel Stage*, has stressed the care applied to the grin in the making up of minstrel "end men": "Most performers exercised great care in fixing their mouths, for there was a rather widely accepted superstition among them that they would be unable to work properly in their acts unless this part of their make-up was perfect. These big lips and the distended mouth helped to accentuate their shining white teeth."[29] In Ellison's *Invisible Man*, the grin is another of those identities that haunts the protagonist:

> Then near the door I saw something which I'd never noticed there before: the cast-iron figure of a very black, red-lipped and wide-mouthed Negro, whose white eyes stared up at me from the floor, his face an enormous grin, his single large black hand held palm up before his chest. It was a bank, a piece of early Americana, the kind of bank which, if a coin is placed in the hand and a lever pressed upon the back, will raise its arm and flip the coin into the grinning mouth. For a second I stopped, feeling hate charging within me, then dashed over and grabbed it, suddenly as enraged by the tolerance or lack of discrimination, or whatever, that allowed Mary to keep such a self-mocking image around, as by the knocking [on the radiator pipes].[30]

Ellison's example of early Americana is perhaps the Jolly Black Man from Buffalo, New York (1882), included in the collection of the Philadelphia Toy Museum; for little girls, the collection contains a Dinah Bank, into whose wide, red-lipped mouth little girls could push their precious coins.

TOYS AND DOLLS AND PICTURE POSTCARDS

Blacks in the nineteenth century confronted not only the distorting verbal images of the plantation tradition but also exaggerated graphic images. All the realism of the occasional blacks in the photographs of a Mathew Brady could do little to counterbalance these graphic images of "happy darkies." They were encountered early, in significant contexts. Toys and dolls, for example, are extremely important in psychological life histories.[31] An example from Victorian England reminds us of how often the play of children is, unfortunately, children playing at growing up. In H. G. Wells's book on *Floor Games* published in 1913, his little Edwardians (or post-Edwardians) were permitted to aggrandize the parlor floor. There, in play modeled after their elders' more serious pursuits, they brought the blessings of civilization to the four corners of the room. Wells describes the Game of Wonderful Islands: "We land and alter things and build and rearrange and hoist paper flags on pins, and subjugate populations and confer all the blessings of civilization upon these lands."[32] Antonia Fraser, from the perspective of a more analytical, and troubled, age, comments, "Here is no introspection about the British Empire, pacifism, what is or is not good for the children's souls, but a careless confidence that children play with what amuses them, and that this in turn must be the best possible thing for their future happiness."[33]

Young southern children, and possibly northern, could people their worlds, or perhaps their past, with little black dolls. Janet Pagter Johl's *The Fascinating Story of Dolls* includes photographs of two such groups. One set is apparently intended to represent types and includes a mammy, a washerwoman (with scrub board and bundle on her head), an elderly "uncle" (with chicken under his arm), a city Negro named Mr. Palmetto (well dressed, a posie in his buttonhole), a plantation worker, a convict in stripes (complete with ball and chain), a preacher, a banjo strummer, and a cotton picker. The dolls are crudely made, one head indistinguishable from the next. Into each face are stuck two eyes, a nose, and a mouth. The eyes and mouth start out whitely against the uniform backdrop of dark skin, but at least the mouth is not exaggeratedly large, as it is in most nineteenth-century representations. In the second group, the Southern Darky Dolls made by Helen Siebold Walter, a grinning half-moon mouth dominates the faces of Aunt Peachy, Uncle Hannibal, and that of one of their four "Pickaninnies," a girl named

Watermelon. Watermelon and her three sister siblings, Alabaster, Peaches, and Hallelujah, are all characterized by white pop eyes and "kinks of hair . . . hand wrapped with cord."³⁴ Johl's text reveals much about the dolls' appeal to tradition and to the author:

> Many dolls represent these faithful and loyal Americans, revealing the types of work in which they are engaged, and the happy nature that is so characteristic of the colored race, and so enviable. . . .
> "Southern Darky Dolls" originated in Staunton, Virginia under the skillful hand of Helen Siebold Walter. The little Pickaninnies are hand made in brown and black sateen, and the kinks of hair are hand wrapped with cord exactly the way Mammy wraps the hair of her little ones. To perpetuate a phase of the south fast disappearing there are also other colored dolls,—Aunt Peachy and Uncle Hannibal, who were dearly be-loved by all the little white "chillun" they raised in Virginia.
> Miss Walter has made her old time "Southern Darkies" as authentic as possible in make-up and costumes and sought to bring to life the characteristics of sweetness and faithfulness.³⁵

One doll which originated in the 1890s and is, according to an informant, still being sold is the golliwogg.³⁶ The golliwogg first appeared in England in 1895 as a character in *Two Dutch Dolls and a Golliwogg*, an illustrated children's book by Bertha and Florence Upton. According to Margery Fisher, the original was "a tattered old 'nigger doll' from America that Florence Upton's aunt lent to her" and is "now preserved in a glass case at the British Prime Minister's home, Chequers."³⁷ Twelve volumes followed in the next fourteen years with the golliwogg assuming center stage, as suggested by titles such as *The Golliwogg's Bicycle Club* (1896), *The Golliwogg at the Sea-Side* (1898), *The Golliwogg in War!* (1899), etc.

In appearance, the golliwogg is a black minstrel with a fright wig. An illustration from *Two Dutch Dolls and a Golliwogg* pictures the golliwogg in the primary colors of fire engine—red trousers, sky-blue jacket, bright red bow tie, bright red lips, white pop eyes, and black fright wig. Fright would seem to be one of the reactions the doll evoked, according to Antonia Fraser's *A History of Toys*:

> Psychologists sometimes question the giving of golliwogs to young children on the grounds that the black face, pop eyes and big red mouth

are the unconscious source of many childish nightmares. Lady Mary Clive, describing her Edwardian childhood in *A Day of Reckoning*, certainly gives a horrifying picture of the giant child-size golliwog which her mother bought for her eldest brother, and which was universally feared by the children, who preferred the more welcoming and cosy teddy bear.[38]

And fright is also the reaction to the golliwogg on the part of the other dolls at its first appearance. In *Two Dutch Dolls and a Golliwogg*, one Dutch doll awakens in a shop on Christmas Eve and helps another out of her box. The two of them are dancing and playing leapfrog when "the blackest gnome Stands there alone, / They scatter in their fright." The response to the doll must have been, at the very least, ambivalent. Fisher has argued that with certain minor alterations the doll became "a toy beloved by small children."[39]

Picture postcards in the United States began with the souvenir issues sold at the Columbian Exposition in Chicago in 1893. They soon furnished another form for portraying the stereotyped black image. "Watermelon Jake," for example, is a photograph copyrighted in 1901 by the Detroit Photographic Company of a black ragamuffin grinning out at the viewer above his half-eaten slice of watermelon, the half-moon slice of melon a mocking simulacrum of the grinning, turned-up mouth poised above it. Dorothy B. Ryan, in *Picture Postcards in the United States 1893–1918*, describes the portrayal of blacks:

> Although undeniably racist in nature, Negroes on cards are sought by many collectors and provide valuable insight into the popular conception of the black man at the time. Repeatedly portrayed as lazy, unintelligent, and impoverished . . . the Tuck Oilette black studies by H. Dix Sandford were apparently distributed in this country as well as in England; the repeated use of the noun "coon" on the Tuck cards, as well as on those of other publishers, is regrettable. . . . "Dixie Land" . . . includes a fine portrait of "Ole Mammy," several scenes in the cotton fields, the traditional watermelon feast ("We's in heben"), and a particularly racist card of a black man with a watermelon under each arm eyeing a loose chicken ("Dis am de wist perdickermunt ob mah life!").[40]

Postcards used for advertising similarly reinforced images, as in Ryan's example of the advertising postcard for Korn Kinks Malted

Flakes, featuring a gawky young Kornelia Kinks (in kinky, berib-
boned hair, exaggerated mouth) walking on stilts while pressing
a box of Korn Kinks under one arm, trying to remain balanced as a
young black urchin determinedly pulls at one of her stilts, which
has become entangled in her kite string; Kornelia's legend declares,
"You smash dem Kinks / I'll spoil you' face chile."[41]

THE LITHOGRAPH

The lithograph, the nineteenth century's democratic art form, did
not neglect the grin. In 1828 and 1829, Edward Williams Clay began
a series of etchings, later lithographed, which satirized free blacks
in Philadelphia. His *Life in Philadelphia* series depended for its humor on the incongruity of blacks dressed up in the height of exotic
fashion, "imitating" whites. The example included in William Murrell's *A History of American Graphic Humor (1747–1865)* shows "a
couple of overdressed darkies" (Murrell's prose) learning the paces
of a new dance. A legend spoken by the man is intended to heighten
the incongruity: "I reckon I've cotcht de figure now!"[42]

In keeping with the comic stereotypes, the activities of politically
empowered blacks in other countries of the Western Hemisphere are
portrayed as laughable and deflated through burlesque. Everything
they do is overdone. Their attempts to imitate the forms of "white"
civilization reveal them as comic buffoons, as poor players upon
the world's stage. Several lithographs included in Murrell's study
reflect these views; revealing, too, is Murrell's unreflective prose
commentary:

> Nicaragua furnished an occasion for an American cartoonist in 1839
> when its negro "Emperor" received the protests of the United States
> minister on the detention of the American owned steamer "Prome-
> theus" by the English brig-of-war "Express." Mr. Chatfield is seen in
> conversation with the "Emperor," who, seated on a rum barrel, is pre-
> sented as wearing a military coat and plumed hat but no trousers, and
> only one boot. He has a bottle in his left hand, and his "unmention-
> ables" are hung over his right arm. It is a very gay little lithograph . . . ,
> and the whole scene looks like one out of a comic opera. The same year
> saw the introduction to President Van Buren of the Haytian Envoy; and

H. R. Robinson published a print . . . showing the ubiquitous Major Jack Downing presenting "the Marquis De Quashipompo, Envoy Extraordinary." The Major hides his grin behind his hand, and a grotesque looking negro in the court costumes of an earlier century makes an exaggerated bow before the plainly dressed Van Buren. . . .

In Soloque, *Emperor of Hayti, Creating a Grand Duke* . . . we have a capital though savage satire on the mushroom empires founded by megalomaniac negroes who possessed sufficient martial and executive cunning. And quite possibly the anonymous draughtsman intended an oblique thrust at Napoleon III and Dom Pedro of Brazil. But there actually was a negro, Soulouque, who proclaimed himself Faustin I and who held power and maintained a burlesque imperial state in Hayti from 1849 to 1858; and it is not at all unlikely that the grotesque scene in this print is closer to such incidents it ridicules than even the artist supposed. In any case, it is an excellent and most amusing drawing: the amazingly proportioned and arrogant Emperor, his bloated consort, his imbecilic Prime Minister, the bullying and giggling courtiers, the awed expectant Grand Duke, and the diplomatic representatives of the United States, Great Britain, and France—all are most felicitous characterizations.[43]

The "felicitous characterizations" of the "diplomatic representatives of the United States, Great Britain, and France" are sickened by the spectacle. One holds his stomach and talks of throwing up; another holds a bottle of scent to his nose while telling the American, "They smell very disagreeable." The tall American replies, "Why yes the ceremony & the stink is so Great I shall be compelled to take a very large Chaw of Tobacco on the strength of it as a disinfecting agent. No wonder they have the yellow fever here. These Niggers would Breed a Pestilence anywhere. As to coupling Niggers & Republic Principals together, you might as well try to match an owl with a Bird of Paradise. They'd mate as well."

It is in the Currier & Ives Darktown lithographs of Thomas Worth that the absurdity of freed blacks is most strongly stated in graphic form for the 1880s and 1890s. Currier & Ives, who styled themselves publishers of "Colored Engravings for the People," sold their seven thousand hand-colored lithographs for prices ranging from five to twenty-five cents and never for more than three dollars apiece (for the large folios). In their heyday "Currier prints were to be found adorning the walls of barrooms, barbershops, firehouses, and hotels, as well as the homes of rich and poor alike."[44]

Thomas Worth belonged to the group of artists Harry T. Peters has identified as contributing most to the success of Currier & Ives. Earlier, the firm had featured blacks in occasional lithographs and in group scenes in political cartoons dealing with the "irrepressible conflict." In these scenes, the black figure tends to be somewhat comic, apart from, even though with, others, as reflected in his comment while sailing with ten other figures in the 1860 Republican rowboat "ship of state": "If de boat and all hands sink, dis Nigger sure to swim. Yah! Yah!"[45] Another 1860 Currier & Ives print, *An Heir to the Throne, Or the Next Republican Candidate*, features a noble tribune and an admirable Lincoln (leaning on a split rail) introducing the new candidate. Lincoln declares, "How fortunate! that this intellectual and noble creature should have been discovered just at this time, to prove to the world the superiority of the Colored over the Anglo Saxon race, he will be a worthy successor to carry out the policy which I shall inaugurate." The candidate, an undersized black man who appears more feeble-minded than grotesque, leans on a spear and responds to the speech of Lincoln and the similar grandiloquence of the tribune, "What, can dey be?" On the wall in the background are the words "Barnum's What Is It / Now Exhibiting."[46] But Currier & Ives was a business, always attentive to the market, as reflected in its 1868 *Reconstruction of "A White Man's Government,"* meant to chide the uncooperative South. A realistic, and sympathetically drawn, black man holds onto the "Tree of Liberty" with one hand while extending his other hand to a Southerner, caught in a rushing stream and about to be dashed over a waterfall. Not only is the drawing warmly human, but the black man's diction is "white": "Give me your hand master, now that I have a good hold of this tree I can help you out of your trouble," to which the Southerner replies, "You go to thunder! do you think I'll let an infernal Nigger take Me by the hand?,—no sir-ree this is a white man's government." A sober citizen standing on the bank, looking a little like Grant out of uniform, observes, "My friend I think you had better use all means to get ashore; even if it is a black man that saves you."[47]

Such sentiments were out of place by the 1880s and 1890s. Reconstruction had ended. Federal troops no longer garrisoned the South. The Yankee schoolmarms were a memory; most of the schools they had staffed were either closed or closing. Sharecropping bound the former slave to the land in endless cycles of cotton growing and debt peonage. Those who went to the cities found many of the crafts they had performed as slaves closed to them. The vote was increasingly restricted by ingenious means or crude. Difference—between whites and blacks—was asserted by Jim Crow laws, night riders, ropes, and firebrands. The Darktown lithographs of Thomas Worth were a comic expression of a "necessary" difference.

The Darktown prints picture a world off center, a world in which comical "darkies" play at being white folks. The effect is absurdity. The message is clear: a free black is imaginable, and, with the war, inevitable, but his attempts to ape his betters must—as his speech— continually express his comic incapacity. Strong, sinewy, noble white firemen, for example, will act heroically in the Currier & Ives lithographs of an L. Maurer[48] in an age hungry for the graphic representation of shipwrecks, earthquakes, and fires; but the Darktown Fire Brigade will do everything wrong. In the 1884 *The Darktown Fire Brigade—Saved* lithograph, the fireman plays his hose on a black figure stuck in a hole in the roof while the fire goes unattended; a woman dressed in a nightshirt fans herself as she jumps into a net, which is a quilt filled with holes. The poses of the figures are antic, in no way heroic, and they are all graced with disproportionately large feet (a comic device exploited also by minstrels). Time does not improve the Darktown Fire Brigade; an 1887 print, *The Darktown Fire Brigade—Hook and Ladder Gymnastics*, pictures a "rescued" woman (again in a nightshirt) flying through the air at the top of a ladder. One of two firemen attempting to keep the ladder from falling cries out, "Brace her up dar! and cotch her on de fly!" to another fireman, who will apparently "cotch her" by spearing her with a harpoon. Meanwhile, two others play hoses on the hook and ladder rather than on the fire.[49]

In other activities, the viewer is always aware that Darktown is an imitation, and a poor imitation, of the real world. Just as the minstrels will portray blacks who are inappropriately overdressed, the Darktown prints will feature blacks engaging in "white" leisure-class activities. In *The Darktown Yacht Club—Hard Up for a Breeze. / The cup in danger* print, black sailors will try to create a breeze with bellows and a fan. Even after they have won the race, another print shows them dancing victoriously, but their yacht is sinking. The new game of lawn tennis is featured in two prints; the "scientific player" delivers his "scientific stroke" by falling over the net and knocking it down. The "champion" in the rowing competition is in danger in one print but succeeds in the follow-up print by rowing over his opponent. Two Darktown hunt prints present the posture and the reality. The reality is the patch in the pants, under the hunting coat; the runaway horse, its rider hanging from a branch; sweating nags, ready for the glue factory; and bedraggled, comic dogs, their splayed limbs unrecognizable in the noble context of hunting. A dapper bicyclist in *On His Style* approaches a railroad crossing declaring, "Take a mity smart lokymoky to kotch dis coon!" In the next print, *Off His Nut,* he and his bicycle are wrapped around the locomotive's smokestack and the legend reads, "Gracious Massy, I'se struck de comet!"[50]

The world of Worth's lithographs was rich and varied. Peters has commented on the variety: "The Darktowns provide a humorous treatment of almost every activity of Negro life, real and imagined, from the cradle to the grave. They include burlesques of all kinds of sports—baseball, . . . tennis, . . . yachting, . . . fox hunting, . . . and the like. There are comic horse-racing pictures, scenes of watermelon- and oyster-eating contests, foot races, crap games, bicycle outings . . . and races, banjo classes, Darktown fire brigades in action, and a hundred other varied subjects."[51] The power of the Darktown lithographs to create "pictures in our heads" is recognized in a May 1897 review in the St. Louis *Post-Dispatch* of *Darkest America*, an all-black show: "If you are a Southerner and acquainted with the 'brother in black' you will find much entertainment in 'Darkest America.' If you come from the other side of the line and have formed your own ideas of Colored folks from the stage Negro and Darktown sketches, you will be instructed and amused."[52] Murrell's history notes the ubiquitousness of the Darktown prints: "No saloon, poolroom, or barbershop was as it should be in the late eight-

ies unless it had one or more of Thomas Worth's Darktown lithographs."[53] Walton Rawls has stressed the commercial and political
motivations underlying the recurring stressing of difference: "Anti-
Negro feeling was widespread in the North in the decades just before
the Civil War—and, as Messrs. Currier and Ives were profitably to
discover, just as rampant in the remaining decades of the century.
They issued hundreds of prints (listed in their catalogs as *The Darktown Series*) that crudely ridiculed the aspirations of American Negroes to a better life. In the same sense that bucolic scenes of cot-
tages in the woods were appealing and salable to the row-house and
tenement dweller, caricatures of Negroes comically failing to master even the rudiments of life in the white man's world were just the
right thing to adorn the workingmen's saloons and hiring halls—
symbolic icons of safe containment of this black threat to their
livelihoods."[54]

THE MINSTREL PERFORMANCE

The minstrel performance was the consummate fleshing out of the
black stereotype—the caricature made flesh and acted out upon the
public stage. It combined both the plantation tradition from the literature (along with what might be called its antitradition, the grotesque, comic doings of freed blacks) and the graphic impact of such
representational forms as dolls and lithographs. It created a frame
within which whites could look on at the doings of colored folks
and be amused by their foibles and reassured by their difference.
Their malapropisms, mispronunciations, and puns were the verbal
equivalents of the social mismatching that cast blacks as free and,
somehow, in our midst. Their incapacity in both these regards was
regularly, and ritually, celebrated in the most popular form of theater
in the nineteenth century: the minstrel performance.[55]

   In the performance, it was difference that was at center stage. Earlier I quoted Wittke's comments on the care performers took in making up their mouths. Robert C. Toll has observed that "like the
Cheshire Cat in the topsy-turvy world through the looking glass, the
minstrel show, long after it disappeared, left its central image—
the grinning black mask—lingering on, deeply embedded in [the]

American consciousness."[56] The grin, and the shining white teeth, were, like an art object, set in skin blackened and, as noted earlier, without natural highlights. The eyeballs by contrast seemed unnaturally white. All this was topped by a wig, ranging from the typical endman's three-pointed wig to the grotesque fright wigs.

Difference, too, was central to costuming and stage business. Toll has stressed that every "facet of minstrels' appearance emphasized the differences between blacks and whites":

> The early minstrels' visual impact only began with their bizarre black masks. They wore baggy, mismatched patchwork clothes and huge shoes, adding the stereotype of big feet to their facial stereotypes of Negroes. Once on stage, the Virginia Minstrels erupted into continual motion, contorting their bodies, cocking their heads, rolling their eyes, and twisting their legs. Even before the entertainment began, they could not sit still. When the music started, they exploded in a non-stop, rapid-fire flurry of frenetic motion, wild hollering, bursts of laughter, catchy songs, salty jokes, and stomping dances that did not stop until the curtain fell.[57]

Carl Wittke, the acknowledged dean of minstrel history, has described the change in what he calls "the plantation type" to "the Negro type" of minstrelsy:

> The genuine darky has been depicted as "the folk-figure of a simple, somewhat rustic character, instinctively humorous, irrationally credulous, gifted in song and dance, interesting in spontaneous frolic, endowed with artless philosophy." In the process of adapting this type to the theatre, the stage Negro became quite a different person from the model on which he was formed. More specifically, the plantation type which got into minstrelsy apparently was calculated to give the impression that all Negroes were lazy, shiftless fellows, careless of the morrow. The stage Negro loved watermelons and ate them in a peculiar way. He turned out to be an expert wielder of the razor, a weapon which he always had ready for use on such special social occasions as crap games, of which the stage Negro was passionately fond.
>
> In minstrelsy, the Negro type had all these characteristics and many more. He always was distinguished by an unusually large mouth and a peculiar kind of broad grin; he dressed in gaudy colors and in a flashy style; he usually consumed more gin than he could properly hold; and he loved chickens so well that he could not pass a chicken-coop without

falling into temptation. In minstrelsy, moreover, the Negro's alleged love for the grand manner led him to use words so long that he not only did not understand their meaning, but twisted the syllables in the most ludicrous fashion in his futile efforts to pronounce them. This, in the main, was the Negro of the joke-book tradition and more especially of the minstrel tradition, and undoubtedly he was a somewhat different individual from the one to be found in real life in the Southern states. But it was this type of darky that the white minstrels strove to imitate or, better stated perhaps, created and perpetuated.[58]

Wittke's description raises the question, how true was the minstrel type? From the perspective of the 1980s, the question can be easily dismissed, but earlier statements reveal how complicated this question is and touch on its implications for presumptions about the nature of the black self. Problems exist, for example, even in the description just cited, in Wittke's apparent acceptance of Francis Pendleton Gaines's characterization of the "genuine darky" from Gaines's *The Southern Plantation*. In addition, Wittke believed that the earlier minstrel productions more accurately depicted the Negro and that the minstrel performance was corrupted over time both by gigantism (the increase in the number of cast, props, and effects) and its absorption of other forms (in its attempts to compete with vaudeville and variety shows):

> Even the first part frequently was put on in Oriental splendor and with an ever-growing personnel, a far cry from the simple imitations of the early black face actors. . . . Caricaturing supplanted carefully studied plantation types. . . .
> There was little similarity between the performance of the last two decades of minstrelsy and those of the earlier period. From a simple, and fairly truthful imitation of Negro folkmusic and Negro folkways, as practiced by the pioneers of the burnt cork profession, minstrelsy had developed into a mixture of comic opera, burlesque, variety acts and buffoonery.[59]

However, from Wittke's own description, as in his recounting of the grotesque gyrations and raggedy costuming of pioneer Thomas Dartmouth ("Jim Crow") Rice, the earlier "realism" was very much in the eye of the beholder. But beholders were often, apparently, ready to credit the type, as in the report by a New York critic on the Negro impersonation by Rice in the summer of 1840: "Entering the theatre, we found it crammed from pit to dome, and the best representative of our American Negro that we ever saw was stretching every mouth in the house to its utmost tension. Such a natural gait!—such a laugh!—and such a twitching-up of the arm and shoulder! It was *the* Negro, par excellence. Long live James Crow, Esquire!"[60]

In Russel Crouse's nostalgic retrospective *It Seems Like Yesterday*, no question is raised about the realism in the representation. Rather, Crouse traces the type to its origins in the plantations of the South, where "they danced and sang, when their work was finished, with an abandon not comparable with any of the world's ideas of slavery." Regarding some of the form's verbal qualities, Crouse noted that the minstrel show was "the first form of entertainment to make use of the Negro's amusing gift for bad grammar and for mispronunciation."[61] Crouse's study is clearly superficial, but even so thoughtful a writer as Constance Rourke argued in *American Humor* that "the Negro minstrel was deeply grounded in reality, even though the impersonators were white, even though the figure was a myth."[62] The evidence suggests, too, that the burnt cork performers themselves did not believe they were misrepresenting a people. Frank Dumont, in his 1899 *The Witmark Amateur Minstrel Guide and Burnt Cork Encyclopedia*, observed that "minstrelsy is the one American form of amusement, purely our own, and it has lived and thrived even though the plantation darkey, who first gave it a character, has departed. The dandy negro has supplanted him, but the laughable blunders are still incorporated in the negro of the present time."[63] And Dailey Paskman and Sigmund Spaeth, in their *"Gentlemen, Be Seated!": A Parade of Old-Time Minstrels*, assume realism in the minstrels' comic use of language: "Malapropisms have always flourished in the minstrel show, particularly when imitating the speech of the negro, who loves big words and lots of them, and can mispronounce them and get their meanings tangled with grace, facility, and generally comic effect."[64]

It is clear from the reports and the commentary that the audiences who flocked to the minstrel shows in the nineteenth century did not go to see the unreal staged. It is unlikely there was much questioning of the reality of the representations when even sophisticated observers assumed their verisimilitude and when the representations set in motion upon the stage were so like other current representations, both from other graphic forms and from the world of plantation literature. But if the stage minstrel representation of blacks was so unrealistic, why was the form so popular? Various reasons have been considered: sheer entertainment and emotional release; the appeals to the common man, nostalgia, and curiosity; and the form's stress on the difference between whites and blacks.

The form apparently appealed to an uncomplicated love of sheer fun, an appeal which had earlier been responded to primarily by the circus (one of minstrelsy's forebears) and by the western tall tale (which often merged with the early minstrel patter, as when blackface minstrels assumed the persona of the western roarer). A predilection for the amusing, unleavened by the didactic and the moralistic, was no doubt encouraged by the needs of a growing urban population, somewhat removed from the folk and open to the stimulus of new entertainment forms. (The early presence in the minstrel performances of Irish elements, for example, reflects the Irish immigrations of the 1840s.) So there was a market for this new form. Wittke has described the popular entertainment then available:

> Minstrelsy was born in a decade when the fashionable American public had not yet become addicted to the theatre-going habit, and when the average American preferred to attend lectures on such subjects as mesmerism, animal magnetism, phrenology, and the new phenomenon of the electric telegraph. Religious revivals were flourishing, and the public was devoted to circuses, pantomimes, gorgeous displays of fireworks, and museums of natural wonders.[65]

Compared with these generally sedate forms of entertainment, the minstrel shows were a rousing form of emotional release with an emphasis on crowd pleasing. Toll has stressed these qualities:

> Unequivocally committed to pleasing the new common man audiences, the minstrel show was housed in its own show places which gave no hint of being "aristocratic opera houses"; it was performed by middling Americans, focused on humble, folk characters, and featured earthy, robust song, dance, and humor. Every part of the minstrel show, from its

format to its content, grew out of minstrels' attempts to please their audiences. "I've got only one method," explained J. H. Haverly, the greatest minstrel promoter, in a classic statement of the popular entertainer's creed, "and that is to find out what the people want and then to give them that thing. . . . There's no use trying to force the public into a theater." Minstrels certainly did not have to force anyone into their theaters. Their only problem in this regard was to accommodate everyone that wanted to see their exciting shows. . . .

Their performances seemed more a wild, uninhibited party than a professional show, which projected Negroes as impulsive and uncontrolled, even as it recaptured the feelings of the country hoedowns that many newly urban residents must have surely missed. Minstrels not only seemed to be having a great time, they also got their audience to join in the fun until the entire minstrel house shook with foot-stomping, hand-clapping, whistling, shouting, laughing, singing, dancing people.[66]

The minstrel show was at home in a Jacksonian world; and as a vehicle for emotional release, as well as in its encouragement of audience participation (patrons might sing along with the old, familiar songs or even yell out requests that some crowd-pleasing element be repeated), it responded to needs sometimes served by religious revivals.

The minstrel show's appeal to the common man, an appeal which was central to western humor, is stressed in Gary D. Engle's discussion of the form: "The tradition of minstrel burlesque . . . was not just an expression of anti-European sentiments. It was one manifestation of a deeper psychological dynamic inherent in a democratic society. When a person is not convinced of his own personal worth regardless of his social status, he tends to develop a desire to annihilate any person, role, institution, or tradition that can conceivably be thought of as superior. The entertainments which such a person turns to tend to be, like minstrelsy, those which consistently deflate the 'highbrow' and thus affirm the image of the common man." Engle stresses "the anarchical spirit of burlesque": "Fair game was anything associated with the formal American theater, which as an institution was a European cultural offspring. Melodrama, romance, opera, ballet, extravaganza, indeed any form which succeeded on the American stage quickly found a grotesque version of itself in minstrelsy."[67] Toll, in discussing some of the qualities of the form, suggests some of the ways in which it differed from more formal, elite forms: "It was not concerned with developing characterization, unraveling a plot, playing a complex, unified musical score, or building slowly to climactic moments."[68] More traditional theater forms often suffered in competition with the minstrels; not uncommon was the February 5, 1858 report in the *Evening Dispatch* of Augusta, Georgia that "a splendid company presenting *The School for Scandal* in that city had no audience 'in consequence of the Campbell Minstrels.'"[69]

The minstrel show's appeal to nostalgia has received little attention, but the propensity to make icons of the institutional forms of our past is ignored by those approaches which concentrate on the various listings of lacks—whether by Winthrop, Cooper, or James—which are cited to prove how nontraditional America is. In the form in which it evolved on the minstrel stage, the plantation tradition became an American tradition, and Stephen Foster's celebrations of loss became the migrants' and immigrants' touchstones. Further, the stability of the plantation relationships appealed to people caught up in change and in the shifting, materialistic, often anonymous embrace of the cities. The machine, identified by Leo Marx, was in the garden, but so also were treeless streets and crowded tenements, relationships based on cash and temporal advantage, the jostle of foreign accents and dark skins. The plantation tradition furnished a still point in our history, which all too often has been a history of our maladaptation to change.

We sometimes forget how much of the history of the first half of the nineteenth century was the history of sectional strife, brought on by the question of the extension of slavery. But despite the strife, many people had had little direct contact with blacks and fewer still with the peculiar institution. Northern curiosity regarding the lives of Negroes was, paradoxically, responded to by both the realism and naturalism of the slave narratives and the caricatures of the minstrel shows. "Negro impersonators" began to appear in circuses in the early nineteenth century. Wittke attributes the increasing popularity of George Washington Dixon during the summer of 1829 to "the growing interest of the public in Negro impersonations." He notes that "for a full decade before the first minstrel show was presented, individual actors blacked up and staged their specialities, either as single acts or during the intermission between acts of a regular play," and that "'Negro specialists' everywhere were much in demand."[70] At the same time, so were former slaves much in demand among the audiences who attended the abolitionists' lectures. The two figures—on the one hand, sober, "noble," dignified exslaves, recounting the hell of slavery, and, on the other, comic, cavorting buffoons, embracing the plantation tradition—could hardly have been more different, and in their unresolvable images might be viewed a forewarning of "the irresistible conflict."

As slavery evolved into segregation, to separate by law what had previously needed no separation, pictorial representation became caricature: to fix, to separate, to assert unequivocal difference. In a world of change; in a world where traditions and values were threatened; in a world of etiquette books, blue-backed spellers, and prescriptive grammars; in a world of neighbors not privy to your past, however rich that past may have been in its sense of place and its traditions of family; in a world where you are simply what you appear to be—in such a world, the art of the minstrels, of the caricaturists, created a stable, unthreatening, unambiguous image, none of that "now you see it, now you don't" sort of persona from the world of mulattoes. The mulatto was often unwelcome, even distrusted; his/her presence confounded the need for order, the need to place the other and, thus, one's self. This need probably accounts for the comment by mulatto actress Mabel Whitman in an article which appeared in the Baltimore *Afro-American* in December 1931: "As a matter of fact . . . you never have a real light colored star on the white stage. When we get too light . . . they won't really welcome you."[71]

The role of the minstrel show in asserting difference must be distinguished from its role in appealing to the common man, a distinction not always made. Engle's analysis, for example, tends to view the blackface minstrel as a symbol for the audience's class frustrations. The way in which the black persona becomes a vehicle for class analysis can be seen in Engle's shift from focusing on the black to focusing on what he represented for his audience, an audience buffeted by the perplexities of a mobile society:

> During the mid-nineteenth century the minstrel clown was America's favorite fool. The figure was a grotesque and cruel caricature of American blacks. He was intended by the white mentality that created him to serve as a comic representative of the racial minority which was forced to occupy the lowest class in American society. In the minstrel show the blackface clown played out his role as fool in two ways. First, he manifested the weaknesses which inhibit success in a socially mobile culture. He was lazy, ignorant, illiterate, hedonistic, vain, often immoral, fatalistic, and gauche. Secondly, the figure suffered in absurdly comic ways the indignities and embarrassments that can occur when a person's ambitions lead him into roles that he cannot adequately fulfill.[72]

Engle's discussion (as well as his comments quoted earlier on the burlesque functions of the minstrel stage) moves through the persona to the world of the audience's troubles; but stressing difference focuses on the persona while not denying other possible symbolic uses. It is significant that it was the black who assumed center stage in minstrel productions, not some other ethnic group such as the Irish, or some other category such as the greenhorn or country bumpkin. And on center stage the blackface minstrel's very blackness acted to defy the translucence of symbol; rather, it grounded judgment like a lightning rod, absorbed analysis like a scapegoat. It was, in itself, the answer; the questions would have to find another medium.[73]

Paul Lawrence Dunbar and the Plantation Tradition

The plantation tradition was both a boon and a curse to an aspiring writer like Paul Lawrence Dunbar. The young black writer need not invent a self or craft a form: the tradition provided all. But for Dunbar the tradition both tempted and limited. His dialect poems made him one of the most popular poets of the period, and yet he viewed his achievement with some ambivalence. James Weldon Johnson quotes Dunbar's reservations, expressed during a six-week visit to

Johnson's home in Jacksonville, Florida in 1901: "You know, of course, that I didn't start out as a dialect poet. I simply came to the conclusion that I could write it as well, if not better, than anybody else I knew of, and that by doing so I should gain a hearing. I gained the hearing, and now they don't want me to write any thing but dialect."[74] This ambivalence is expressed, too, in his reference in "The Poet" to a "jingle in a broken tongue."[75]

It is ironic that William Dean Howells's praise of Dunbar's dialect poems, which helped to launch his career, is also a major document in the literature of limitation. It is questionable whether Howells was at all aware how patronizing was his praise; and it is a testimony to the power of stereotypes when so cosmopolitan a critic can err so greatly. Alluding to earlier comments, Howells wrote:

> Yet it appeared to me then, and it appears to me now, that there is a precious difference of temperament between the races which it would be a great pity ever to lose, and that this is best preserved and most charmingly suggested by Mr. Dunbar in those pieces of his where he studies the moods and traits of his race in its own accent of our English. We call such pieces dialect pieces for want of some closer phrase, but they are really not dialect so much as delightful personal attempts and failures for the written and spoken language. In nothing is his essentially refined and delicate art so well shown as in these pieces, which, as I ventured to say, described the range between appetite and emotion, with certain lifts far beyond and above it, which is the range of the race. He reveals in these a finely ironical perception of the negro's limitations, with a tenderness for them which I think so very rare as to be almost quite new.[76]

Dunbar's dialect poetry has been strongly criticized by a number of recent critics. Jean Wagner, for example, writes that "Dunbar's dialect is at best a secondhand instrument irredeemably blemished by the degrading themes imposed upon it by the enemies of the black people."[77] But many black people, both in Dunbar's time and later, did not seem to feel degraded by Dunbar's work; rather, they committed it to memory, quoted it on social and public occasions, even named their public schools, and an occasional apartment house and bank, after this poet who, they felt, was one of their own. Were these readers simply deluded, victims of a false consciousness, gulled by reputation, regardless of potential political content? A careful reading of Dunbar's dialect poems supports the critics' charge that Dunbar exploited the conventions of plantation literature, but it also illustrates a countervailing politics that is often ignored.

Those who have criticized Dunbar have often faulted him for failing to be this or that other kind of poet. He was not a James M. Whitfield, whose "America," published in 1853, revealed the divisions underlying the "national" homilies:

America, it is to thee,
Thou boasted land of liberty,—
It is to thee I raise my song,
Thou land of blood, and crime, and wrong.
It is to thee, my native land,
From which has issued many a band
To tear the black man from his soil,
And force him here to delve and toil;
Chained on your blood-bemoistened sod,
Cringing beneath a tyrant's rod,
Stripped of those rights which Nature's God
    Bequeathed to all the human race,
Bound to a petty tyrant's nod,
Because he wears a paler face.[78]

Nor was he a Du Bois, penning his troubled "A Litany of Atlanta" on the train, returning to Atlanta after the riot of 1906.[79] But if Dunbar was neither a Whitman nor a Du Bois, he was a more complex poet than either, whose politics, except in such poems as "We Wear the Mask," has gone largely unremarked.

Dunbar's genius lay in his ability to master a multitude of forms/ styles: "He wrote in almost every prevailing style—the greatest black exploiter of English poetic techniques between Whitman and Cullen. Sonnet, madrigal, couplet, ballad, spiritual, pre-blues, songs (including use of musical notation in some instances)—Dunbar seems to have tried them all."[80] And within these forms sound a multitude of voices. Mark Twain had declared to the reader of *Huckleberry Finn* that the differences in the voices of his characters were not authorial errors but dialectical differences; in Dunbar's poems sound the dialects of plantation-era blacks, country whites, Scottish whites, Irish whites, as well as standard English whites.

With his mimic's ear he heard, as Whitman before him, the play of voices in the land, but, unlike Whitman, he did not attempt to infuse the voices but simply to record them. Dunbar assumes the voices, but he also assumes the personae and the conventions, both metrical and social.

It is the voicing of the social conventions that has drawn the greatest criticism.[81] The southern "redeemers" had set out to undo the reforms of the Reconstruction period (which lasted so pitifully short a time) and to restore the power of the former slaveholders; on the literary front, the postwar plantation literature was intended to recall the good old days of the plantation South and to erase the images of the slave narratives and abolition literature—Uncle Remus had replaced Uncle Tom. In this context, a poem such as Dunbar's "The Deserted Plantation" must be viewed as a part of plantation literature. It is a retrospective poem, the black narrator, a former slave, nostalgically recalling the good old days. In language that recalls the Currier & Ives print of the happy, fiddling, dancing slaves before their cabin, Dunbar writes, "Whah's de da'kies, dem dat used to be a dancin' / Evry night befo' de ole cabin do'? / Whah's de chillun, dem dat used to be a-prancin / Er a rollin' in de san' er on de flo'?" (67). The poem concludes with two of the most "loyal" stanzas in all of plantation literature:

> Dey have lef' de ole plantation to de swallers,
>   But it hol's in me a lover till de las';
> Fu' I fin' hyeah in de memory dat follers
>   All dat loved me an' dat I loved in de pas'.
>
> So I'll stay an' watch de deah ole place an' tend it
>   Ez I used to in de happy days gone by.
> 'Twell de othah Mastah thinks it's time to end it,
>   An' calls me to my qua'ters in de sky.

In Dunbar's defense it is not sufficient to say that the nostalgic mode was one that Dunbar cultivated and that the mode was very popular, as evidenced by many of the gift books published at the time. "Speakin' O Christmas," for example, nostalgically recalls the Christmases of time past; but plantation days and Christmases past

are not comparable. And other poems exploit other plantation stereotypes. "The Delinquent" portrays a trifling black man, coming
home at dawn after drinking all night. "A Coquette Conquered" de-
means black love in its depiction of a black girl whose resistance
melts away at the prospect of getting a possum. (The effect of this
poem is magnified by the fact that it is followed by "Nora: A Sere-
nade," a poem in standard English which is an idealized appeal to an
idealized white woman.) "Accountability" places the speaker in one
role dear to the hearts of the slave masters: the chicken thief.

The stereotypes can be found, too, in *Lyrics of the Hearthside*
(1899). In "The News" an old, blind slave is bereft at news of the
death of his old master on the battlefield; he was too weak to go
with him when he went off to war but will follow him in death:
"'P'omised yo' pappy I'd allus tek keer / Ov you,—yes, mastuh,—I's
follerin',—hyeah'" (137). In "Chrismus on the Plantation" the freedmen rally around their kind old former master, who can't afford to
pay them and must give up the old homestead:

> Er in othah wo'ds, you wants us to fu'git dat you's
>   been kin',
> An ez soon ez you is he'pless, wes to leave you
>   hyeah behin'.
> Well, ef dat's de way dis freedom ac's on people,
>   white er black,
> You kin jes' tell Mistah Lincum fo' to tek his
>   freedom back. (138)

"A Back-log Song" (143) includes a smiling master; and in "A Cabin
Tale: The Younger Master Asks for a Story" the old storytelling is
accompanied by lessons on manners for those born to rule: "'Set up
nice now. Goodness lan's! / Hol' yo'se'f up lak yo' pa. / Bet nobidy
evah saw / Him scrunched down lak you was den— / Hightone boys
meks hightone men'" (154).[82]

Such poems, as various critics suggest, tend to legitimize the master-slave relationship by their silence regarding its complexity and
its violence. But these poems do not reflect the full range of the
response to slavery in Dunbar's dialect poems. "Parted" (145) is a

poem in black dialect whose speaker has been sold down the river, parted from his love, whom he hopes will be faithful. It is certainly true, of course, that "Parted" is a muted protest and is all but lost among the poems in black dialect that either legitimize the master-slave relationship or simply portray the day-to-day life of the slave or freed black. A poem in black dialect from *Lyrics of Sunshine and Shadow* (1905), "The Old Cabin" (260–261), speaks quite realistically of the evils of slavery but at the same time reflects a characteristic tendency for Dunbar's poetry to turn to "somep'n joyful":

> In de dead of night I sometimes,
>   Git to t'inkin of de pas'
> An' de days w'en slavery helt me
>   In my mis'ry—ha'd an fas'.
> Dough de time was mighty tryin',
>   In dese houahs somehow hit seem
> Dat a brightah light come slippin'
>   Thoo de kivahs of my dream.
> An' my min' fu'gits de whuppins
>   Drops de feah o block an' lash
> An' flies straight to somep'n joyful
>   In a secon's lightnin' flash.

Two of his poems written in black dialect recognize the black soldier's role in the Union army. In "Whistling Sam" Sam enlists: "At de call fu' col'ed soldiers, Sam enlisted 'mong de res' / Wid de blue o' Gawd's great ahmy wropped about his swellin' breas', / An' he laffed an' whistled loudah in his youfful joy an' glee / Dat de govament would let him he'p to make his people free" (157). Dunbar recognizes that their souls were already free: "An' de da'kies all was happy; souls an' bodies bofe was freed. / Why, hit seemed lak de Redeemah mus' 'a' been on earf indeed" (157). The speaker in "When Dey 'Listed Colored Soldiers" recalls the sentiments of her man, 'Lias: "Oh, I hugged him, an' I kissed him, an' I baiged him not to go; / But he tol' me dat his conscience, hit was callin' to him so, / An' he couldn't baih to lingah w'en he had a chanst to fight / For de freedom dey had gin him an' de glory of de right" (183). 'Lias is killed: "Den dey tol' me dey had laid him some'r's way down souf to res', / Wid de flag dat he had fit for shinin' daih acrost his breas' " (183).

These last two poems help to illustrate differences between Dunbar's poems in black dialect and those in standard English. He has been criticized for seeming to "reserve the 'serious' subjects for standard English."[83] But this criticism is only partly accurate and must be considered in the context of the conventions for dialect poetry. But it also ignores the specific worlds the poems create. Dunbar's poems in black dialect are rarely abstract. The concepts in the line "For de freedom dey had gin him an' de glory of de right" are exceptional. More typical is the concrete representation, from the same poem, of a rather subtle epistemological awareness: "Bofe my mastuhs went in gray suits, an' I loved de Yankee blue, / But I'tought dat I could sorrer for de losin' of 'em too; / But I couldn't, for I didn't know de ha'f o' whut I saw, / 'Twell dey 'listed colo'ed sojers an' my 'Lias went to wah" (183). Rather than "reserve the 'serious' subjects for standard English," Dunbar is attempting to be true to the voices for which he is acting as a medium, and the voices, including those that speak in various white dialects, express themselves concretely. This concreteness is often lacking in his poems in standard English. In his love poems, for example, those featuring black characters and speakers reflect a concrete world of the cabins and plantations, with their animals and implements, sounds and smells. Those in standard English tend to depict abstractions (personified Love, for example) or idealized relations or idealized women. His black characters "walk on the ground," not on some thin, idealized air. They speak in earthy, simple language that reflects their day-to-day experience; characters in the poems in standard English rarely speak—they are spoken of. This comparison also draws attention to an important quality of the dialect poems: neglected in the criticism is the political importance of Dunbar's many portrayals of simple black humanity, engaged in the common, day-to-day tasks and emotions in which all mankind engage, portrayals that reflect an implicit politics at a time when the prevailing images stressed the black-as-child or black-as-beast/animal.[84]

Du Bois wrote in *Dusk of Dawn* that he was familiar with Dunbar's work but that, until they met, had not realized he was a black man;[85] Dunbar later complained of having to play the part of a "black white man." It would seem that what Dunbar objected to was not black dialect but the critical tendency to limit his expression to black dialect, just as he would have objected to any limitation on his choice of forms.[86]

Dunbar was a mask wearer throughout his brief career. Artistically, he assumed the voices of his various models, even when they encouraged his tendency to exploit the most sentimental of magazine conventions. He set out, for example, industriously to "dismantle" James Whitcomb Riley's poetic "devices,"[87] and in his poem "James Whitcomb Riley" (287) he praises the poet because "he sings the simple songs that come / The closest to your heart." It is in this context, perhaps, that the often-cited lines from "The Poet"—"But ah, the world, it turned to praise / A jingle in a broken tongue" (191)—can best be understood.

The Black Self's Support
through Family, Religion, Spirituals

What I have been discussing are the influences that have been brought to bear upon the black self. In view of the complex psychological warfare waged against the self—by plantation literature, by graphic forms of representation, by the minstrel stage, as well as by the day-to-day pressures of survival and getting a living in the pre— and post–Civil War periods—it would not be unreasonable to argue for a dispersed, weakened, almost nonexistent self. Further, such a damaged self could hardly be expected to craft undamaged institutions; thus, a damaged black family would seem to be a natural product of such presumed damaged selves.

A number of observers have developed arguments based on these assumptions. Stanley Elkins, for example, has developed his "Sambo thesis," arguing from analogies with data on victimization from the concentration camp literature that the self under slavery was infantilized, that the power of the masters developed attitudes of dependency, and that blacks looked to masters for models of conduct.[88] For E. Franklin Frazier, too, imitation was central, since he believed there was little survival of cultural traits in America, and since he did not credit the growth or persistence of adaptive institutional structures in the face of the disorganizing pressures of slavery: "The pattern of behavior and ideals which he took over from the white man were acquired through formal imitation of people outside his social world. In their social isolation the majority of [plantation] Negroes were forced to draw upon the meager social heritage which they had acquired during slavery." In the absence of slavery and the master "things fall apart":

> What authority was there to take the place of the master's in regulating sex relations and maintaining the permanency of marital ties? Where could the Negro father look for sanctions of his authority in family relations which had scarcely existed in the past?. . . When the yoke of slavery was lifted the drifting masses were left without any restraint upon their vagrant impulses and wild desires. The old intimacy between master and slave, upon which the moral order of the slave regime had rested, was destroyed forever.[89]

And, more recently, Daniel Patrick Moynihan has described a "tangle of pathology" at the heart of Negro society, brought on by the weakening of the family structure during slavery.[90]

The social theorists cited above may have been influenced by black writers who have stressed the impact of the environment on the individual; Richard Wright, for example, has written about the time when he realized he was powerless, when he realized that there were men who "could violate my life at will."[91] In *Black Boy* and other works Wright has told us much about the workings of power in black-white relations, but it would be a mistake to view Wright's world as a mirror of the whole of black existence. *Black Boy*, for example, is not simply a remembrance of things past but a recrafting of a past, which is not to argue that the recrafting is not "true" in many important ways. The stress on aloneness, terror, hunger, and power is a response, though heightened, to his existential reality but also a response to his later awareness that "words could be weapons" and to the influence of the "Chicago school of sociology," which, in the writings of Robert Park, Ernest W. Burgess, and Louis Wirth (and through anthropologist Robert Redfield) stressed the impact of the environment upon the person. It was his stress on the limited, victimized self, a prey to the hostile world, not simply the promptings of parricide, that evoked the criticism of James Baldwin and Ralph Ellison.[92]

In view, then, of the history of pressures—psychological and physical—upon the black self, as well as the portrayal of the pressures of the environment upon the self in the writings of such black writers as Wright, Ann Petry, Chester Himes, and others, the view of the person and his institutions in the writings of Elkins, Frazier, and Moynihan might seem eminently unexceptionable. However, too much slips through their nets of assumptions. The black self has evidenced an amazing resilience under extreme conditions, a performance that overshadows those momentary acts of heroism typically commended by our histories. Simple survival has daily required so much more than the Sambo thesis would credit, and again and again the historical accounts permit us to glimpse here a man, there a woman in their moments of luminous transcendence, as in these accounts of escapees cited by Leon Litwack:

> No less persistent was a Maryland servant who tried to join others in a mass escape despite the fact that his hands and feet had been amputated some years before because of severe frostbite. "Well, I got him back and had him tied up," the owner told a visiting Englishman, "for I thought he must be mad. But it was no use, he got away again, and walked to Washington." How, asked the curious visitor, could he have managed such a remarkable deed? . . . "Oh, he just stumped along. He was always a right smart nigger, and he could do many things after he lost his limbs."

.   .   .   .

> Near Vicksburg, where slaves had been deserting in substantial numbers, a planter went out to the quarters and asked the "patriarch" among his slaves, "Uncle Si, I don't suppose you are going off to those hateful Yankees, too, are you?" "O no, marster," he replied, "I'se gwine to stay right here with you." When the planter visited the quarters the next morning, he found that every one of his slaves had left that night, including Uncle Si and his wife. Searching the nearby woods for them, he came across Uncle Si, bending over the prostrate body of his wife, weeping. The planter wondered why he had subjected her to such a difficult

and now fatal journey. "I couldn't help it, marster," the old man replied; "but then, you see, she died free."[93]

These and countless others—many of whom were engaged in the unspectacular heroism of daily survival, both before and after "freedom"—argue against a too reductive, a too damaged view of the black self. Jaqueline Jones, considering the role of the commonplace in the lives of the post–Civil War slaves, argues for what we might term a politics of the ordinary: "For the outcast group, the preservation of family integrity served as a political statement to the white South. To nurse a child, send a daughter to school, feed a hungry family after a long day at work in the fields, or patch a shirt by the light of a flickering fire—these simple acts of domesticity acquired special significance when performed for a people so beleaguered by human as well as natural forces."[94] Observing these simple acts, and many others, Jones and other recent historians such as Eugene D. Genovese, Herbert G. Gutman, Lawrence W. Levine, and Leon F. Litwack have provided considerable evidence for a richer, more complex view of the black self. Their findings will help us to understand the role of such institutions as the family and religion and such expressive forms as the spirituals in the crafting of black self-images, self-images much at variance with those crafted for blacks by whites.

FAMILY

"It is difficult to get a clear picture of the family relations of slaves, between the Southern apologist and his picture of cabin life, with idyllic devotion and careless toil, and that of the abolitionist with his tale of family disruption and cruelty, adultery, and illegitimate mulattoes."[95] Du Bois's perception of the problem in 1909 will hold true for many years thereafter. The one-dimensionality in the portrayals was a product of the propagandistic intent, but the effects continued long after the abolition of slavery. It was in the interests of the southern apologists, of course, to picture slavery as a happy state. But the post–Civil War "friends of the Negro," with their theories of "uplift" and the work ethic, also distorted reality. It was they, for example, who both neglected and denied the existence of secular folk songs; they collected, rather, the spirituals, which corresponded to their own views on the seriousness and decorum of slaves and ex-slaves. It was the northern missionary schoolteachers at such institutions as Hampton and Tuskegee who worked to suppress manifestations of the sensual and to inculcate sobriety and Puritan work habits. And it will be the attempt to respond to that dry white eye looking on that will influence the conduct of countless members of the black middle class; that will help to explain the social theorists of the diminished self; and that will account in part for the emphases described earlier in Wright and other writers, as well as for some of the rhetoric of victimization from the civil rights movement.

Jacqueline Jones has written:

> In their devotion to family ties—a devotion that encompassed kin and ultimately the whole slave community—black women and men affirmed the value of group survival over the slaveholders' base financial and political considerations. Slave family life, as the cornerstone of Afro-American culture, combined an African heritage with American exigencies, and within the network of kin relations black women and men sought to express their respect for each other even as they resisted the intrusiveness of whites. Thus when it emerged from bondage, the black family had a highly developed sense of itself as an institution protective of the community at large.[96]

Jones and a number of other contemporary historians have considered the black family from the point of view of blacks. While this might seem a natural perspective, Gutman has criticized a broad range of historians for their preoccupation with "what enslavement did to Afro-Americans": "Too much attention is given in their works to slave 'treatment'; too little attention to slave culture and to the development of distinctive slave feelings, beliefs, and especially institutions."[97] A number of historians have also criticized the bias introduced into the study of the black family by viewing it, implicitly or explicitly, from the perspective of the white middle-class family; this bias makes one insensitive, for example, to the role of kin, and "fictive" kin, networks. Those historians criticizing

the views of Frazier, Elkins, and Moynihan argue that, despite oppression, blacks were often able to develop families that served the
important needs of their members and that these families were not
dependent on white models.

The importance attributed to the black family by its members is
repeatedly stressed in the historical record. There are perhaps no
more moving historical accounts than those describing the attempts
by family members to locate each other at the end of the Civil War:

> Each reunion had its own incredible story, revealing the extraordinary
> resourcefulness with which husbands and wives, parents and children,
> brothers and sisters sought each other out in the immediate aftermath of
> Union occupation and emancipation. Family members embarked on
> these searches, a much-impressed Freedmen's Bureau officer reported,
> "with an ardor and faithfulness sufficient to vindicate the fidelity and
> affection of any race—the excited joys of the regathering being equalled
> only by the previous sorrows and pains of separation." . . . "They had a
> passion, not so much for wandering, as for getting together," a Freed-
> men's Bureau agent in South Carolina wrote of the postwar migrations
> of blacks; "and every mother's son among them seemed to be in search
> of his mother; every mother in search of her children. In their eyes the
> work of emancipation was incomplete until the families which had been
> dispersed by slavery were reunited." In North Carolina, a northern jour-
> nalist encountered a middle-aged freedman—"plodding along, staff in
> hand, and apparently very footsore and tired"—who had already walked
> nearly six hundred miles in his determination to reach the wife and
> children he had been sold away from four years before.

The search for missing relatives would continue long after emancipation: "Until well into the 1870s and the 1880s, the newly established black newspapers, both in the South and in the North,
abounded with advertisements in which relatives requested any information that might assist them."[98]

The unions which could generate such loyalty and emotion have
been intensively scrutinized. The issues involved in historically re-
constructing the postwar black family are many, complex, and subtle; but a paragraph from Gutman's important study, *The Black
Family in Slavery and Freedom 1750–1925*, helps to clarify the interrelations. Gutman is commenting on data from the Virginia

Freedmen's Bureau regarding the registration of slave marriages in three Virginia counties in 1866. The data reveal not only the prevalence of double-headed households but also long-lasting unions. Gutman stresses the implications for much conventional theory:

> Most of the registrants, moreover, were unskilled laborers and farm hands, not servants and artisans, a fact that contradicts the assertion that double-headed households had existed mostly among "elite" slaves. Much that flaws the study of slaves and ex-slaves flows from this belief: the alleged inadequacy of the slave father and husband, the absence of male "models" for young slave children to emulate, the prevalence of the "Sambo" personality, the insistence that slave marriage usually meant little more than successive polygyny, and the belief that the "matrifocal" household (a "natural" adaptation by most blacks to the "realities" of slavery) prevailed among the mass of illiterate plantation field hands and laborers. These misconceptions accompany another erroneous belief: that when slaves did honor the two-parent household they did so either as a result of the encouragement offered to "favored" slaves by owners or because daily contact between whites and slave servants and artisans (as contrasted to slaves living in the "quarters") permitted these few slaves to "imitate" marriage "models" common among owners and other whites. Implicit in such arguments, none of which rests on significant evidence, is the assumption that such "models" were infrequent among the slaves themselves, an assumption that has encouraged simplified and misleading descriptions of slave socialization and slave culture.

Gutman finds evidence of long marriages in "all slave social settings in the decades preceding the Civil War."[99]

In addition to the prevalence of the double-headed household, extended kin networks furnished an institutional form largely ignored by many critics, but one which has persisted and performed important roles into the present. Gutman has observed that kin networks "broke out of the boundaries fixed by ownership and thereby connected men, women, and children of similar and different slave generations who belonged to different owners":

> Exogamy, by ramifying kin networks throughout a region, served as an extremely effective cultural agency for the diffusion and exchange of slave social beliefs that had no direct connection to marital taboos. Gift-

transfer together with short-distance sale, paradoxically, fed this socially expansive thrust. A slave sold or hired to a planter or farmer nearby, given as a gift to an owner's son or daughter, or allowed to marry a mate belonging to a different owner retained kin ties to a family of origin and to the kin groups associated with it. But the same slave could also form new kin ties that supplemented the older ones. Gift-transfer and especially sale had harsh economic origins and cut slaves and their families painfully, but enlarged slave-kin networks spread over physical space, and enlarged slave communities took shape over the entire South. Communication networks were built upon these enlarged kin networks and undercut the dependence of slaves upon those who owned them.[100]

The institutional forms—long-lasting, double-headed unions and kinship networks—fostered important qualities of respect, loyalty, imitation, and affection. Slaves were not socialized simply by overseers and masters; there was no cultural vacuum, forcing them to look to the "big house" for their models: "Most Good Hope [a South Carolina plantation] marriages lasted for many years, and parents and children in these settled immediate families also increasingly became a part of expanding kin networks. . . . Slave children born in the 1840s or the 1850s grew up in a slave community made up of interrelated but well-defined immediate families. Such ties rooted them in a shared Afro-American past and helped define the identity of particular men, women, and children, allowing slave children to absorb values from parents, grandparents, other adult kin, and adult non-kin."[101]

Intergenerational families, kin and nonkin networks, and the size and complexity of the plantations furnished models for the growing slaves. Jones has studied the division of labor within households. Women often had to work in the fields and assume "primary responsibility for children and for operations involved in daily household maintenance—cooking, cleaning, tending fires, sewing and patching clothes. Wives and mothers completed these tasks either very early in the morning, before the start of the 'regular' work day on the plantation, or at night, after other family members had gone to sleep."[102] Jones has pointed out that slave fathers would try to keep their wives out of the fields, a form of authority more easily exercised after emancipation, when it would often be viewed by whites as "putting on airs."[103] Because the slave father was owned and could not himself be a possessor of property, his authority within the family could not rest on his economic superiority, which encouraged a kind of equality between husband and wife within a structure of differential responsibility:[104]

> Fathers shared the obligations of family life with their wives. In denying slaves the right to own property, make a living for themselves, participate in public life, or protect their children, the institution of bondage deprived black men of access to the patriarchy in the larger economic and political sense. But at home, men and women worked together to support the father's role as provider and protector. In the evenings and on Sundays, men collected firewood; made shoes; wove baskets; constructed beds, tables, chairs, and animal traps; and carved butter paddles and ax handles. Other family members appreciated a father's skills; recalled Molly Ammonds, "My pappy made all de furniture dat went in our house an' it were might' good furniture too," and Pauline Johnson echoed, "De furn'chure was ho-mek, but my dady mek it good an' stout." Husbands provided necessary supplements to the family diet by hunting and trapping quails, possums, turkeys, rabbits, squirrels, and raccoons, and by fishing. They often assumed responsibility for cultivating the tiny household garden plots allotted to families by the master. Some craftsmen, like Bill Austin's father, received goods or small sums of money in return for their work on nearby estates; Jack Austin, "regarded as a fairly good carpenter, mason, and bricklayer," was paid in "hams, bits of cornmeal, cloth for dresses for his wife and children, and other small gifts; these he either used for his small family or bartered with other slaves."[105]

Genovese, whose approach has tended to view plantation slavery as a "paternalistic" system, has argued that the owners were placed in the contradictory position of encouraging strong male models:

> This division of labor and the strengthened male role within it, which so many planters encouraged, helped shape the kind of men who might prove more independent than slaves were supposed to be. The slaveholders, therefore, here as elsewhere, had to live with a contradiction: dispirited slave men could not keep the good order necessary for efficiency and, besides, might become troublesome in their very irresponsibility; spirited slaves with a sense of being men would help keep good order

and render the plantation more efficient, but they too, in different ways, might become troublesome in their very responsibility.[106]

It is impossible to do justice to so complex and important an institution as the black family in this brief discussion. Many areas of activity—such as the force of the family bond in deterring runaways; the importance of elders; and the insistence on sharecropping by blacks in the post–Civil War period as an expression of family strength—must be ignored. My focus, too, has necessarily been limited to slavery and to the postslavery period. However, Gutman's study extends the discussion back into the eighteenth century, and both Gutman and Jones extend their analyses into the twentieth century. A brief note on their findings will permit us to appreciate the persistence of a stable black family throughout the period covered here. Jones, comparing census data from the Cotton Belt for 1880 and 1900, found that "the 'typical' Afro-American household retained certain structural characteristics throughout this twenty-year period. At the core of this household were both a husband and wife (89.6 percent of all households in the 1880 sample, and 87.8 percent in 1900, were headed by a man; 86.4 percent and 82.5 percent, respectively, included both spouses). The typical household remained nuclear, although extended families (that is, those that included blood relations) increased in importance over time (from 13.6 percent in 1880 to 23 percent in 1900). The average household had between four and five members. Significantly, a crude index of local kinship networks suggests that at least one-third of all families lived near some of their relatives."[107] Gutman studied (with Laurence A. Glasco) the New York State manuscript census schedules for 1855, 1875, 1905, and 1925 and, later, 13,924 New York City black households for 1905 and 1925, years which include the great migration into Harlem. In both cities lower-class households, generally considered to most clearly reflect the "weakness in the Negro family," were studied. In Buffalo, the "double-headed kin-related household always was the characteristic Buffalo Afro-American household, ranging from 82 to 92 percent of all households. The double-headed household did not decline in importance over time." Among the important findings for New York City in 1925: "85 percent of New

York City kin-related black households were double-headed. Thirty-two of these 13,934 were father-absent households and subfamilies headed by women under thirty. . . . Between 7 and 8 percent of females aged twenty-five to forty-four headed male-absent households and subfamilies. Twenty years earlier, the percentage had been higher (10 percent)."[108]

RELIGION AND THE SPIRITUALS

It is difficult to discuss religion and the spirituals separately, just as it is not always easy to separate sermon from song at a black service. Both sermon and song well up to express the spiritual geographies of black lives. The spirituals are the "good news" of God's grace, the "sorrow songs" of man's estate. They share with religion generally and with the black family important psychological roles. They provide a space, symbolic or actual, that is not the white man's space; they create areas which blacks can control; and they furnish alternatives to white evaluations, permitting one to consider a different self and a different fate. Thomas Wentworth Higginson, who had commanded a black regiment during the war, commented later that "we abolitionists had underrated the suffering produced by slavery among the negroes, but had overrated the demoralization. Or rather, we did not know how the religious temperament of the negroes had checked the demoralization."[109]

Communal prayer meetings and services have been at the center of the black religious experience. Genovese has described the pride, self-respect, and "astonishing confidence in their own spiritual quality" expressed in the prayer meetings and has pointed out that "the meetings provided a sense of autonomy—of constituting not merely a community unto themselves but a community with leaders of their own choice."[110] Jones has stressed the solace and support found at the services:

The impulse for mutual solace and support among rural Afro-Americans culminated in their religious institutions and worship services. At monthly meetings women and men met to reaffirm their unique spiritual heritage, to seek comfort, and to comfort one another.

Black women found a "psychological center" in religious belief, and the church provided strength for those overcome by the day-to-day business of living. For many weary sharecroppers' wives and mothers, worship services allowed for physical and spiritual release and offered a means of transcending earthly cares in the company of one's friends and family. Faith created "a private world inside the self, sustained by religious sentiment and religious symbolism . . . fashioned to contain the world without."[111]

The continuance of the service's role in black lives is suggested by Maya Angelou's description:

> Down to the right, Mr. and Mrs. Stewart, who only a few hours earlier had crumbled in our front yard, defeated by the cotton rows, now sat on the edges of their rickety-rackety chairs. Their faces shone with the delight of their souls. The mean whitefolks was going to get their comeuppance. Wasn't that what the minister said, and wasn't he quoting from the words of God Himself? They had been refreshed with the hope of revenge and the promise of justice. . . .
>
> America's historic bowers and scrapers shifted easily and happily in the makeshift church. . . .
>
> The congregation lowed with satisfaction. Even if they were society's pariahs, they were going to be angels in a marble white heaven and sit on the right hand of Jesus, the son of God. The Lord loved the poor and hates those cast high in the world. Hadn't He Himself said it would be easier for a camel to go through the eye of a needle than for a rich man to enter heaven?[112]

The spirituals have had a significance probably greater even than the sermons in the religious lives of blacks. This is probably in part due to the informality of the authority of the early religious leader; he was often simply "one of us," given leadership often by circumstance. In any case, his role was often shared with others who felt compelled to testify. Speaking out, testifying, shouting were the logical acts of people who felt they needed no intermediary to speak to God, who was an immediate, felt presence. As one northern missionary reported: "They believe simply in the love of Christ, and they speak of Him and talk to Him with a familiarity that is absolutely startling. They pray as though they thought Christ himself was standing in the very room."[113] This attitude was expressed, too, in their worship. A black woman defended the black form of worship to some northern white visitors shortly after the war: "I goes ter some churches, an' I sees all de folks settin' quiet an' still, like dey dunno what de Holy Sperit am. But I fin's in my Bible, that when a man or a 'ooman gets full ob de Holy Sperit, ef dey shold hol' dar peace, de stones would cry out; an' ef de power ob God can make de stones cry out, how can it help makin' us poor creeturs cry out, who feels ter praise Him fer His mercy."[114]

The spirituals differed from the sermons, too, in that they belonged to the mass; in fact, they could be viewed as simply sermons in song. And as the possession of the mass, they were wherever the mass was; they were not contained within the prayer meeting but could act to shape, to reshape, the slaves' world in both field and cabin. Lawrence W. Levine has noted that "neither the slaves nor their African forebears ever drew modernity's clear line between the sacred and the secular. The uses to which spirituals were put are an unmistakable indication of this. They were not sung solely or even primarily in churches or praise houses but were used as rowing songs, field songs, work songs, and social songs."[115]

I have described the spirituals with the seemingly contradictory phrases "good news" and "sorrow songs." Just as the spirituals were sung in prayer meeting, field, and cabin, they furnished frames for the range of black emotions. Levine has observed that the spirituals have been "referred to as 'sorrow songs,' and in some respects they were," but that "these feelings were rarely pervasive or permanent; almost always they were overshadowed by a triumphant note of affirmation":

> For all their inevitable sadness, slave songs were characterized more by a feeling of confidence than of despair. There was confidence that contemporary power relationships were not immutable: "Did not old Pharaoh get lost, get lost, get lost, . . . get lost in the Red Sea?"; confidence in the possibility of instantaneous change: "Jesus make de dumn to speak. . . . Jesus make de cripple walk. . . . Jesus give de blind his sight. . . . Jesus do most anything"; confidence in the rewards of persistence: "Keep a' inching along like a poor inchworm, / Jesus will come by'nd bye"; confidence that nothing could stand in the way of the justice they would receive: "You kin hender me here, but you can't do it

dah," "O no man, no man, no man can hinder me"; confidence in the prospects of the future: "We'll walk de golden streets / Of de New Jerusalem." Religion, the slave sang, "is good for anything, . . . Religion make you happy, . . . Religion gib me patience, . . . O member, get Religion, . . . Religion is so sweet."[116]

Levine has described a number of themes which recur in the spirituals. "The most persistent single image the slave songs contain is that of the chosen people"; the songs affirmed personal worth in a world where economics defined a person's value. A recurring theme is that of the intimate or personal God, one more like that of the African past than that of the white Protestant present. Another theme Levine examines is the certainty of ultimate justice, of revenge, of retribution, of the "tables turned." Finally, there is the theme of change, of new beginnings, of the possibility of choice, with the attendant attitude of confidence.[117] The spirituals performed at least two important functions in the lives of blacks, functions shared with the family and with other elements of the expressive folk culture, such as secular songs, moralizing tales, and animal tales: they affirmed the community and denied aloneness, and they created a space between blacks and whites:

> The spirituals . . . placed the individual in continual dialogue with his community, allowing him at one and the same time to preserve his voice as a distinct entity and to blend it with those of his fellows. Here again slave music confronts us with evidence which indicates that, however seriously the slave system may have diminished the central communality that had bound African societies together, it was never able to destroy it totally or to leave the individual atomized and psychically defenseless before his white masters. . . .
>
> Slave music, slave religion, slave folk beliefs—the entire sacred world of the black slaves—created the necessary space between the slaves and their owners and were the means of preventing legal slavery from becoming spiritual slavery.[118]

CONCLUSION

The family, religion, and the spirituals served to counter the image of the black created by plantation literature, the graphic forms of representation, and the minstrel stage. At the same time, economic needs, the traditional communal orientation, and extended kin and nonkin networks helped to foster attitudes that Jones has referred to as "corporatism" and "mutuality":

> Within black families and communities . . . public-private, male-female distinctions were less tightly drawn than among middle-class whites. Together, black women and men participated in a rural folk culture based upon group cooperation rather than male competition and the accumulation of goods. . . .
>
> Even rural communities that lacked the almost total isolation of the Sea Islands possessed a strong commitment to corporatism and a concomitant scorn for the hoarding of private possessions. As government researcher J. Bradford Laws wrote disapprovingly of the sugar workers he studied in 1902, "They have an unfortunate notion of generosity, which enables the more worthless to borrow fuel, food, and what not on all hands from the more thrifty." It is clear that these patterns of behavior were determined as much by economic necessity as by cultural "choice." If black household members pooled their energies to make a good crop, and if communities collectively provided for their own welfare, then poverty and oppression ruled out most of the alternative strategies. Individualism was a luxury that sharecroppers simply could not afford.[119]

Too many blacks, according to Freedmen's Bureau agent John De Forest, "felt obliged to look after a 'horde of lazy relatives' and neighbors, thus losing a precious opportunity to get ahead on their own."[120]

De Forest's views reflect the white individualistic ethic of the nineteenth century, but they sublimely ignore the black reality. Blacks have drawn their strength from the community; whites have been emboldened by the mythic promise of success, individually achieved. The two views, rooted in their different histories, also imply different views of the self. The white may cherish "rugged individualism"; the black more closely approaches the view attributed to the African villager by Huggins that I quoted earlier—the "concept of individual freedom was the fantasy of a lunatic."

But writing, as distinct from preaching or other forms of oratory, is an individualistic activity; writing gets done in some form of Hawthorne's "dismal chamber," not through communal call and response. In some respects, the division in Dunbar between dialect poetry (with which he entertained large audiences from the public stage) and poetry in standard English symbolizes the movement from the folk to the elite. For the black writer, in view of the history of forced illiteracy, the poem in standard English, the short story, the novel can be said to be expressions of the literate elite, whereas folklore is the expression of the mass. To become a writer becomes, in a sense, a way of leaving the black mass; as, in Nigeria, to go to school in England, to be schooled to work within the imperial bureaucracy, was to be alienated from the tribe. And in a similar fashion, to be a mulatto, or a member of the black bourgeoisie, is often to leave the black mass.

But the black masses, the historical source of strength, have exerted an almost irresistible pull on the black psyche, so that he/she who would leave them—either through class mobility or passing—often suffers from terrible ambivalence. But even in the absence of ambivalence, the evaluations of whites—their attitudes toward color, for example—will profoundly affect characters and their authors. The result of the contradictory pressures from the two cultures, from the impulses toward acceptance and denial, and from the ambivalence on the part of the characters is the literature which I described earlier as "a literature of dissimulation, of masking, of self-hatred, of racial ambivalence, and even, for some writers, a literature of disappearance."

In Dunbar's frustration we can see the difficulties faced by black writers who would oppose conventional expectations regarding their voice and subject matter. As cosmopolitan a figure as William Dean Howells, who could be so sensitive to the qualities of foreign writers, will enunciate the black writer's limitations. Charles Chesnutt will attempt to alter whites' perceptions of mulattoes, to argue—in the face of a century's insistence on difference—that mulattoes are "just like white folks," but his argument will have little effect. The publication of his last novel will follow shortly after his 1903 observation, quoted above, to the effect that the Negro's rights were at their lowest ebb in thirty-five years; and then, silence. James Weldon Johnson will reflect Du Bois's view of the "talented tenth" in the responses of his protagonist, who will ultimately choose to "pass" for white, a gain which he will view as a probable loss in the closing pages. Thurman will be the first to satirize the valuing of lighter skin, a theme subsequently treated in such works as *The Black Bourgeoisie, Maud Martha,* and *The Bluest Eye.* In *Quicksand* and *Passing,* Larsen will create case studies in ambivalence, as her characters yearn for whiteness, yearn for blackness. Finally, Toomer, too, reflects through *Cane* the ambivalence that rends Larsen and her characters, while at the same time expressing the mass/elite division, which will later be a major theme in *Invisible Man.*

All the writers cited above reflect the contradictory pulls upon the black self at the end of the nineteenth century and the beginning of the twentieth. Their characters reflect ambivalence, uncertainty, the terrible awareness of the white other. It is with such writers as Langston Hughes, who will draw upon black music and later create that twentieth-century "folk" hero Jesse B. Simple; Claude McKay, who will record the lives of peasant, lower class, and working class; and Zora Neale Hurston, who will turn, through folklore, to black culture that we will have writers who are, at last, easy in their bones, at home—as was Marcus Garvey—with the black mass, the traditional source of black strength.

CHAPTER TEN

Charles W. Chesnutt

THE "problem of the twentieth century is the problem of the color-line," wrote W. E. B. Du Bois in 1903.[1] Several years earlier Charles Chesnutt published his second volume of short stories titled *The Wife of His Youth and Other Stories of the Color Line* (1899). The problem of the color line will be Du Bois's preoccupation throughout a long, varied, and distinguished career. The color line will also preoccupy Charles Chesnutt, but in his writings the line will grow ragged and breached. The categories of black and white will lose their simple fixity. Blacks will even cross the line to live as whites; and the forbidden theme of miscegenation will be explored.

In a rather formal statement, included in his journal for 1880, Chesnutt viewed the existence of the caste system, or color line, as furnishing a purpose for his writing: "The object of my writings would be not so much the elevation of the colored people as the elevation of the whites—for I consider the unjust spirit of caste which is so insidious as to pervade a whole nation, and so powerful as to subject a whole race and all connected with it to scorn and social ostracism—I consider this a barrier to the moral progress of the American people; and I would be one of the first to head a determined, organized crusade against it."[2] But the "formal" purpose was mixed with his own personal experience as a mulatto whose lightness of skin color could permit him to pass for white; and his writing will reflect the mix of public purpose and personal experience. William L. Andrews has observed that "when Chesnutt became an author, he struck back at those who questioned his moral worth or individual capabilities merely because he shared the blood of whites and blacks." Chesnutt's first published essay will criticize those laws which "make mixed blood a *prima facie* proof of illegitimacy":

"It is a fact that at present, in the United States, a colored man or woman whose complexion is white or nearly white is presumed, in the absence of any knowledge of his or her antecedents, to be the offspring of a union not sanctified by law." And years after his literary career had ended Chesnutt will still lament the "persistence of 'the old theory, so pleasant to the superior race, that a mixture of blood simply results in combining the worst qualities of the parent strains.' "[3]

However, in choosing to write about the color line, in choosing to write about the lives of blacks and mulattoes, in ascribing to them simple, ordinary human responses of the kind that William Dean Howells depicted in the lives of whites, Chesnutt had to consider prevailing images and literary strategies:

> Chesnutt saw the Afro-American stereotyped in American fiction as 1) "the bad Negro" (a law breaker or one who demands his rights too vociferously); 2) "the good Negro" (the faithful retainer); 3) "the modern 'white man's nigger'" (a fawning client, preacher, or politician); 4) "the wastrel type" (one who "squandered his substance in riotous living"); and 5) "the minstrel type" (one who "tried to keep the white folks in good humor by his capers and antics").[4]

The second and fifth of these traits derive largely from the plantation tradition (though the third part of the minstrel show often presented an urban setting), which, in the writings of Thomas Nelson Page, Thomas Dixon, Joel Chandler Harris, and others, pictured the world of the South for both northern and southern readers. These writers generally placed blacks in the only space (despite the migrations to southern and northern cities) that white readers could comfortably imagine for them: the plantation setting. Any other setting was a deviation from the ideal and a falling away from the ideal personal relationship: of child to father, servant to master, peasant to aristocrat. Loss of this relationship—of the sentiments, standards, restraints, paternalism—was experienced as unhappiness, anomie, malaise and is reflected in types one and four and in the appearance of type three, who substituted for the old contentment with paternalism a new opportunism and manipulation.[5]

For Charles Chesnutt, considering writing as a career yet needing to support his family and not wanting to be viewed as an extremist, the question of literary strategies became central. The writers of slave narratives, with their "privileged" access to the exotic and the morally controversial, could write for the curious and the committed; a realism verging on naturalism was the expected mode for their subject matter. But a realistic portrayal of black lives in the postwar world would have presumed a humanity and an equality that few readers, north or south, really accepted. Further, it would have drawn attention to the persistence of a "problem," and few retained the patience to consider "niggers' problems." Thus a writer with the integrity of a Chesnutt faced the question of how to deal honestly with black characters in black settings. The most popular literary models were the sentimental caricature of plantation literature, its antitype the "bad nigger," and the comic caricature of the stage minstrel. Chesnutt adopted two general strategies for his early, major fiction. First, for personal and professional reasons much of his fiction focused on the lives of mulattoes. Though distrusted by some, their way of life would not be foreign to others, since their culture was modeled after that of the white middle and upper classes. As one of the mulatto members of the dancing class in "Her Virginia Mammy" explains to the teacher, "'The most advanced of us are not numerous enough to make the fine distinctions that are possible among white people; and of course as we rise in life we can't get entirely away from our brothers and our sisters and our cousins, who don't always keep abreast of us. We do, however, draw certain lines of character and manners and occupation. . . . we must have standards that will give our people something to aspire to.'"[6] The often-expressed views of Mr. Ryder, the protagonist of "The Wife of His Youth," express an even stronger view of intraracial differences: "'We people of mixed blood are ground between the upper and the nether millstone. Our fate lies between absorption by the white race and extinction in the black. The one doesn't want us yet, but may take us in time. The other would welcome us, but it would be for us a backward step.'"[7]

Chesnutt's other general strategy was to adopt for literary purposes the black survival strategy of masking. Earlier, slaves had had to live lives separate from and more complex than the reductive masks that presumed to be their lives. Now, a black writer such as Chesnutt, in order to have his characters admitted into the Victorian drawing room, where morality, propriety, and order held sway, would adopt the strategy of masking.[8] The technique of masking is evident in Chesnutt's first book, *The Conjure Woman* (1899), where Chesnutt assumes a white mask, which serves as a decorous frame for the black folk reality of the tales: "Behind the mask of a southernized northern white man he ushers his readers into the newly mythologized, 'progressive' South. However, once the reader is maneuvered into the familiar and definable place and time and fellowship of the frame story, Chesnutt, Janus-faced, turns to the reader behind the mask of Uncle Julius and leads him unexpectedly into the strange and disquieting world of the Old South."[9]

Chesnutt's *The Wife of His Youth and Other Stories of the Color Line*, rushed into publication by Houghton Mifflin for the 1899 Christmas market, further illustrates Chesnutt's consciousness of the need to disarm his potential reader. Although he introduced the collection with "The Wife of His Youth," a story of mulattoes, "knowledgeable and respectable people had spoken of it . . . as stylistically well-wrought, emotionally well-balanced, and morally admirable."[10] "The Wife of His Youth" is followed by two stories, in both of which the protagonist's relationship to the black race is concealed. In "Her Virginia Mammy" the black blood of the dancing teacher is revealed only in the closing pages. Even then it is only intuited by her suitor, both lover and gentleman, who chooses not to reveal the identity of the teacher's self-sacrificing mother; the mother, for the sake of her child's future happiness, chooses, rather than to be reunited with her daughter, to mask herself as her child's former mammy. In the next story in the collection, "The Sheriff's Children," it is only revealed in the closing pages (though to both readers and sheriff) that the sheriff's mulatto prisoner, accused of murdering a white man, is his own son. His son had been sold as a child, along with his son's mother, to a speculator on his way to Alabama. But the sheriff is not presented as vicious or cruel; rather, Chesnutt stresses his uprightness, his sense of duty and responsibility. He had served during the war, rising to rank of colonel; following the war he was the "most available" candidate for the office of sheriff. When the mob arrives to "lynch the nigger," he tells them, "'You know *me*. I've got powder and ball, and I've faced fire before now, with nothing between me and the enemy, and I don't mean to surrender this jail while I'm able to shoot.'"[11] It is under such a cover of respectability that we are surprised by the fact of miscegenation.

Chesnutt's choice of these three stories to introduce his collection suggests his consciousness of the need to disarm his reader. This is suggested, too, by his choosing to place "The Web of Circumstance" last, a story which illustrates the fragility of the American Dream if your skin is black. Ben Davis (blacksmith, property owner, representative of the virtues of thrift and success), upon the false accusation of having stolen a buggy whip, is brought to trial and given the "'light sentence of imprisonment for five years in the penitentiary at hard labor.'" (In an earlier sentencing a white man had received one year—for manslaughter.) By the end of the five-year period Davis has been brutalized; his wife has taken up with Davis's former employee, a man who had planted the false evidence; his daughter has drowned; his son has been lynched; and his property, according to the woman next door, "'wuz sol fer de mortgage, er de taxes, er de lawyer, er sump'n,—I don' know w'at. A w'ite man got it.'" The woman next door, while unsure of the exact circumstances, calls up the threat that hovered at the edges of every black success in the postwar period. Moments earlier, the couple currently living in his house, not knowing Ben Davis, had ventured that he had been sent to the penitentiary for "sheep stealin'," said the wife, "hoss stealin'," said the husband. Just as his reputation and the fate of his property dissolve in the imprecision of the reports, the solidity of his past achievements assumes the quality of dream. Little remains for Ben Davis but to be shot by a white man who has mistaken his intentions, which occurs in the closing paragraphs of the story. The coda appended to the story, in which Chesnutt expresses his hope for "another golden age, when all men will dwell together in love and harmony," does little to temper this "most pessimistic of his color line stories."[12] It is, as Andrews asserts, a "record of the way in which economic, social, and psychological conditions can unite to throttle human aspirations and quash human dignity."[13]

If Chesnutt had hoped to disarm his readers, he was only partially successful: "While some might praise Chesnutt's depiction of Afro-American life as both interesting and socially constructive, others would denounce his stories as false, his themes 'repulsive,' and purposes invidious. These attacks usually came from reviewers north and south who detected in *The Wife of His Youth* a barely concealed brief for 'legal sanction' of miscegenation."[14] The color line had all but vanished in some of the stories, and many reviewers apparently feared such a Humpty-Dumpty could not be put back together again. Despite Chesnutt's general sobriety and the relative conventionality of his vision, his imaginative crossings of the color line lent a surreal quality to those seemingly solid categories of white and black. What could be more subversive, for example, than the dancing teacher's observations in "Her Virginia Mammy" regarding her first "colored" class: "She was somewhat surprised, and pleasantly so, when her class came together for their first lesson, at not finding them darker and more uncouth. Her pupils were mostly people whom she would have passed on the street without a second glance, and among them were several whom she had known by sight for years, but had never dreamed of as being colored people."[15] We will, of course, eventually learn (though the speaker will not) that she too is colored. This learning and other lessons (Chesnutt's subversive "sermons") were not palatable to many critics; these were not Blake's angels under the masks of the children of the poor, toward whom one must exercise care so as not to drive them from your door. These were people who undermined one's perceptions; who put in jeopardy one's assumptions regarding being and the self; who, to pursue the sometimes unstated reasoning, threatened the race with mongrelization and one's daughter with marriage.

Such writings threatened the principle of difference, asserted by plantation literature, by graphic images, and by the minstrel stage. Chesnutt's first novel, *The House behind the Cedars* (1900), will also threaten that principle, but it will not elicit the kind of criticism cited above. The major reason for this probably lies in Chesnutt's tempering his subversive "sermon" by including in the second half of the novel the theme of "the tragic mulatto": Roweena Walden will suffer for her attempt to "pass"; her death will restore, to art and to life, its proper balance.[16] William L. Andrews has commented on the interplay between Chesnutt's narrative strategy and his audience's assumptions: "If the second half of *The House behind the Cedars* had not ended so comfortably for white social prejudices and so melodramatically for popular literary sentiments, the social and moral implications of the first part of the novel might have impressed Chesnutt's audience more. On the other hand, it is possible that without the bow in the direction of convention, the novel might never have been published at all."[17] Perhaps Chesnutt's narrative strategy should be viewed as the consummate masking, the "sermon" made palatable. Clearly it is the "sermon" which most interested Chesnutt, and it is to this half of the novel that he devotes his greatest care; the melodramatic second half serves best to emphasize the greater skill of the first. In considering the novel, I will limit my own discussion to the first half.

In *The House behind the Cedars* Chesnutt employed a narrative strategy similar to that employed to disarm the reader in *The Conjure Woman*. The reader is again presented with a white narrator, but something unexpected occurs. The reality the reader had thought fixed becomes unstuck almost midway through the novel. The narrator, it turns out, is not white but black. It is at this point that the author addresses the reader regarding the character of mulattoes:

> If there be a dainty reader of this tale who scorns a lie, and who writes the story of his life upon his sleeve for all the world to read, let him uncurl his scornful lip and come down from the pedestal of superior morality, to which assured position and wide opportunity have lifted him, and put himself in the place of Reena and her brother, upon whom God had lavished his best gifts, and from whom society would have withheld all that made these gifts valuable. To undertake what they tried to do required great courage. Had they possessed the sneaking, cringing, treacherous character traditionally ascribed to people of mixed blood— the character which the blessed institutions of a free slave-holding republic had been well adapted to foster among them; had they been selfish enough to sacrifice to their ambition the mother that gave them birth, society would have been placated or humbugged, and the voyage of their life might have been one of unbroken smoothness.[18]

It is a point of view which Chesnutt hopes the reader will accept, having been disarmed by his narrative strategy. Chesnutt has insinuated these "black" characters into our drawing room and, in turn, has shown us, or tried to show us, how absurd are our attitudes toward mulattoes through the portrayal of these two exemplary mulattoes, John Warwick and Roweena Walden. What begins as fiction becomes, also, an exercise in social justice and a lesson in manners. For Chesnutt was an early "spy in the enemy's country," but his was not the "darky act" of the protagonist's grandfather in *Invisible Man*. His was the act that presumed likeness, only to reveal the difference that was really likeness.

Chesnutt's strategy is to create two exemplary mulattoes whose characters are noble: who, in fact, recall characters from the South's favorite novelist, Sir Walter Scott. They are beings from the medieval courtly love tradition: suggested through their names, through the allusions to literature, and through Roweena's being chosen Queen of Love and Beauty at the medieval-style tournament staged in Patesville.[19] They are stripped of any suggestions of the complex web of black culture; they are whiter than white. But in a novel set in the postwar South, how was Chesnutt able to conceal from the reader, for approximately one hundred pages, such an important fact as race? In general, he was able to do this by assuming the mask of the white man, and by so knowing that role, and being so sensitive to the subtle and complex process of perceiving the other and to the functioning of stereotypes within that process, that he is able, as the magician is able, to misdirect our attention.[20] He manipulates our expectations, knowing both that they *are* our beliefs and that they *become* our beliefs, and that they determine much of what we see along the way. By considering the complex process of misdirection in *The House behind the Cedars*, we will have a clearer understanding of the times in which Chesnutt wrote, as well as of the structure of the novel and of Chesnutt's own preoccupations.

The reader must first be made to assume that John Warwick is white.[21] From the first page the author refers to him as a "gentleman," a term the character also applies to himself in the scene in which his mother asks who is at the door. His features are "white" features: "In appearance he was tall, dark, with straight, black, lustrous hair, and very clean-cut, high-bred features" (4). (Later the portraits of Warwick's wife's white ancestors will be described as "high-featured, proud men and women" [58].) He arrives at the hotel "by carriage," dressed in a "suit of linen duck—the day was warm—a panama straw hat, and patent leather shoes" (4). Those in a position to "know" people respond to him as to a white man: The day clerk at the Patesville Hotel reflects on his signature in the register: "'One of the South Ca'lina bigbugs, I reckon—probably in cotton or turpentine'" (4). At Judge Straight's a colored man lifts his hat politely, paying him the deference due white gentlemen; the colored man's dialect contrasts sharply with Warwick's precise speech. He is picked to manage a plantation during the war and he later marries the owner's daughter (20). Judge Straight extends his hand to him warmly, even after learning who he is (31). That staunch, correct Southerner George Tryon "would have maintained against all comers that Warwick was the finest fellow in the world" (63).

His sister Reena/Roweena's features are, likewise, "white": The woman walking before Warwick was of "a stately beauty seldom encountered. . . . Her abundant hair, of a dark and glossy brown, was neatly plaited and coiled above an ivory column" (8); "a singularly pretty face" (10); "her hair was long and smooth and glossy, with a wave like the ripple of a summer breeze upon the surface of still water." (Only in retrospect will these remarks on Reena's hair, including her mother's response, "'her hairs b'n took good care of, an' there ain't nary gal in town that's got any finer'" [20], take on significance in the context of the "good hair"/"bad hair" distinction.) On the steamboat, in the chapter ironically titled "Down the River," Reena keeps to her cabin; the black stewardess observes, "'W'ite folks has deir troubles jes' ez well ez black folks,'" and adds, perhaps ironically, "'an' sometimes feels 'em mo', 'cause dey ain't ez use' ter 'em'" (38). At the tournament, Roweena is chosen by "all the best people" to be the Queen of Love and Beauty, and, in true courtly love tradition, George Tryon loses his heart to her. He responds to her beauty: "His heart had thrilled at first sight of this tall girl, with the ivory complexion, the rippling brown hair. . . . He discovered that she had a short upper lip . . . this stately dark girl" (64, 65). In sum, "she represented in her adorable person and her pure heart the finest flower of the finest race God had ever made" (90).

These descriptive passages are surely intended to throw us off the scent, to direct our eyes to the wrong shell while the dark pea is spirited into our consciousness. But Chesnutt is not through; he has other, more complex techniques. He intends that we be thoroughly at home with the assumption that this is a novel about whites, that we have admitted into our drawing room a tale we can be comfortable with—not some pathetic, sordid account of the doings of the colored race. No, these are estimable characters: gentlemen, gentle ladies.

In their consciousnesses, and in the reflections of observers, they will be distanced from the lives of blacks. In Warwick's first stroll through Patesville, he looks upon the changes, including the black policeman, as a distanced white observer might. When Reena stops to help a black woman set a laundry basket on her head, Aunt Zilphy acknowledges her aid in language that supports the reader's assumption, which is in keeping with the verbal context, that this is an act of *noblesse oblige*: "'You wuz alluz a good gal, and de Lawd love eve 'body wa't he'p de po' ole nigger'" (10). When the black man Frank from across the street wonders aloud at Warwick's pausing outside the house behind the cedars, his father recalls him to his work in language meant to stress their difference: "'An' you need n' 'sturb you 'se'f 'bout dem folks 'cross de street, fer dey ain't yo' kin'" (13). Shortly thereafter, the author develops further this distancing of difference when he writes of the "women in the house behind the cedars, who, while superior in blood and breeding to the people of the neighborhood in which they lived, were yet under the shadow of some cloud which clearly shut them out from the better society of the town" (29). This difference is further emphasized in a later exchange. Reena's mother suggests, "wistfully," that Reena will be so homesick in a month that she'll be willing to walk home. Frank replies that he would fetch her home in his cart. This amuses Reena's mother: "Her daughter was going to live in a fine house, and marry a rich man, and ride in her carriage. Of course a Negro would drive the carriage, but that was different from riding with one in a cart" (37). Reena is pictured viewing the black deckhands: "the excited Negroes, their white teeth and eyeballs glistening in the surrounding darkness" (39). In discussions on the steamboat, Warwick is "sound on the subject of Negroes, Yankees, and the righteousness of the lost cause" (39). When asked if his people lost any niggers, he responds: "'My father owned a hundred,' he replied grandly" (40).

This distancing is an element, too, in authorial commentary. Early in the novel, as Warwick walks down the street, it is noted that the junction of two streets is known as Liberty Point, "perhaps because slave auctions were sometimes held there in the good old days" (8). What might seem ironic—the phrasing "in the good old days"—in an ironic context or in retrospect was simply an attitudinal assumption of many readers, accustomed to such phrases in the plantation literature of the period. The narrator notes that the young woman's (Roweena's) speech had a touch of the old black woman's speech and comments, "The current Southern speech, including his [Warwick's] own, was rarely without a touch of it. The corruption of the white people's speech was one element—only one—of the Negro's unconscious revenge for his own debasement" (10).

The single most complex element of narrative manipulation is the obscuring of the reason for dissimulation. The language employed is that used to describe some scandal from the past, a scandal so great that, if revealed, it would unmask Warwick's class pretensions; but it is not the language one would use to speak of race. An early remark by Warwick's mother illustrates Chesnutt's method: "'You've grown so tall, John, and are such a fine gentleman! And you *are* a gentleman now, John, ain't you—sure enough? Nobody knows the old story?'" (17). His mother does not note that he is now a white man but that he is now a gentleman. His past is described as an "old story," as though race were not a condition but, rather, an addition to a life, as a story or scandal might be. Warwick replies in a similar vein: "'I haven't felt under any obligation to spoil it by raking up old stories that are best forgotten'" (17). Such terms as *story* and *secret* are used frequently thereafter.

His account to his mother and sister of his life during his absence reinforces the reader's assumptions. The language recalls the language of a knight's tale: "He had gone out into a seemingly hostile world, and made fortune stand and deliver" (20). His opportunities (freed from the story, the scandal) are apparently unlimited: "With the whole world before him, he had remained in the South, the land of his fathers, where, he conceived, he had an inalienable birthright" (20). This birthright and his father's are touched on in a later comment (which extends the knight's tale language) regarding his choice of the name "Warwick": "From Bulwer's novel, he had read the story of Warwick the kingmaker, and upon leaving home had chosen it for his own. He was a new man, but he had the blood of an old race, and he would select for his own one of its worthy names" (27). Finally, deceptive too is the comment that "by some good chance he had escaped military service in the Confederate army," a remark that reinforces the assumption that he is white since blacks did not serve in the Confederate army, except as workers in labor battalions.

This complex web of misdirection unravels once the secret is out. It is the whisking away of the cloth, the display of the interior of the hat—which is empty or full, depending on your sensibilities. Chesnutt's "magic" makes the point that James Weldon Johnson's publishers make more prosaically in the 1912 preface to *The Autobiography of an Ex-Coloured Man*: "These pages . . . reveal the unsuspected fact that prejudice against the Negro is exerting a pressure which, in New York and other large cities where the opportunity is open, is actually and constantly forcing an unascertainable number of fair-complexioned coloured people over into the white race."[22]

Chesnutt has magicked a black man and a black woman into our drawing room, our study, our private meditations. He has revealed that things are not necessarily what they seem, an ungluing of reality which was part of an emerging pattern in America. This was the message, whether intended or not, of western humorists, wearing their masks of dead-pan expressionless faces; of confidence men of various sorts, traveling from place to place in the highwayless purlieus of the South and Midwest (as the Duke and the Dauphin in *Huckleberry Finn*); of the great revivalists, expanding, often implicitly, upon Anne Hutchinson's argument for a distinction between sanctification and justification (a theme reflected in the welter of mask wearers that people Hawthorne's pages); of the new advertising, hinting at the possibilities latent in the alteration of the appearance of things; and in the affront to settled convictions by the confrontation of different cultures—in the mix and jostle of immigrants to the shore, wanderers to the plains, and migrants to the cities. From this larger perspective, Chesnutt's argument is rather modest and restrained, unlike George S. Schuyler's 1931 novel *Black No More*, in which a black doctor develops a treatment that turns blacks into whites: "The entire nation became alarmed. Hundreds of thousands of people, North and South, flocked into the Knights of Nordica. The real white people were panic-stricken, especially in Dixie. There was no way, apparently, of telling a real Caucasian from an imitation one."[23] Chesnutt's hope, so clearly expressed by his statement to the reader cited earlier, is that readers will have the grace to re-see what they have seen and, more narrowly, to be open to the merits of mulattoes, who, on the evidence of John Warwick and Roweena Weldon, would seem to be, as James Weldon Johnson's protagonist will later argue, "just like white folks."

CHAPTER ELEVEN

James Weldon Johnson

CHARLES CHESNUTT'S PUBLISHER did not publicize his race until 1899.[1] When James Weldon Johnson published his novel of passing, *The Autobiography of an Ex-Coloured Man* (1912), he published it anonymously. Johnson's effacement as writer is mirrored in the novel by the disappearance of his protagonist—into the white race. But the protagonist's decision to pass, his *personal* disappearance, becomes amplified by his attitude toward the race: the protagonist's solution to the problem of racial conflict is to champion blacks who are "just like white folks," which implies the disappearance of both blacks and black culture.

This "solution" had been latent in various earlier arguments which espoused the "uplift" of the race. And it had been latent in the insecurity experienced by the emerging middle and upper classes—for these it was often the conduct of the masses which was felt to "hold back" the race, to limit opportunities, to provide substance for the grossness and unselectivity in white stereotypes. Such blacks often tended to see activities of "the race" through the presumed eyes of whites, now overseeing their souls as they had once overseen their bodies. This is the message of the "short yellow woman with a pince-nez on a chain," crying out in "blazing hate" to the protagonist in *Invisible Man* when he tries to put the grinning black-man bank into her garbage can: "'We keep our place clean and respectable and we don't want you field niggers coming up from the South and ruining things.'"[2] And this is included in the "double-consciousness" earlier described by Du Bois: "this sense of always looking at one's self through the eyes of others, of measuring one's soul by the tape of a world that looks on in amused contempt and pity."

The theme of uplift emerged naturally from the experience of slavery. It figured in "An Address to the Colored People of the

United States" which Frederick Douglass participated in drafting at the Colored National Convention of 1848: "'As one rises, all must rise, and as one falls all must fall. Having now, our feet on the rock of freedom, we must drag our brethren from the slimy depths of slavery, ignorance, and ruin.'" Douglass and others saw the need for unity, "because all black people would be forcibly lumped together regardless of individual preferences or personal merits."[3]

This sense of unity, however, will not persist. It will, paradoxically, dissolve in the very forms of the argument that will give it voice: those who criticize the state of the masses will, almost ineluctably, both formalize difference and promulgate difference. In the views of black minister Alexander Crummell, we can now see how early some of the later differences surfaced. Crummell's approach to racial uplift after the war "presupposed ... that blacks were oppressed because of some flaw in themselves, and not only because of a moral flaw in the hearts of their oppressors," an attitude which will be expressed later in an 1897 American Negro Academy *Occasional Paper* by Du Bois, where he "opined that the way to alleviate 'the present friction between the races' was to correct the 'immorality, crime and laziness among the Negroes themselves.'" Crummell's position, according to Wilson Jeremiah Moses, "amounted to a denial of the political importance of moral suasion, agitation, and propaganda. It signified an acceptance of the idea that blacks should be more concerned with mastering the culture of the Anglo-American gentry than with protesting political and educational injustices either of the past or the present." Blacks should "turn their attention to strengthening 'three special points of weakness in our race,' which he apprehended as, 'The Status of The Family'; 'The Conditions of Labor'; 'The Element of Morals.'" As this approach suggests the later Frazier and Moynihan arguments, he also anticipates Du Bois's later view of the role of the "Talented Tenth": "The uplift of black people was seen as being dependent upon character building and the elevation of moral life. The program of character building and moral regeneration was to be carried out through the work of an educated black elite."[4]

Du Bois's 1897 listing of "immorality, crime, and laziness" suggests the strength of this view and its general acceptance in the period. Du Bois had written that "we believe that the first and greatest step toward the settlement of the present friction between the races—commonly called the Negro Problem—lies in the correction of the immorality, crime and laziness among the Negroes themselves, which still remains as a heritage from slavery. We believe that only earnest and long continued efforts on our own part can cure these social ills." Moses has observed that "while such a statement reveals definite concern for the welfare of the masses and a commitment to uplifting them it does not reveal a willingness to accept the masses on their own terms."[5] The approach of the National Association of Colored Women, founded in 1896 and serving as the major national organization of middle-class black women until 1935, similarly denied black culture in its focus on the culture-to-be, its slogan being "lifting as we climb." Moses has described their approach: "Uplift is the key word, for the middle-class Afro-American woman, like her white counterpart, viewed the masses as victims of cultural and social retardation. She had little sense of fellowship or identity with the masses. Her attitude was often one of crusading, uplifting zeal. The masses were to be prepared for the responsibilities of citizenship; they were to be Anglo-Americanized, it was hoped; they would be assimilated into mainstream American life."[6]

This emphasis on uplift and assimilation, this derogation of the culture—and thus the lives—of the black masses, is expressed in the early attitudes of James Weldon Johnson. Two events reveal his views: his experience teaching in 1891 at a rural Georgia school after his first year at Atlanta University; and his winning the Atlanta University Quiz Club Contest in English Composition and Oratory in 1892.

Forty-two years after his experience in rural Georgia, Johnson reflected upon the black masses in his autobiography *Along This Way*. The reflections, matured and retrospective, considerably mute the ambivalence experienced by Johnson in 1891 and later by his protagonist in *The Autobiography of an Ex-Coloured Man*. The mature Johnson reflects upon the understanding of identity gained from the experience: "As I worked with my children in school and met with their parents in the homes, on the farms, and in church, I found myself studying them all with a sympathetic objectivity, as though

they were something apart; but in an instant's reflection I could realize that they were me, and I was they; that a force stronger than
blood made us one." And he expresses a faith in the masses that
would seem, again, to reflect the more mature Johnson rather than
the youthful college student:

> I was anxious to learn to know the masses of my people, to know what
> they thought, what they felt, and the things of which they dreamed; and
> in trying to find out, I laid the first stones in the foundation of faith in
> them on which I have stood ever since. I gained a realization of their
> best qualities that has made any temptation for me to stand on a little,
> individual peak of snobbish pride seem absurd. I saw them hedged for
> centuries by prejudice, intolerance, and brutality; hobbled by their own
> ignorance, poverty, and helplessness; yet, notwithstanding, still brave
> and unvanquished. I discerned that the forces behind the slow but per-
> sistent movement forward of the race lie, ultimately, in them; that
> when the vanguard of that movement must fall back, it must fall back
> on them.[7]

However, Eugene Levy has pictured a more callow twenty-year-old:

> This identification did not spring into existence in the summer of 1891.
> The young student teacher of 1891 was still very much the educated
> city dweller; he was now aware of how the other seven-eighths lived,
> but it was years before he saw much of value in the culture of the rural
> Negro. . . . While he adjusted to the low living standard in both homes,
> he did not accept it willingly. He insisted, for example, on a private
> room in a two-room cabin; he could not stomach the coarse fare of fat
> pork, greens, and corn bread put before him; and he clung firmly to
> those symbols of civilization, the toothbrush and the bath. It was not
> young Johnson's duty, after all, to preserve a folk culture; rather, he was
> to do what he could to bring middle-class standards to his students. In
> this vein, he lamented the lack of order, beauty, and community pride in
> the nearest village. Conversely, he took considerable pride in the order
> and discipline he brought to his own classroom.[8]

A poem from this period, written in Johnson's school copybook and
included in Levy's biography, is revealing:

> It is the job of jobs to teach,
> A colored country school;

I almost side with men who say
The Negro is a fool.

He never seems to understand,
A single thing that is said;
O' if there's anything opaque
It is a "nigger's" head.

O' give me back my city life,
And everything it means;
Even though I board at old A.U.
And weekly dine on beans.[9]

But at the same time that Johnson's experience might take such a form, it will also further complicate his knowledge and contribute later to the mass/elite ambivalence reflected both in his life and in the life of his character. A similar experience of the lives of the rural black masses will contribute to an ambivalence central to both Du Bois's *The Souls of Black Folk* and Jean Toomer's *Cane*.[10]

It would be expecting too much to look for the wisdom of the later autobiography in Johnson's oration of 1892. His winning address, "The Progress of the South and of the Country, as Dependent on the Elevation of the Negro," echoed the uplift philosophy of such "race leaders" as Crummell and the views of the National Association of Colored Women:

> Since the core of the problem was the belief in black inferiority, the obvious solution was to remove the belief by removing the fact of inferiority. This task Johnson assigned to blacks themselves. The white man had to acknowledge advancement as it occurred; it was up to the Negro, however, to prove his mental, moral, and physical equality. Johnson found nothing in the Afro-American past to aid him in proving his worth. He told his audience that they had to overcome their heritage of slavery, which crushed "manhood, intelligence, and virtue" and engendered "vice, superstition, and immorality." Education of the masses, above all else, would correct these weaknesses, for it would raise the ignorant above "animal passion" and consequently improve morality. It would bring in its wake enlightened wealth and power, which, in turn, would generate both self-respect and respect from others. When the white man realized the race's advancement, then caste would be at an end.

Self-help was stressed in his address, and he "made no attempt to discover any positive values in black culture. There is no sign in the Quiz Club oration of his later emphasis on the race's contribution to American culture or of his other efforts to create a usable past for the black American. In 1892 the only task of blacks was to lift themselves out of vice, superstition, and immorality into Victorian America."[11]

Not until the 1920s will Johnson view wholly in its own right even so large an element of black culture as black music. Earlier, when he was writing "coon songs" with Bob Cole and his brother J. Rosamund, he had "wanted somehow to maintain the racial identity of the music he was helping to produce, and at the same time 'refine' and 'elevate' it, bringing it into conformity with conventional musical and moral standards." Levy has observed that "his own musical achievements pointed to an ultimate loss of racial identity. The lyrics for the most popular Cole and Johnson songs largely succeeded in avoiding the obnoxious racial stereotypes of the coon song, but replaced them with the equally stereotyped, though essentially nonracial, emotions of Tin Pan Alley."[12] By the time Johnson wrote *The Autobiography* his character seemed to reflect an ambivalence toward black music that probably suggests a larger ambivalence in Johnson's life. On the one hand, he determines he will take black music and transform it, which would seem to echo the refining impulse reflected in his own songwriting; his character observing another man at the piano declares, "I sat amazed. I had been turning classic music into rag-time, a comparatively easy task; and this man had taken rag-time and made it classic. The thought came across me like a flash—It can be done, why can't I do it? From that moment my mind was made up. I clearly saw the way of carrying out the ambition I had formed when a boy" (142). On the other hand, he is later profoundly moved by the spirituals and declares, "The day will come when this slave music will be the most treasured heritage of the American Negro" (182), a view which he will expand upon in the 1920s: "It is a fact beyond question that the Negro in the United States has produced fine and distinctive folk-art. Aframerican folk-art, an art by Africa out of America, Negro creative genius working under the spur and backlash of American conditions, is unlike anything else in America and not the same as anything else in the world; nor could it have been possible in any other place or in any other times."[13]

Johnson's ambivalence, his character's ambivalence, is a recurring element in both the experience and the literature of the twentieth century. It is a response to attitudes toward class, status, color, and power and has so powerfully influenced both the culture and the literature that the Black Power and Black Arts movements of the 1960s and 1970s can be viewed largely as responses to an implicit ideology of self-diminishment contained in the ambivalence; thus, the ambivalence is present even in its negation. But long before this period, before even the self-assertion of the 1920s, Johnson's protagonist was making his separate peace with ambivalence and racism: his disappearance will be his individualistic solution. But the solution highlights the problem for the black masses when reflecting upon their selves. If their nonuplifted selves are not to be valued, and if society fails to create the economic plenty that makes a middle-class existence possible, where are they to stand, where are they to be somebody? These questions will preoccupy black literature in the twentieth century. An examination of *The Autobiography of an Ex-Coloured Man* will furnish us with an early formulation of some of the questions.

Johnson's protagonist has reached the age of eleven before he is even aware that he is "coloured." The awareness makes him more solitary. "I do not think my friends at school changed so much toward me as I did toward them. I grew reserved" (22). At the same time that he anticipates slights from the white children, he does not identify with "other coloured children": "I had had no particular like or dislike for these black and brown boys and girls ... but I do know that when the blow fell [the realization that he is not "white"], I had a very strong aversion to being classed with them" (23).

The protagonist's "aversion," seemingly sourceless and unfocused, is manifested, over the course of the novel, as an aversion for lower-class blacks, as in his reaction to a restaurant in Atlanta: "The place was smoky, the tables were covered with oilcloth, the floor with sawdust, and from the kitchen came a rancid odour of fish fried over several times, which almost nauseated me. . . . The food was not badly cooked; but the iron knives and forks needed to be scrubbed, the plates and dishes and glasses needed to be washed and well dried" (57). He inquires of his companion: "I then wanted to know why somebody didn't open a place where respectable coloured people who had money could be accommodated" (57). The protagonist and his money are soon parted, but Johnson does not intend irony; rather, the protagonist's remarks about "respectable coloured people" signal an attitude toward class that recurs throughout the novel.

His first identification with blacks, for example, is an identification with *certain* blacks: "Through my music teaching and my not absolutely irregular attendance at church I became acquainted with the best class of coloured people in Jacksonville. This was really my entrance into the race" (74). The protagonist identifies three classes of blacks in Jacksonville; but it is significant, in view of his tendency to look upon blacks from the perspective of the white man he ultimately "becomes," that the classifying is from the perspective of the whites: "The coloured people may be said to be roughly divided into three classes, not so much in respect to themselves as in respect to their relations with the whites" (76).

> There are those constituting what might be called the desperate class—the men who work in the lumber and turpentine camps, the ex-convicts, the bar-room loafers are all in this class. . . . This class of blacks hate everything covered by a white skin, and in return they are loathed by the whites. The whites regard them just about as a man would a vicious mule, a thing to be worked, driven, and beaten, and killed for kicking. . . . The second class, as regards the relations between blacks and whites, comprises the servants, the washerwomen, the waiters, the cooks, the coachmen, and all who are connected with the whites by domestic service. These may be generally characterized as simple, kind-hearted, and faithful. . . . Any white person is "good" who treats them kindly, and they love him for that kindness. . . . The third class is composed of the independent workmen and tradesmen, and of the well-to-do and educated coloured people. (76–78)

It is with the third class, the "refined coloured people," that the protagonist identifies. He believes they experience racial invidiousness more deeply, despite his earlier comments about the "desperate class": "The position of the advanced element of the coloured race is often very trying. They are the ones among the blacks who carry the entire weight of the race question; it worries the others very little" (81). It is this class that tries to better itself, though whites think they are putting on airs or "going through a monkey-like imitation" of them (80), and it is this class which in cities "where the professional and well-to-do class is large . . . have formed society— society as discriminating as the actual conditions will allow it to be" (82). He strongly approves society and its discriminations and finds it most complexly developed in the city of Washington, D.C.: "This is on account of the large number of individuals earning good salaries and having a reasonable amount of leisure time to draw from. There are dozens of physicians and lawyers, scores of school-teachers, and hundreds of clerks in the departments" (153).[14]

The protagonist both identifies with this class and views the rest of the race from the perspective of this class. The Washington doctor the protagonist meets on board ship illustrates this dual process:

> Washington shows the Negro not only at his best, but also at his worst. As I drove round with the doctor, he commented rather harshly on those of the latter class which we saw. He remarked: "You see those lazy, loafing, good-for-nothing darkies; they're not worth digging graves for; yet they are the ones who create impressions of the race for the casual observer. It's because they are always in evidence on the street corners, while the rest of us are hard at work, and you know a dozen loafing darkies make a bigger crowd and a worse impression in this country than fifty white men of the same class. But they ought not to represent the race. We are the race, and the race ought to be judged by us, not by them. Every race and every nation should be judged by the best it has been able to produce, not by the worst." (155–156)[15]

This "best" class can be viewed quite literally as whites in black/ brown face. They even speak more like whites: "There are none of that heavy-tongued enunciation which characterizes even the best-educated coloured people of the South" (153). His attitude is perhaps most clearly suggested by a passage in which the protagonist comments on the failure of whites to distinguish among the classes: "His efforts to elevate himself socially are looked upon as a sort of absurd caricature of 'white civilization.' A novel dealing with coloured people who lived in respectable homes and amidst a fair degree of culture and who naturally acted 'just like white folks' would be taken in a comic-opera sense" (168).[16]

It is as "white folks" that the protagonist seems to move among other blacks. It is appropriate that he moves into the "interior" as a collector of folk music. His stance is distanced; he is the anthropologist, the observer, and the observer could as easily be white. It is only to the music and its performance that he responds sympathetically; when considering the masses, which are the source of the art (as originators, bearers, and, ultimately, performers), he does not probe beneath the stereotypes. His impressions of rural blacks go no deeper than his earlier observations regarding the "desperate class" and the "domestic service" class of Jacksonville:

> This was my first real experience among rural coloured people, and all that I saw was interesting to me; but there was a great deal which does not require description at my hands; for log-cabins and plantations and dialect-speaking "darkies" are perhaps better known in American literature than any other single picture of our national life. Indeed, they form an ideal and exclusive literary concept of the American Negro to such an extent that it is almost impossible to get the reading public to recognize him in any other setting; so I shall endeavor to avoid giving the reader any already overworked and hackneyed descriptions. This generally accepted literary ideal of the American Negro constitutes what is really an obstacle in the way of the thoughtful and progressive element of the race. His character has been established as a happy-go-lucky, laughing, shuffling, banjo-picking being. (167–168)

The protagonist doesn't question the prevailing "literary concept"; what troubles him is the white failure to recognize efforts to "elevate himself socially," to notice the black others. He observes blacks on foot on their way to a church meeting: "It was amusing to see some of the latter class trudging down the hot and dusty road, with their shoes, which were brand-new, strung across their shoulders" (173). Even at the lynching, which he observes while gathering material in a small rural town, the black victim is viewed in words strangely like those a white observer might have used: "There he stood, a man only in form and stature, every sign of degeneracy stamped upon his countenance" (186).

It is this event that determines the protagonist, finally, to pass: "All the while I understood that it was not discouragement or fear or search for a larger field of action and opportunity that was driving me out of the Negro race. I knew it was shame, unbearable shame. Shame at being identified with a people that could with impunity be treated worse than animals" (190–191). He seeks a "white man's success": "I had made up my mind that since I was not going to be a Negro, I would avail myself of every possible opportunity to make a white man's success; and that, if it can be summed up in any one word, means money" (193). He is attracted to, and ultimately marries, a woman who is a vision of whiteness: "She was as white as a lily, and she was dressed in white. Indeed, she seemed to me the most dazzlingly white thing I had ever seen" (198).

Even after her death, he remains "white." He is comfortable as a white man; his children will not have the "brand . . . placed upon them." Only at moments does he regret his choice, but this regret is not the yearning that anguished Nella Larsen's characters, for whom separation from Negroes is felt as a separation from whatever gives life its vividness and without which life—rooms, persons, events, both for *Quicksand*'s Helga Crane living among white people in Denmark and for *Passing*'s Clare Kendry passing for white in America— is characterized by the recurring colorless adjective "pale." For Johnson's protagonist, regret is an infrequent efflorescence of vainglory— it is the loss of self-importance, not the loss of self: "They [that small but gallant band of coloured men who are publicly fighting the cause of their race] are men who are making history and a race. I, too, might have taken part in a work so glorious. . . . when I sometimes open a little box in which I still keep my fast yellowing manuscripts, the only tangible remnants of a vanished dream, a dead ambition, a sacrificed talent, I cannot repress the thought that, after all, I have chosen the lesser part, that I have sold my birthright for a mess of pottage" (211).[17]

CHAPTER TWELVE

Wallace Thurman

I<small>F</small> "racial uplift" often resulted in denying black culture as it espoused self-criticism (perhaps self-denial), self-help, and self-improvement, it also contributed to separating black from black by further encouraging distinctions of color and class and by valuing those with lighter skins over those with darker skins. These distinctions and invidiousness had begun in the pre–Civil War plantation South, where mulattoes tended to figure disproportionately as house servants and artisans.[1] Both roles exposed them to skills and contacts which could be exploited after the war. But, in addition, mulattoes were more readily "emancipated by their white fathers and formed the basis of the free Negro population that grew up in the South before the Civil War. In 1850, mulattoes or mixed-bloods constituted 37 per cent of the free Negro population but only 8 per cent of the slave population."[2] The often unspoken acknowledgment that a southern family contained both a white family and a black family continued well into the twentieth century. Those who were emancipated had an early advantage in securing those positions of privilege which were scarce in a racist economy of status. Thus, the valuing of lighter skin color, so prominent a feature of the black psyche in the early decades of the twentieth century, had a firm basis in class privilege and was exacerbated both by the solemn injunctions of "racial uplift" and by the unsubtle denigration of graphic caricature and other forms of racism.

Distinctions based on color, though apparent to everyone, were largely unacknowledged. A Chesnutt might describe the "Blue Vein Society" and the lives of well-mannered mulattoes, but there is little recognition that anyone is hurt by all this; and in such a story as "The Wife of His Youth" the protagonist, from the security of his position and the abundance of his virtues, is able to practice the generous *noblesse oblige* implicit in his recognition of the black wife of his youth. But that people were hurt, that blood might be drawn in these distinctions, was recognized by the folklore, that "living newspaper" of the unlettered, as in the folk verse "If you're white, you're alright, / If you're black, stay back, / If you're brown, stick around" and in the song cited by Wallace Thurman in *The Blacker the Berry* ... : "*A yellow gal rides in a limousine, / A brown-skin rides a Ford, / A black gal rides on an old jackass, / But she gets there, yes my Lord.*"[3] Although the folkloric evidence is mixed, Lawrence Levine has recorded a recurring denigration of blackness:

> Every collection of early twentieth-century Negro songs included at least several with this theme:
>> Stan' back, black man,
>> You cain't shine;
>> Yo' lips is too thick,
>> An' you hain't my kin'.
> Frequently, frustration with the configurations of blackness focused upon women. In 1919 a Negro on a freight train in North Carolina sang: "I don't want no jet black woman for my regular." A decade earlier black children in the Deep South sang: "I marry black gal, she was black, you know. / For when I went to see her, she look like a crow-ow / She look like a crow-ow-ow."[4]

But folklore is underground, intraethnic; not until Thurman's novel will readers, black and white, be exposed to a novel whose central theme is the hurt caused by the absorption by blacks of white ideals of color.

But the hurt was there, however unadmitted. Color distinctions both rewarded those "blessed" with "bright skin" and "good hair" and limited the access of others to marriage, the professions, and social position. More than simply years will have to pass before the publication of such a book as James A. Farabee's 1983 *A Guide to Beautiful Skin for Black Men and Women*, which begins: "We can no longer accept the fact that dark skins should follow the accepted rules for Anglo-Saxon skin care. The dark complexion requires new moods, new feelings, and, above all else, new complexion standards from its own ancient beauty heritage for its Western way of life."[5]

One measure of the impact of color on access is its effect on acceptability into "society," a measure that has a broader impact on the culture, when the upper and upper-middle classes establish the acceptable tone. Frazier has argued that until at least the First World War and later in such cities as Charleston, Atlanta, and New Orleans, light skin was the dominant characteristic in social mobility and acceptance by "society." Gerri Majors, society columnist for *Jet* and author of *Black Society*, has written that "'Light bright and damned near white' was one of the prerequisites for admission to black society in the old days," and that the "'paper bag test'" prevailed "wherein a woman whose skin was darker than a Kraft paper bag was not admitted to the most exclusive societies and social clubs." Psychiatrists Abram Kardiner and Lionel Ovesey in their 1951 study of the black personality, *The Mark of Oppression*, declared that "gradations of color became [during slavery] a fixed method of determining status which persists to this day."[6]

The pain from color prejudice experienced by Thurman's Emma Lou has been expressed by countless characters since, a testimony to the pervasiveness of the phenomenon (reflected, too, in the predominance of light-skinned models in such magazines as *Ebony* and the proliferation of ads for skin bleaches and hair straighteners) and the need for the consciousness raising of the 1960s and 1970s. A few examples from the literature will suggest its persistence. Maud Martha, in Gwendolyn Brooks's 1951 novel, reflects on the idea of "pretty": "I am still, definitely, not what he [Paul Phillips] can call pretty if he remains true to what his idea of pretty has always been. Pretty would be a little cream-colored thing with curly hair. Or at the very lowest pretty would be a little curly-haired thing the color of cocoa with a lot of milk in it. Whereas, I am the color of cocoa straight, if you can be even that 'kind' to me." She and Paul Phillips are contemplating marriage, and their reflections on their mutual suitability become a dialogue on the desirability of white features:

> "I am not a pretty woman," said Maud Martha. "If you married a pretty woman, you could be the father of pretty children. Envied by people. The father of beautiful children."
>
> "But I don't know," said Paul. "Because my features aren't fine. They aren't regular. They're heavy. They're real Negro features. I'm light, or at

least I can claim to be a sort of low-toned yellow, and my hair has a teeny crimp. But even so I'm not handsome."[7]

Toni Morrison's *The Bluest Eye* is, among other things, a profound meditation on the child's pondering of the nature of the pretty and the ugly. It is the substance of Pecola Breedlove's secret self-inquiries: "Long hours she sat looking in the mirror, trying to discover the secret of the ugliness, the ugliness that made her ignored or despised at school." It is the secret revealed and concealed in the taunts of the light-skinned Maureen Peal: "'I *am* cute! And you ugly! Black and ugly black e mos. I *am* cute!'" And it is the subject of the protagonist's most anguished brooding:

> We were sinking under the wisdom, accuracy, and relevance of Maureen's last words. If she was cute—and if anything could be believed, she *was*—then we were not. And what did that mean? We were lesser. Nicer, brighter, but still lesser. Dolls we could destroy, but we could not destroy the honey voices of parents and aunts, the obedience in the eyes of our peers, the slippery light in the eyes of our teachers when they encountered the Maureen Peals of the world. What was the secret? What did we lack? Why was it important? . . . And all the time we knew that Maureen Peal was not the Enemy and not worthy of such intense hatred. The *Thing* to fear was the *Thing* that made *her* beautiful, and not us.[8]

Such feelings of unworthiness help to explain the psychological element in Marcus Garvey's appeal in the 1920s. He brilliantly articulated the masses' feelings of political and psychological inadequacy. As a people blacks had celebrated the return and march down Fifth Avenue of the all-black "Hell Fighters" of the 369th Regiment—attached to the French army due to American reluctance to permit black combat troops, they were in the trenches 191 days, saw 171 of their officers and men cited for the croix de guerre and the Legion of Honor for "exceptional bravery in action," and were chosen "as the French High Command's supreme mark of honor, the regiment . . . among all Allied forces to lead the march to the Rhine."[9] These same people later saw their streets filled with white-robed Ku Klux Klansmen, those mute, striding testimonials to the triumph of hate, the evanescence of celebration and hope, and other streets filled with rioters in the bloody summer of 1919. Marcus Garvey's grand parades must have seemed cleansing, almost sacramental, as they filled the streets with panoply and power. E. David Cronon has described the parade on August 2, 1920, on the occasion of the first international convention of the Universal Negro Improvement Association:

> The convention opened on Sunday, August l, with three religious services and a silent march of members and delegates through the streets of Harlem. This was but a prelude for the huge parade the next afternoon, which was the talk of Harlem for months to come. For the first time all of the components and massed units of the U.N.I.A. were revealed to an astonished and admiring black world. In addition to numerous bands, choruses, and contingents from the various local U.N.I.A. divisions, there were units of the new African Legion, smartly dressed in dark blue uniforms with red-striped trousers, some mounted on horseback and others marching with well-drilled precision. Although the Legionnaires were unarmed except for the dress swords of their officers, many were veterans of the recent World War, and their existence as a paramilitary organization suggested that Garvey believed the redemption of the race might require force. Another uniformed group was the Black Cross Nurses, neatly garbed in white, ready to back their men in the African Legion or to aid stricken peoples anywhere in the world. The parade, stretching several miles through Harlem, was an impressive show of organizational strength.[10]

Jervis Anderson has written of Garvey's parades that "riding at the head of this spectacle, in the most impressive of the limousines was the Provisional President of Africa himself, attired—as Rogers saw him—'in raiment that outdid Solomon in all its glory.'"[11] As the African "government in exile," the Universal Negro Improvement Association appealed strongly to the disillusioned of both the South and the West Indies, who could all too clearly foresee their tomorrows now that they had arrived at the "promised land."[12] Richard Wright, who treats a Garvey parade somewhat ironically in *Lawd Today*, still conveys the visionary aspect of the marchers ("Their shoulders were straight, their faces up, and their eyes gazed into the far distance, as though piercing concrete and steel, as though entranced by some strange mirage upon the horizon") and the excitement experienced by the viewing crowds: "Young brown-skinned high school girls with dirty stockings and rundown heels stood on curbstones, clapping their hands. Scrawny waifs scurried in and out of the crowd, yelling encouragement to the musicians. Clerks in hotdog stands, drugstores, grocery stores, and drygoods stores craned their necks over counters to get a glimpse."[13]

From the New Orleans funeral march, with its celebration of community and joy, denying the privacy of death and the loneliness of sorrow; to James Reese Europe leading the 369th Regiment's band down Fifth Avenue to 130th Street to break into "Here Comes My Daddy"; to Marcus Garvey's marching bands declaring to all the adrift and spurned, laboring under the cloud of Mr. Charlie's displeasure, that, yeah, Ethiopia is gonna spread its wings, there's a new day a comin', the black marching band was a signature written upon the air, an assertion of a reality against reality. The assertion was political *and* psychological. The marching band was a metaphor for the intertwining of power, space, and psyche. Another metaphor, suggested by Claude McKay's discussion of Marcus Garvey and one that will recall the emotional appeal of community control in the 1960s and 1970s, was the control by blacks of ships:

> American Negroes had never beheld a steamship with a Negro crew and owned and officered by Negroes. Even the smallest excursion boat chartered by a church for a summer's day vacation was owned and officered by whites. . . . Summer after summer most of them had taken excursion trips, organized by churches or clubs. But it was always a "white" boat and not always were they treated considerately and politely by officers and crew.
>
> Now, in this first boat of the Black Star Line, owned by the Universal Negro Improvement Association, they saw something different. They saw themselves sailing without making any apology for being passengers. It was their own ship, a Negro ship.[14]

McKay's comments appreciate the yearnings of the powerless, an appeal missing in those reports that focus largely only on the unseaworthiness of the ships of the Black Star Line.

It is difficult to separate psychology from politics in Garvey's appeal, but his keen awareness of color prejudice within the black community helps to explain his impact upon the black masses. The masses knew all too well how their blackness was viewed. "Black" and "ugly" were often used interchangeably as epithets, even among blacks themselves. Susy, in Claude McKay's *Home to Harlem*, says of herself: "'Yes, mam, I done larned about mah own self fust. Had no illusions about mahself. I knowed I was black and ugly and no-class and unejucated.'"[15] Madame C. J. Walker had become the first female black millionaire from her discovery of a hair-straightening formula that would take the kinks out of "bad hair."[16] Richard Wright catches the appeal, and the surreal, in the processed hair and bleached skin of a woman gazed upon by Jake Jackson and his friends, a vision ironically following their viewing of Garvey's parade:

> They passed a beauty parlor and the scent of burning hair stung their nostrils. From a doorway a black woman stepped to the sidewalk and came briskly forward. Her hair was shining jet, and was brushed straight back, plastered to her head. The contrast between the overdose of white powder and the natural color of the skin was so sharp that she looked like two people instead of one; it was as if her ghost were walking in front of her.
> "She's ready!"
> "She's mellow!"
> "She's pig meat!"
> "Naw, she gnat's liver!"
> "Laaaaawd, today!"[17]

Marcus Garvey preached the message that black is beautiful; that blacks were a people in exile; that black men had created great civilizations long before the white man; that Africa had developed great cultures and great people; that Ethiopia stretched forth her wings. "Thousands of New York's domestics, janitors, and postal employees, for whom Africa and blackness but a short time before were synonyms for barbarism and pariah status, accepted the Garveyite vision of a renascent Mother Africa, united and mightier than in the days of the great pharaohs, her ancient arts and sciences the envy of the planet."[18] Garvey, a *black* man, had no problems with such words as "Negro" or "black." By contrast, John Daniels's 1914 study notes a far different attitude among Boston's upper-class blacks: "In the upper gradations of the Negro community, and generally speak-

ing in measure proportioned to the elements of superior education, refinement, Northern rearing, lightness of complexion, and an
admixture of white blood, objection to the word [Negro] becomes
deep-seated, positive, and even vehement."[19] Garvey named his
organization the Universal Negro Improvement Association, his
newspaper the *Negro World*. He taunted mulattoes, as wanting to
be white, declared that Du Bois was "trying to be everything else
but a Negro."[20] He wrote of the need to see God as black ("Whilst
our God has no color, yet it is human to see everything through
one's own spectacles, we have only now started out [late though it
be] to see our God through our own spectacles");[21] the Madonna as
black; of the need to manufacture black dolls for black children.
To many in the upper classes he was an embarrassment: "Upper-
class Harlem regarded the pageantry of Liberty Hall and the global
schemes of its owner with a mixture of chagrin and derision. In 'respectable' circles, Garveyites were commonly referred to as 'out-
laws' and UNIA rendered as 'ugliest Negroes in America.'" But, as
David Levering Lewis has noted, "None of this disturbed Garvey.
His watchword was never 'caution,' but 'up, you mighty race.'"[22] To
their contempt he was indifferent; to their preachments of integra-
tion he preached separation. And no one, not even Du Bois, wrote
more trenchantly on the phenomenon of color prejudice within the
black community.[23] He criticized other black newspapers for their
extensive advertising of skin-whiteners and hair-straighteners and
refused to carry such ads in the *Negro World*:

> I severely criticized "The Chicago Defender" for publishing humiliating
> and vicious advertisements against the pride and integrity of the race. At
> that time the "Defender" was publishing full page advertisements about
> "bleaching the skin" and "straightening the hair." One of these adver-
> tisements was from the Plough Manufacturing Company of Tennessee
> made up as follows:
> There were many degrading exhortations to the race to change its
> black complexion as an entrant to society. There were pictures of two
> women, one black and the other very bright and under the picture of the
> black woman appeared these words: "Lighten your black skin," indicat-
> ing perfection to be reached by bleaching white like the light woman.
> There were other advertisements such as "Bleach your dark skin,"

"Take the black out of your face," "If you want to be in society lighten your black skin," "Have a light complexion and be in society," "Light skin beauty over night," "Amazing bleach works under skin," "The only harmless way to bleach the skin white," "The most wonderful skin whitener," "Straighten your kinky hair," "Take the kink out of your hair and be in society," "Knock the kink out," "Straighten hair in five days," etc. These advertisements could also be found in any of the Negro papers published all over the country influencing the poor, unthinking masses to be dissatisfied with their race and color, and to "aspire" to look white so as to be in society. I attacked this vicious progaganda.[24]

The division between such figures as Du Bois and Garvey was paralleled by the perhaps less rancorous division between those who preferred that black writers chronicle the activities of the middle and upper classes and those writers such as Langston Hughes, Claude McKay, and Zora Neale Hurston who delighted in the lives of the masses. Jessie Fauset's characters won the approbation of the first group; they were highly praised, for example, by Du Bois. Her characters, mulatto children of "old families of Boston, Charleston, New Orleans, and Philadelphia . . . impressively represented by her character Van Meier (modelled on DuBois) . . . [are e]qual to whites in every respect (save money)."[25] Angela Murray, her heroine in *Plum Bun*, blends "racial uplift" and *noblesse oblige* in her discussion of class and color: "'Our case is unique,' the beautiful, cultured voice intoned; 'Those of us who have forged forward, who have gained the front ranks in money and training, will not, are not able as yet to go our separate ways apart from the unwashed, untutored herd. We must still look back and render service to our less fortunate, weaker brethren.'"[26]

Hughes, McKay, and Hurston turned to the black masses, both lower class and peasantry, for their characters and themes. Hughes early turned to folklore, such as the blues in his "The Weary Blues," written when he was only eighteen. His sympathy for the underclass of workers is reflected in such poems as "Song to a Negro Washwoman." In an interview with Dewey Jones of the Chicago *Defender*, Hughes explained that his *Fine Clothes to the Jew* was "limited to an interpretation of the 'lower classes,' the ones to whom life is least kind. I try to catch the hurt of their lives, the monotony of their 'jobs,' and the veiled weariness of their songs. They are the people I know best."[27] McKay's identification with the masses dates from his early studies of the Jamaican peasantry. His portrayals of their labor are often detailed and empathic accounts of pride and striving against almost unbearable burdens of taxes, exploitation, illness, and hunger. As Jean Wagner notes, McKay "associates the good with the black race and the soil" and points out that "it is highly significant that all these country folks are blacks, excluding the mulattoes whom McKay implicitly rejects as all too eager to see in their white ancestry a justification for disdaining the blacks."[28] *Home to Harlem*, McKay's major novel, explores the world of working-class blacks:

> *Home to Harlem* was a bombshell. Where Van Vechten had offended by intruding the underclass into a novel about High Harlem, McKay sinned far more grievously by totally ignoring the upper classes. It was as though the residents of Edgecombe Avenue and the Dunbar had drowned in the Harlem River. No graduates of Harvard and Howard discourse on literature at the Dark Tower; there are no easily recognized imitations of Du Bois, Jessie Fauset, or James Weldon Johnson—and no whites at all. When he mentions the unavoidable fact of class distinctions, McKay draws the illustration from the society of Pullman car cooks and waiters.[29]

Zora Neale Hurston, too, ignored the upper classes, the literati. She wandered the South gathering folklore for the work she was doing in anthropology with Franz Boas, work later collected in *Of Mules and Men*, work that carried her from front porches to turpentine camps to the French Quarter in New Orleans; and she later wrote a novel, *Their Eyes Were Watching God*, set in her all-black Florida hometown.

The portrayal of unexemplary lives was disturbing to many middle- and upper-class blacks. Such portrayals furnished no models for "racial uplift." In addition, such portrayals could "tar all blacks with the same brush"; that is, whites might not be able to discern their own superiority and progress in the unflattering representations drawn from the lives of the masses. This concern was expressed publicly, often in the press, and the targets of their criticism, generally the younger writers, responded in turn. A major, and very conservative, statement was George S. Schuyler's "The Negro-Art Hokum," published in the *Nation* in 1926, in which Schuyler ridiculed even the concept of a Harlem Renaissance, despite the annual *Crisis* and *Opportunity* contests, the increasing publication of black writers, and the publication only the year before of the Alain Locke–edited *The New Negro*: "Eager apostles from Greenwich Village, Harlem, and environs proclaimed a great renaissance of Negro art just around the corner waiting to be ushered on the scene by those whose hobby is taking races, nations, peoples, and movements under their wing. New art forms expressing the 'peculiar' psychology of the Negro were about to flood the market. In short, the art of Homo Africanus was about to electrify the waiting world. Skeptics patiently waited. They still wait." Schuyler declared "the Aframerican is merely a lampblacked Anglo-Saxon," that "the Aframerican is subject to the same economic and social forces that mold the actions and thoughts of the white Americans." Thus, there is no distinctive black American culture and art.[30]

Freda Kirchway, managing editor of the *Nation*, sent Langston Hughes proofs of the Schuyler article, and he responded by writing "The Negro Artist and the Racial Mountain." The "mountain" in Hughes's title was the "urge within the race toward whiteness, the desire to pour racial individuality into the mold of American standardization, and to be as little Negro and as much American as possible." He identified this urge as underlying a young Negro poet's once declaring, "I want to be a poet—not a Negro poet," and went on to describe the milieu of the middle and upper classes, who deny blackness and yearn for whiteness:

> But let us look at the immediate background of this young poet. His family is of what I suppose one would call the Negro middle class: people who are by no means rich yet never uncomfortable nor hungry—smug, contented, respectable folk, members of the Baptist church. The father goes to work every morning. He is a chief steward at a large white club. The mother sometimes does fancy sewing or supervises parties for the rich families of the town. The children go to a mixed school. In the home they read white papers and magazines. And the mother often says "Don't be like niggers" when the children are bad. A frequent phrase from the father is, "Look how well a white man does things." And so

the word white comes to be unconsciously a symbol of all the virtues. It holds for the children beauty, morality, and money. The whisper of "I want to be white" runs silently through their minds. This young poet's home is, I believe, a fairly typical home of the colored middle class. One sees immediately how difficult it would be for an artist born in such a home to interest himself in interpreting the beauty of his own people. He is never taught to see that beauty. He is taught rather not to see it, or if he does, to be ashamed of it when it is not according to Caucasian patterns.

For racial culture the home of a self-styled "high-class" Negro has nothing better to offer. Instead there will perhaps be more aping of things white than in a less cultured or less wealthy home. The father is perhaps a doctor, lawyer, land-owner, or politician. The mother may be a social worker, or a teacher, or she may do nothing and have a maid. Father is often dark but he has usually married the lightest woman he could find. The family attend a fashionable church where few really colored faces are to be found. And they themselves draw a color line. In the North they go to white theatres and white movies. And in the South they have at least two cars and a house "like white folks." Nordic manners, Nordic faces, Nordic hair, Nordic art (if any), and an Episcopal heaven. A very high mountain indeed for the would-be racial artist to climb in order to discover himself and his people.

He describes the prominent Philadelphia clubwoman who would pay eleven dollars to hear Andalusian popular songs but not think of going to hear Clara Smith sing Negro folksongs. He describes, too, the questions asked by his own people: "Do you think Negroes should always write about Negroes? I wish you wouldn't read some of your poems to white folks. How do you find anything interesting in a place like a cabaret? Why do you write about black people? You aren't black. What makes you do so many jazz poems?" Because the Philadelphia clubwoman believes that "white is best" she dislikes the spirituals and anything distinctly racial, even an art that is truthful: "She doesn't care for the Winold Reiss portraits of Negroes because they are 'too Negro.' She does not want a true picture of herself from anybody. She wants the artist to flatter her, to make the white world believe that all Negroes are as smug and as near white in soul as she wants to be. But, to my mind, it is the duty of the younger Negro artist, if he accepts any duties at all from outsiders, to change through the force of his art that old whispering 'I want to be white,' hidden in the aspirations of his people, to 'Why would I want to be white? I am a Negro—and beautiful!'"[31]

The savage criticism of the white Carl Van Vechten's *Nigger Heaven* (1926) was the next significant action in a conflict that might be termed a small-scale battle of the books. Du Bois's review declared the book "a blow in the face. It is an affront to the hospitality of black folk and to the intelligence of white. . . . I find this novel neither truthful nor artistic."[32] Various newspapers refused to advertise the book. Van Vechten was hung in effigy on 135th Street,[33] and he found himself barred from certain clubs "until one night, flanked by the redoubtable Zora Hurston, he successfully braved the ban." Arnold Rampersad writes that for young black writers "Van Vechten's troubles were their own":

> The attack on him was an attack on what they themselves stood for— artistic and sexual freedom, a love of the black masses, a refusal to idealize black life, and a revolt against bourgeois hypocrisy. In July, Hughes received a frightening reminder of black snobbishness when the old poet George M. McClellan wrote to tell him that while he liked the poems in *The Weary Blues*, he had scissored from the dustjacket "that hideous black 'nigger' playing the piano."[34]

The young black writers would counterattack. The "Niggerati," so named by Hurston, would publish a magazine to be titled *Fire* that would scorch their critics. Its intent is suggested by the opening lines of the foreword, a free-form verse by Hughes and Thurman:

> FIRE . . . flaming, burning, searing and penetrating
>   far beneath the superficial items of the
>   flesh to boil the sluggish blood . . .[35]

Some critics responded, so they claimed, by throwing it *into* the fire.

Soon the guardians of the proprieties would have another opportunity upon the publication of Hughes's *Fine Clothes to the Jew* (1927):

> Under a headline proclaiming Hughes a "SEWER DWELLER," William M. Kelley of the New York *Amsterdam News*, who once had sought his work, denounced *Fine Clothes to the Jew* as "about 100 pages of trash. . . .

It reeks of the gutter and sewer." The regular reviewer of the Philadelphia *Tribune* adamantly refused to publicize it; Eustace Gay confessed that *Fine Clothes to the Jew* "disgusts me." In the Pittsburgh *Courier*, historian J. A. Rogers called it "piffling trash" that left him "positively sick." The Chicago *Whip* sneered at the dedication to Van Vechten, "a literary gutter-rat" who perhaps alone "will revel in the lecherous, lust-reeking characters that Hughes finds time to poeticize about. . . . These poems are unsanitary, insipid and repulsing." Hughes was the "poet 'low-rate' of Harlem." The following week, refining its position, the *Tribune* lamented Langston's "obsession for the more degenerate elements" of black life; the book was "a study in the perversions of the Negro."[36]

Hughes failed to wilt under the attack. To the Cleveland *Plain-Dealer* "curious about the hubbub in the black press over poetry, of all things, he explained that the black reviewers still thought that 'we should display our "higher selves"—whatever they are,' missing the point 'that every "ugly" poem I write is a protest against the ugliness it pictures.' " Invited to reply in his defense, he wrote in the Pittsburgh *Courier* that there were four reasons for the attack on his work: "the low self-esteem of the 'best' blacks; their obsession with white opinion; their *nouveau riche* snobbery; and the lack of artistic and cultural training 'from which to view either their own or the white man's books or pictures.' " Of his own work he wrote: " 'My poems are indelicate. But so is life.' " He "wrote about 'harlots and gin-bibers. But they are human. Solomon, Homer, Shakespeare, and Walt Whitman were not afraid or ashamed to include them.' "[37]

When Wallace Thurman's *The Blacker the Berry . . .* was published in 1929 it was welcomed as another big gun in the continuing battle: "Jackman and Hughes kept score of Renaissance intramural competition, and, by their count, the genteel letters team was losing badly by 1929. Relishing the mischief of *The Blacker the Berry*, Hughes praised Thurman's 'gorgeous book' and predicted it would 'complicate things immeasurably' for all the associations, leagues, and federations, as well as for the 'seal-of-high-and-holy approval of Harmon awards.'" The book could not but be controversial, as the first novel to treat color prejudice within the race as a central theme. *Opportunity*'s Eunice Hunton wrote that "the immaturity and gaucherie of the work of the young man from the West strikes one with a force that is distinctly disheartening." Whether or not Emma Lou was Thurman, as Lewis and others have suggested, color prejudice within the race could never again go unrecognized. Thurman detailed its many facets uncompromisingly in a book of which Lewis has written, "Seldom has so much misery, masochism, and misunderstanding been crammed into one small novel."[38]

Emma Lou, Wallace Thurman's protagonist in *The Blacker the Berry . . .* , is in certain respects the female counterpart to Johnson's protagonist. Her perspective, too, is that of the white "other," so that she judges herself and the actions of other blacks by presumed white standards. She, too, exhibits an aversion to lower-class blacks, having early absorbed such terms as "the right sort of people" and "people who really mattered," but in her case considerations of class are inextricably mixed with her preoccupation with color. Johnson's protagonist could pass for white; Thurman's Emma Lou is her family's black berry, her mother's "niggerish-looking child." Johnson's protagonist could view race rather dryly, abstractly; his criticism focuses on black behavior. Emma Lou is so obsessed by color that all other issues are as though seen through her glass darkly.

Thurman gathers into the person of Emma Lou all the hurts, defensive reactions, and dramatic situations which play out the theme of color prejudice. She is a sad diorama of all the possibilities, slowly unrolling, cumulatively indicting. It begins in the family. Emma Lou's light-skinned mother and grandmother were embarrassed by her dark skin:

> Her mother had hidden her away on occasions when she was to have company, and her grandmother had been cruel in always assailing Emma Lou's father, whose only crime seemed to be that he had had a blue black skin. . . .
> Everything possible had been done to alleviate the unhappy condition, every suggested agent had been employed, but her skin, despite bleachings, scourgings, and powderings, had remained black—fast black. . . .
> She should have been a boy, then color of skin wouldn't have mattered so much, for wasn't her mother always saying that a black boy could get along, but that a black girl would never know anything but sorrow and disappointment? (194, 4)

People remarked to her mother on her color: "'What an extraordinarily black child! Where did you adopt it?' or else, 'Such lovely unniggerish hair on such a niggerish-looking child.' Some had even been facetious and made suggestions like, 'Try some lye, Jane, it may eat it out. She can't look any worse'" (15). Even in play, her color became a source of pain: "Then there had been her childhood days when she had ventured forth into the streets to play. All of her colored playmates had been mulattoes, and her white playmates had never ceased calling public attention to her crow-like complexion. Consequently, she had grown sensitive and had soon been driven to play by herself, avoiding contact with other children as much as possible. Her mother encouraged her in this, had even suggested that she not attend certain parties because she might not have a good time" (194–195).

In the world outside her family and outside the streets of childhood, the judgments are as casual and as cruel:

"She's hottentot enough to take something. . . . Thank God, she won't be in any of our classes." (33)

"Fats" was looking at Emma Lou, too, but as he passed, he turned his eyes from her and broadcast a withering look at the lad who had spoken: "Man, you know I don't haul no coal." (92)

"Oh, she [Emma Lou] probably works for them. It's good you danced with her. Nobody else would."
"I didn't see nothing wrong with her. She might have been a little dark."
"Little dark is right, and you know when they comes blacker'n me, they ain't got no go." Braxton was a reddish brown aristocrat, with clear-cut features and curly hair. His paternal grandfather had been an Iroquois Indian. (110–111)

She [Emma Lou] remembered too vividly how, on ringing the bell of a house where there had been a vacancy sign in the window, a little girl had come to the door, and, in answer to a voice in the back asking, "Who is it, Cora?" had replied, "Monkey chaser wants to see the room you got to rent." (111)

Wanted: light colored girl to work as waitress in tearoom. . . . Wanted: Nurse girl, light colored preferred (children are afraid of black folks). . . . "It's like this, Emma Lou, they don't want no dark girls in their sorority.

They ain't pledged us, and we're the only two they ain't, and we're both black." . . . "Mr. Brown has some one else in mind." . . . "We have nothing here." (118–119)

"The only thing a black woman is good for is to make money for a brown-skin papa." (132)

He [Alva] did not wish to risk losing her before the end of summer, but neither could he risk taking her out among his friends, for he knew too well that he would be derided for his unseemly preference for "dark meat," and told publicly without regard for her feelings, that "black cats must go." (138)

And at a black performance before a black audience, including Emma Lou and Alva, a ritual denigration of identity is acted out that ironically recalls the antics of nineteenth-century white minstrels in blackface:

Then a very Topsy-like girl skated onto the stage to the tune of "Ireland must be heaven because my mother came from there." Besides being corked until her skin was jet black, the girl had on a wig of kinky hair. Her lips were painted red—their thickness exaggerated by the paint. Her coming created a stir. Every one concerned was indignant that something like her should crash their party. She attempted to attach herself to certain men in the crowd. The straight men spurned her merely by turning away. The comedians made a great fuss about it, pushing her from one to the other, and finally getting into a riotous argument because each accused the other of having invited her. It ended by them agreeing to toss her bodily off the stage to the orchestral accompaniment of "Bye, Bye, Blackbird," while the entire party loudly proclaimed that "Black cats must go."
     Then followed the usual rigamarole carried on weekly at the Lafayette concerning the undesirability of black girls. Every one, that is, all the males, let it be known that high browns and "high yallers" were "forty" with them. (178–179)

Emma Lou absorbs these values and judges herself: "Her Uncle Joe had been wrong—her mother and grandmother had been right. There was no place in the world for a dark girl. . . . It was neither fashionable nor good for a girl to be as dark as she, and to be, at the same time, as untalented and undistinguished. Dark girls could get along if they were exceptionally talented or handsome or wealthy, but she had nothing to recommend her, save a beautiful head of hair" (48, 195). She, in turn, judges others by the same standards:

> She resented being approached by any one so flagrantly inferior, any one so noticeably a typical southern darky, who had no business obtruding into the more refined scheme of things. (26–27)

> But the room had been dark, and so was John. Ugh! (64)

> She [Emma Lou] didn't like black men, and the others seemed to keep their distance. (122)

> Emma Lou had no reason for liking Benson save that she was flattered that a man as light as he should find himself attracted to her. It always gave her a thrill to stroll into church or down Seventh Avenue with him. And she loved to show him off in the reception room of the Y.W.C.A. True, he was almost as colorless and uninteresting to her as the rest of the crowd with whom she now associated, but he had a fair skin and he didn't seem to mind her darkness. Then, it did her good to show Gwendolyn that she, Emma Lou, could get a yellow-skinned man. She always felt that the reason Gwendolyn insisted upon her going with a dark-skinned man was because she secretly considered it unlikely for her to get a light one. (209–210)

Her judgment of the other blacks recalls the attitude of the doctor and many of the views of the protagonist in *The Autobiography of an Ex-Coloured Man*. In addition, she shares with them the attitude expressed by Ellison's protagonist in the early pages of *Invisible Man*; he believed that "only these men [white leaders of the community] could judge truly my ability" (20). An invisible white audience—alert to evidence of "field niggerism," as Ellison's protagonist later wryly expresses it—often shares the black stage. Emma Lou, for example, reflects that "Negroes must always be sober and serious in order to impress white people with their adaptability and non-difference in all salient characteristics save skin color" (42). Emma Lou is terribly conscious of how blacks will look to whites, which is a fear that difference will be showing:

> She wanted the white people who were listening to know that she knew her grammar if this other person didn't. . . . Imagine any one pre-

paring to enter college saying "Is you," and, to make it worse, right before all these white people, these staring white people. (24)

Why she would be ashamed even to be seen on the street with her,
dressed as she was in a red-striped sport suit, a white hat, and white
shoes and stockings. Didn't she know that black people had to be careful
about the colors they affected? (25)

Now Hazel, according to Emma Lou, was the type of Negro who should
go to a Negro college. There were plenty of them in the South whose
standard of scholarship was not beyond her ability. And, then, in one of
those schools, her darky-like clownishness would not have to be paraded
in front of white people, thereby causing discomfort and embarrassment
to others of her race, more civilized and circumspect than she. (31)

Hazel was just a vulgar little nigger from down South. It was her kind,
who, when they came North, made it hard for the colored people already
resident there. It was her kind who knew nothing of the social niceties
or the polite conventions. In her own home they had been used only to
coarse work and coarser manners. And they had been forbidden the
chance to have intimate contact in schools and in public with white
people from whom they might absorb some semblance of culture. (36)

She [Hazel] was a pariah among her own people because she did not
seem to know, as they knew, that Negroes could not afford to be funny
in front of white people even if that was their natural inclination. (42)

The denial of difference, the valuing of white standards in color
prejudice, the mixing of such judgments with the reality of economic advantage—all lead to that ultimate form of masking: the
disappearance of the black self into the white other. For Emma Lou's
mother and her mother's social circle ("the blue vein circle, so
named because all of its members were fair-skinned enough for the
blood to be seen pulsing purple through the veins of their wrists"),
disappearance was a labor of generations: "Their motto must be
'Whiter and whiter every generation,' until the grandchildren of the
blue veins could easily go over to the white race and become assimilated so that problems of race would plague them no more" (11, 12).[39]
For Emma Lou, brooding during her high school graduation ceremony, this disappearance would result in the surfacing of the real

Emma Lou: "High school diploma indeed! What she needed was an efficient bleaching agent, a magic cream that would remove this un-welcome black mask from her face and make her more like her fellow men" (5). Identity is thus, as for the princess in the fairy tale, the revelation of the marvelous under the mask of appearance. Her need, her willingness to believe, is so intense that she is later able to convince herself that her black self is being effaced: "Anyway she wasn't so black. Hadn't she artificially lightened her skin about four or five shades until she was almost brown? Certainly it was all right. She needn't be a foolish ninny all her life" (14). But her students perversely assert what she wishes to conceal; they nickname her "Blacker'n me" (219).

Emma Lou achieves self-knowledge by the end of the novel, but not before her already vulnerable self is exposed to her man Alva's alcoholism, disdain, and use of her as a "black mammy" for his child (by Geraldine); her receipt of the anonymous note (from the other teachers)—"Why don't you take a hint and stop plastering your face with so much rouge and powder"; and the news that her girlfriend Gwendolyn and Benson, a brown-skinned man whom she had dated, had married. This confluence of events is almost too much reality: "She looked up and saw a Western Union office sign shining above a lighted doorway. For a moment she stood still, repeating over and over to herself Western Union, Western Union, as if to understand its meaning. People turned to stare at her as they passed" (224–225). She considers telegraphing home, going home, but resolves instead to begin again.

Her resolution includes a new attitude toward her self: "What she needed to do now was to accept her black skin as being real and unchangeable, to realize that certain things were, had been, and would be, and with this in mind begin life anew, always fighting, not so much for acceptance by other people, but for acceptance of herself by herself. . . . It was clear to her at last that she had exercised the same discrimination against her men and the people she wished for friends that they had exercised against her" (226–227, 238). This new attitude, this new self-knowledge, is modestly phrased. "To accept," "to realize"—these are not Marcus Garvey's ringing declaration that "Black is beautiful." But they are, for Emma Lou, a beginning—as her leaving Alva is a beginning. And in their scale, diminished but honest, they complement the understatement in the closing phrases of the novel: "[She] finished packing her clothes, not stopping even when Alva Junior's cries deafened her, and caused the people in the next room to stir uneasily" (231).

CHAPTER THIRTEEN

Nella Larsen

THE 1920s in black America were a time of ambivalence, toward both skin color and black culture, and perhaps no lives reflected this ambivalence any more profoundly than the real lives of Nella Larsen and Jean Toomer and the fictive lives of their characters: doomed both to be and not to be white. Du Bois had acutely reflected the frustrations for the black "leader" exposed to the countervailing pressures in a political economy of scarcity: "Where in heaven's name do we Negroes stand? If we organize separately for anything—'Jim Crow!' scream all the Disconsolate; if we organize with white people—'Traitors! Pressure! They're betraying us!' yell all the Suspicious. If, unable to get the whole loaf we seize half to ward off starvation—'Compromise!' yell all the Scared. If we let the half loaf go and starve—'Why don't you *do* something?' yell those same critics, dancing about on their toes."[1] Equivalent, though perhaps more subtle, pressures beset the mulatto writer and his/her characters in a period of changing attitudes toward skin color.

It was a time, for example, when many black writers took comfort and joy in the rich shadings of black flesh; when brown skins, and even black skins, were celebrated in the verbal and graphic arts. There were other signs of a diminishing color prejudice. E. Franklin Frazier, for example, has argued that "during a decade or so following the first World War, in both northern and southern cities education and occupation increasingly supplanted family background and a light complexion as a basis for admission to the social elite among Negroes. For example, in New York, Chicago, and Philadelphia, Negroes who had constituted Negro 'society' because they were mulattoes and acted like 'gentlemen' were pushed aside because they were engaged in personal services. The Negro doctors, dentists, lawyers, and businessmen, who could not boast of white ancestors or did not know their white ancestors, were becoming the leaders of Negro 'society.' "² Cedric Dover has cited a study by Cynthia Mathis of seventy-one novels by blacks from 1886 to 1936 that "showed an increasing preference for dark skins, especially after 1920; of 147 beautiful women among their characters, twenty-five were white, fifty-six yellow, fifty-six brown and ten black, the whites being in the earlier, and the blacks in the later, works."³ For mulattoes, especially those light enough to pass, the increasing tendency to value darker skins often made more ambiguous an already ambiguous personal situation. It meant the disordering of a dependable measure of human worth; chance could now figure more prominently in human relationships.

Not only darker skins but all things Negro seemed to be valued more positively. Harlem, already thought of as the "Negro capital of the world," could be viewed variously as the political, literary, and theatrical centers of the black world. And as functions concentrated, they assumed a size, an importance, a blackness that black institutions had never before exhibited. Almost a country within a country, the newly arrived migrant to the city could not but react with surprise, and pleasure, as black cops directed white traffic, bawled out white drivers, as black store clerks served white customers. And Harlem seemed significant not only to Harlemites; it seemed to many to be significant to the city at large—to have to be taken into account by the grandest city in the world.

Not only was Harlem, a black place, significant, but Africa the dark continent was being celebrated as the ancestral home, as the cite of ancient kingdoms and ancient glories, for all those weary and heavy-laden, for all the black exiles in cold, pale, Puritan, oppressive America. And even if its ultimate meaning was questioned, as in the recurring question "What is Africa to me?" in Countee Cullen's poem "Heritage," Africa was being noticed. It was not simply the land of cannibals, as so often pictured in the early comic strips,⁴ and of heathens, patiently awaiting the cross and the missionary. It was the land of art forms that had influenced such Europeans as Matisse, Picasso, Derain, Modigliani, Utrillo, Epstein, Lipschitz, and Guillaume, among others.⁵ And it was not only Marcus Garvey who brought honor and dignity to black Africa by his notice but also the imperious, cerebral Du Bois, who helped organize four postwar Pan-African Conferences—in Paris (1919), London (1921, 1923), and New York (1927).

At the same time that Harlem's star was rising, white America's seemed to be setting—at least this was the majority report of white intellectuals and artists, many of whom lived out the 1920s in Europe, largely abandoning the various Greenwich Villages to the real estate developers. America was the land of Harding, Coolidge, the Chamber of Commerce, and the National Association of Manufacturers. It was the land of the booboisie, the Puritans, the boosters, the Babbitts, the philistines. Small-town America, in Lewis's description, was "dullness made God"; small-city America vied with each other in their claims to be the original of Lewis's Zenith. H. L. Mencken tirelessly compiled manifestations of sterile stupidity, complacency, and emptiness and printed them in the "Americana" section of the *Mercury*; Harold Stearns delivered the page proofs of his *Civilization in the United States*—whose central irony consisted of his contributors' accumulated contention that there *was* no civilization in the United States—to his publisher and took ship for Europe.

Whites who remained in Prohibition-ridden, hypocritical, materialistic America increasingly looked to Harlem for its difference. If the Puritan repressed, blacks did not; if the Anglo-Saxon was inhibited, blacks were not; if Freud had provided the language for understanding the white angst, he obviously did not have the blacks in mind. A transmutation, an alchemy of sorts, took place within the white psyche. All those qualities criticized in the post–Civil War period by the advocates of "moral uplift"—black sensuousness, childlikeness, excess of laughter, present-time orientation—were now salutary qualities. Whites flocked to Harlem to learn how to *be*: how to be natural, how to be instinctive, how to be free. And black intellectuals and artists were not reluctant to articulate a special black spirit sometimes at odds, certainly different from the *Geist* oppressing many whites. Alain Locke, in his essay that introduced *The New Negro*, the 1925 special issue of the *Survey Graphic*, spoke of the "gift of his folk-temperament" to the culture of the

South, of the Negro's "leaven of humor, sentiment, imagination and tropic nonchalance."[6] Earlier Du Bois had established the terms of the contrast: black spirituality/white materialism, black soul/white dollars. When the white New York *Herald Tribune* "announced the Harlem Renaissance a few days after the first *Opportunity* Literary Contest Awards Dinner in May 1925, the newspaper also speculated about what might happen to a 'Nordic' stock, 'so bustling and busy' as sometimes to forget about feelings if touched by an African 'love of color, warmth, rhythm, and the whole of sensuous life.' "[7] Albert C. Barnes, a white contributor to *The New Negro*, articulated the difference, which was beginning to seem commonplace: "The white man in the mass cannot compete with the Negro in spiritual endowment. Many centuries of civilization have attenuated his original gifts and have made his mind dominate his spirit. He has wandered too far from the elementary human needs and their easy means of natural satisfaction. The deep and satisfying harmony which the soul requires no longer arises from the incidents of daily life. The requirements for practical efficiency in a world alien to his spirit have worn thin his religion and devitalized his art."[8] This "romantic racialism" was articulated, also, by black writers, as in the difference described in Countee Cullen's "A Song of Praise": "My love is dark as yours is fair, / Yet lovelier I hold her / Than listless maids with pallid hair, / And blood that's thin and colder."[9]

Black writers expressed difference and praised a dark beauty. Waring Cuney celebrates woman and at the same time comments on the unnaturalness of her urban setting in "No Images":

She does not know
Her beauty,
She thinks her brown body
Has no glory.
If she could dance
Naked,
Under palm trees
And see her image in the river
She would know.
But there are no palm trees
On the street,
And dish water gives back no images.[10]

This unnaturalness of the urban setting, a theme that sounds too in Jean Toomer's *Cane*, is implied in a poem by Edward Silvera:

> There is beauty
> In the faces of black women,
> Jungle beauty
> And mystery
> Dark hidden beauty
> In the faces of black women,
> Which only black men
> See.[11]

As in his "The Negro Speaks of Rivers," Langston Hughes suggests an ancient lineage in his "When Sue Wears Red":

> When Susanna Jones wears red
> Her face is like an ancient cameo
> Turned brown by the ages. . . .
> And the beauty of Susanna Jones in red
> Wakes in my heart a love-fire sharp like pain.[12]

And again and again Hughes, as other black writers, will celebrate dark beauty in terms that will oppose the stereotypes, as in his "To the Black Beloved":

> Ah,
> My black one,
> Thou are not beautiful,
> Yet thou hast
> A loveliness
> Surpassing beauty. . . .
>
> Ah,
> My black one,
> Thou are not luminous,
> Yet an altar of jewels,
> An altar of shimmering jewels,
> Would pale in the light
> Of thy darkness;
> Pale in the light
> Of thy nightness.[13]

The celebration of dark skins went beyond the celebration of dark beauty in the 1920s. The literature celebrated black Madonnas, ebon maids, Negro women, Africa-tinged grandmothers, black mothers, black brothers, brown-faced children, and many more. Responding to Africa, Hughes wrote, "The night is beautiful / So the faces of my people. / The stars are beautiful, / So the eyes of my people. / Beautiful, also, is the sun / Beautiful, also, are the souls of my people."[14] The literature also celebrated the variegated hues of nonwhite skin. Jake, in Claude McKay's *Home to Harlem* (1928), sees beauty in the profuse shadings on the street and in the cabaret:

> The broad pavements of Seventh Avenue were colorful with promenaders. Brown bodies in white carriages pushed by little black brothers wearing nice sailor suits. All the various and varying pigmentation of the human race were assembled there: dim brown, clear brown, rich brown, chestnut, copper, yellow, near-white, mahogany, and gleaming anthracite. Charming brown matrons, proud yellow matrons, dark nursemaids pulled a zigzag course by their restive little charges. . . .
>
> There is no human sight so rich as an assembly of Negroes ranging from lacquer black through brown to cream, decked out in their ceremonial finery. Negroes are like trees. They wear all colors naturally. And Felice, rouged to a ravishing maroon, and wearing a close-fitting, chrome-orange frock and cork-brown slippers, just melted into the scene.[15]

Nella Larsen's Helga Crane in *Quicksand* (1928) is also struck by the variety of colors at a cabaret:

> For the hundredth time she marveled at the gradations within this oppressed race of hers. A dozen shades slid by. There was sooty black, shiny black, taupe, mahogany, bronze, copper, gold, orange, yellow, peach, ivory, pinky white, pastry white. There was yellow hair, brown hair, black hair; straight hair, straightened hair, curly hair, crinkly hair, wooly hair. She saw black eyes in white faces, brown eyes in yellow faces, gray eyes in brown faces, blue eyes in tan faces. Africa, Europe, perhaps with a pinch of Asia, in a fantastic motley of ugliness and beauty, semibarbaric, sophisticated, exotic, were here.

But, unlike Claude McKay's Jake, she resisted its appeal: "But she was blind to its charm, purposely aloof and a little contemptuous, and soon her interest in the moving mosaic waned." Helga Crane's reaction is typical of her ambivalence toward blacks and blackness. Earlier, she had danced and had enjoyed it, but then "a shameful certainty that not only had she been in the jungle, but that she had enjoyed it, began to taunt her. She hardened her determination to get away. She wasn't, she told herself, a jungle creature."[16] Her ambivalence will give her no rest; inevitably it will fall like a shadow across present happiness throughout the novel. Whether she is in Harlem or in Denmark she will long for a different condition: to be away from blacks . . . to be with blacks. Larsen will embody in Helga Crane the conflicting attitudes toward color and race from the 1920s. She is drawn to the order, restraint, and inhibition of white culture but also attracted by the excitement, spontaneity, and disorder of black culture. She appreciates the fact that the masses can enjoy themselves (to be middle class is to be "hincty," she believes), but she resists what she identifies as the appeal of the jungle. Larsen will explore these conflicts in both *Quicksand* (1928) and *Passing* (1929).

Nella Larsen was the recipient of the Harmon Foundation medal "for distinguished achievement among Negroes," following the publication of *Quicksand* (1928), and the first black woman to receive a Guggenheim Fellowship (1930), following the publication of *Passing* (1929). No other black writer, with the possible exception of Jean Toomer, has written more revealingly of the identity struggle, of the anguish and conflict, of characters islanded between two races.

Nella Larsen's *Quicksand* begins:

> Helga Crane sat alone in her room, which at that hour, eight in the evening, was in soft gloom. Only a single reading lamp, dimmed by a great black and red shade, made a pool of light on the blue Chinese carpet, on the bright covers of the books which she had taken down from their long shelves, on the white pages of the opened one selected, on the shining brass bowl crowded with many-colored nasturtiums beside her on the low table, and on the oriental silk which covered the stool at her slim feet. It was a comfortable room, furnished with rare and intensely personal taste, flooded with Southern sun in the day, but shadowy just then with the drawn curtains and single shaded light. Large, too. So large that the spot where Helga sat was a small oasis in a desert of darkness. (23)

These opening lines have the quality of dream-vision. They are a dream of seclusion, privacy, aloneness in a world Helga Crane has created, a world controlled by taste, selection, discrimination. Selection so predominates in the listing of objects that her own feet seem to become objects, as though she has determined their own slimness, their qualities as esthetic objects.[17] But not only her feet—her whole person becomes an object for contemplation:

> An observer would have thought her well fitted to that framing of light and shade. A slight girl of twenty-three years, with narrow, sloping shoulders and delicate but well-turned arms and legs, she had none the less an air of radiant, careless health. In vivid green and gold negligee and glistening brocaded mules, deep sunk in the big high-backed chair, against whose dark tapestry her sharply cut face, with skin like yellow satin, was distinctly outlined, she was—to use a hackneyed word—attractive. Black, very broad brows over soft, yet penetrating, dark eyes, and a pretty mouth, whose sensitive and sensuous lips had a slight questioning petulance and a tiny dissatisfied droop, were the features on which the observer's attention would fasten; though her nose was good, her ears delicately chiseled, and her curly blue-black hair plentiful and always straying in a little wayward, delightful way. Just then it was tumbled, falling unrestrained about her face and on to her shoulders. (24)

The light in which she sits—a "framing of light and shade"—is like the spotlight in a museum, meant to highlight the qualities of the esthetic object—sculpture, painting, tapestry, gem, carving— upon which it falls. But as it illumines the object, it also isolates it (as the pediment the statue, the frame the picture), and isolation, too, is central to these opening paragraphs. Helga sits alone, an aloneness she has chosen: "This was her rest, this intentional isolation for a short while in the evening, this little time in her own attractive room with her own books. To the rapping of the teachers, bearing fresh scandals, or seeking information, or other more concrete favors, or merely talk, at that hour Helga Crane never opened her door" (24). Her aloneness reflects her separation from others at the school, Naxos, where she teaches—a separation that is intellectual, spiritual, esthetic. (Even Margaret Creighton, "to Helga the most congenial member of the whole Naxos faculty," responds to her with diffidence: "'Can I help you?' Margaret offered uncertainly. She was a little afraid of Helga. Nearly everyone was" [41].)[18]

At the same time, the oasis/desert of darkness metaphor contains an element of threat, of potential encroachment. At the edges of Helga Crane's carefully constructed order is disorder. It is significant that on this evening when she has resolved to resign her position at Naxos her agitation is expressed in terms of disorder:

> And after a moment's rest she got hurriedly into bed, leaving her room disorderly for the first time [in two years].
>
> Books and papers scattered about the floor, fragile stockings and underthings and the startling green and gold negligee dripping about on chairs and stool, met the encounter of the amazed eyes of the girl who came in the morning to awaken Helga Crane. (35)

This early suggestion of disorder, which closes chapter 1, is a forewarning of the disorder, some seven years later, at the close of the novel. Helga Crane, for whom order and discrimination, choice and control, are so essential, ends the novel as the wife of a heavy, insensitive, self-satisfied, small-town Baptist preacher: "She, who had never thought of her body save as something on which to hang lovely fabrics, had now constantly to think of it" (203). This is necessary because she is continually pregnant. She, who has spoken again and again against bringing more Negro children into the world, is the mother of three, two of them twins, in a period of twenty months, and she is beset by disorder: "Helga, looking about in helpless dismay and sick disgust at the disorder around her, the permanent assembly of partly emptied medicine bottles on the clock shelf, the perpetual array of drying baby clothes on the chair backs, the constant debris of broken toys on the floor, the unceasing litter of half-dead flowers on the table" (205). She is weakened by childbearing: "Always she felt extraordinarily and annoyingly ill, having forever to be sinking into chairs. Or, if she was out, to be pausing by the roadside, clinging desperately to some convenient fence or tree, waiting for the horrible nausea and hateful faintness to pass" (203). Her mind, formerly a questioning one, sinks into faith: "Faith was really quite easy. One had only to yield. To ask no questions. The more weary, the more weak, she became, the easier it was. Her religion was to her a kind of protective coloring, shielding her from the cruel light of an unbearable reality" (208). It is only after the labor of her fourth childbearing—labor lasting from Sunday to Tuesday—that she determines to leave her house, husband, and children. The determination grows during weeks of recuperation, but the determination is mixed with concern for her three children (the fourth died within a week), with the difficulties in going, with the need for rest. The novel concludes: "And hardly had she left her bed and become able to walk again without pain, hardly had the children returned from the homes of the neighbors, when she began to have her fifth child" (222). By the close of the novel, Helga Crane has lost control of her life.

It is significant that this loss of control is so clearly expressed through childbearing, as though her own physical space is breached by the disorder without, which, through pregnancy, is internalized, only to be further externalized by the imperious demands of the child: by its schedule, by its clutter of things—medicine bottles, baby clothes, broken toys, half-dead flowers. This is a flowering of the sexual, which had earlier figured in that control she had so assiduously exercised. The sexual had been viewed as animal, primitive: "She wasn't, she told herself, a jungle creature" (108). Robert Anderson's kiss had revealed in her "a long-hidden, half understood desire" (174). And the evening following his kiss exposes the potential for disorder in the sexual: "That night riotous and colorful dreams invaded Helga Crane's prim hotel bed. She woke in the morning weary and a bit shocked at the uncontrolled fancies which had visited her. . . . She lived over those brief seconds, thinking not so much of the man whose arms had held her as of the ecstasy which had flooded her. Even recollection brought a little onrush of emotion that made her sway a little" (176).

But the control she had managed to achieve at various moments in her life—as a teacher at Naxos, working for the black insurance company in New York, living with her Danish aunt and uncle in Denmark—always seems tenuous, artificial, forced: the "desert of darkness"—disorder, uncertainty—is always close at hand. In New York: "But it didn't last, this happiness of Helga Crane's. Little by little the signs of spring appeared, but strangely the enchantment of the season, so enthusiastically, so lavishly greeted by the gay dwellers of Harlem, filled her only with restlessness. Somewhere, within her, in a deep recess, crouched discontent" (90). In Denmark: "Well into Helga's second year in Denmark came an indefinite discontent. Not clear, but vague, like a storm gathering far on the horizon" (140).

Helga's discontent grows out of her yearning for a place where she can be herself and an ambivalence regarding what her self really is. Racially, she is the offspring of an affair between her Danish mother and black father. They were apparently never married, and her mother later (when Helga was six) married a white man. Her later ambivalence and yearning have roots in her childhood, a childhood she recalls on the train traveling to Chicago after resigning her position at Naxos:

Memory, flown back to those years following the marriage, dealt her torturing stabs. Before her rose the pictures of her mother's careful management to avoid those ugly scarifying quarrels which even at this far-off time caused an uncontrollable shudder, her own childish self-effacement, the savage unkindness of her step-brothers and sisters, and the jealous, malicious hatred of her mother's husband. Summers, winters, years, passing in one long, changeless stretch of aching misery of soul. Her mother's death, when Helga was fifteen. Her rescue by Uncle Peter, who had sent her to school, a school for Negroes, where for the first time she could breathe freely, where she discovered that because one was dark, one was not necessarily loathsome, and could, therefore, consider oneself without repulsion.

Six years. She had been happy there, as happy as a child unused to happiness dared be. There had always been a feeling of strangeness, of outsideness, and one of holding her breath for fear that it wouldn't last. It hadn't. It had dwindled gradually into eclipse of painful isolation. They had mothers, fathers, brothers, and sisters of whom they spoke frequently, and who sometimes visited them. They went home for the vacations which Helga spent in the city where the school was located.

They visited each other and knew many of the same people. Discontent for which there was no remedy crept upon her. (55–56)

The adult Helga Crane reflects this childhood: alone and lonely; racially ambivalent, which is expressed by her unsettled sense of self/identity; and her continuing discontent with places. Places either contribute to her sense of identity or make her yearn for some other place. Chicago: "She stood intently looking down into the glimmering street, far below, swarming with people. . . . She stood in the doorway, drawn by an uncontrollable desire to mingle with the crowd. . . . There came to her a queer feeling of enthusiasm, as if she were tasting some agreeable, exotic food—sweetbreads, smothered with truffles and mushrooms—perhaps. And, oddly enough, she felt, too, that she had come home. She, Helga Crane, who had no home" (64–65). Harlem: "But, while the continuously gorgeous panorama of Harlem fascinated her, thrilled her, the sober mad rush of white New York failed entirely to stir her" (87).[19]

But her sense of discontent overwhelms place/identity/joy, and the source of her discontent is racial:

Life [in New York City] became for her only a hateful place where one lived in intimacy with people one would not have chosen had one been given choice. . . . Abruptly it flashed upon her that the harrowing irritation of the past weeks was a smoldering hatred. Then, she was overcome by another, so actual, so sharp, so horribly painful, that forever afterward she preferred to forget it. It was as if she were shut up, boxed up, with hundreds of her race, closed up with that something in the racial character which had always been, to her, inexplicable, alien. Why, she demanded in fierce rebellion, should she be yoked to these despised black folk? . . . She didn't, in spite of her racial markings, belong to these dark segregated people. She was different. She felt it. It wasn't merely a matter of color. It was something broader, deeper, that made folk kin. (99, 101, 102)

On the boat to Denmark she even reaches the point where she applies the term *aversion* to blacks, the same term that James Weldon Johnson's protagonist employs: "Leaning against the railing, Helga stared into the approaching night, glad to be at last alone, free of that great superfluity of human beings, yellow, brown, and black, which, as the torrid summer burnt to its close, had so oppressed her. No, she hadn't belonged there. Of her attempt to emerge from that inherent aloneness which was part of her very being, only dullness had come, dullness and a great aversion" (113).

During the voyage, her racial identity seems to slip from her like a discarded garment; she revels "like a released bird in her returned feeling of happiness and freedom, that blessed sense of belonging to herself alone and not to a race" (114). This sense of uniqueness is encouraged by her Danish aunt and uncle, who view her both as niece and objet d'art, capitalizing on her skin coloring by so dressing and bejeweling her as to suggest the primitive and exotic. Her aunt declares, "'You're a foreigner, and different. You must have bright things to set off the color of your lovely brown skin. Striking things, exotic things. You must make an impression'" (120). Their attitude reinforces her own: "It gratified her augmented sense of self-importance" (130). Their view of her as object complements her own and is similar to her earlier view of herself in Naxos. Before leaving America, she had anticipated approval: "She let herself drop into the blissful sensation of visualizing herself in different, strange places, among approving and admiring people, where she would be appreciated, and understood" (105). It is questionable whether she is understood in Denmark, but she is appreciated:

> The day . . . conveyed to Helga her exact status in her new environment. A decoration. A curio. A peacock. Their progress through the shops was an event; an event for Copenhagen as well as for Helga Crane. Her dark, alien appearance was to most people an astonishment. Some stared surreptitiously, some openly, and some stopped dead in front of her in order more fully to profit by their stares. "*Den Sorte*" dropped freely, audibly, from many lips. . . . She was incited to inflame attention and admiration. She was dressed for it, subtly schooled for it. And after a little while she gave herself up wholly to the fascinating business of being seen, gaped at, desired. (129, 130)

But discontent surfaces in Denmark, as it had earlier in America. And again, the source of her discontent is racial. However, aversion is now replaced by yearning, homesickness. The source of her discontent becomes clearer as she attends, with Danish friends, a vaudeville show, whose entertainers include two Negroes who both sing and dance. Unlike the other spectators, she is not amused: "Instead she was filled with a fierce hatred for the cavorting Negroes on the stage. She felt shamed, betrayed, as if these pale[20] pink and white people among whom she lived had suddenly been invited to look upon something in her which she had hidden away and wanted to forget" (43). But she returns "again and again to the Circus, always alone, gazing intently and solemnly at the gesticulating black figures, an ironical and silently speculative spectator. For she knew that into her plan for her life had thrust itself a suspensive conflict in which were fused doubts, rebellion, expediency, and urgent longings" (144). Her feelings crystallize at a performance of Dvořák's *New World Symphony*: "Her definite decision to go was arrived at with almost bewildering suddenness. It was after a concert at which Dvořák's 'New World Symphony' had been wonderfully rendered. Those wailing undertones of 'Swing Low, Sweet Chariot' were too poignantly familiar. They struck into her longing heart. . . . She knew at last what it was that had lurked formless and undesignated these many weeks in the back of her troubled mind. Incompleteness. 'I'm homesick, not for America, but for Negroes. That's the trouble'" (157–158). For the first time she is able to sympathize with her father's desertion of her mother: "She understood his yearning, his intolerable need for the inexhaustible humor and the incessant hope of his own kind, his need for those things, nonmaterial, indigenous to all Negro environments. She understood and could sympathize with his facile surrender to the irresistible ties of race, now that they dragged at her own heart. And as she attended parties, the theater, the opera, and mingled with people on the streets, meeting only pale serious faces when she longed for brown laughing ones, she was able to forgive him" (158).

She returns to New York to luxuriate among her people: "Helga, on her part, had been glad to get back to New York. How glad, or why, she did not truly realize. . . . *These* were her people. Nothing, she had come to understand now, could ever change that. Strange that she had never truly valued this kinship until distance had shown her its worth. How absurd she had been to think that another country, other people, could liberate her from the ties which bound her forever to these mysterious, these terrible, these fascinating, these loveable, dark hordes" (162).

But these feelings, as others, seem overly willed. She cannot still her ambivalence, even though, at times, it is reformulated as a rational calculus of attractions:

> Not that she intended to remain. . . . No. She couldn't stay. Nor she saw now, could she remain away. Leaving, she would have to come back.
>
> This knowledge, this certainty of the division of her life into two parts in two lands, into physical freedom in Europe and spiritual freedom in America, was unfortunate, inconvenient, expensive. (163)

At other times, her ambivalence surfaces in phrases that suggest anxiety, panic: "Yet Helga herself had an acute feeling of insecurity, for which she could not account. Sometimes it amounted to fright almost. 'I must,' she would say then, 'get back to Copenhagen' " (164).

Her existence between the two races will not let her be wholly at peace with either. With whites, she ultimately experiences her objectness, her difference, her incompleteness. With blacks, she ultimately feels engulfed, her uniqueness ignored, her self refracted in the whites' distorting mirror. She experiences her self as the one who is not at ease, while, all about her, others are content. This is most clear in a response in New York: "There were days when the mere sight of the serene tan and brown faces about her stung her like a personal insult. The carefree quality of their laughter roused in her the desire to scream at them: 'Fools, fools! Stupid fools!' " (99).

Her need is to control, but at the same time her need is to surrender to her situation. Her need is to be someone, but her past has permitted her choice. She discovers through the course of the novel that when one can be either, one might be neither; that, where the self is concerned, plenty can be too little. Her choice, ultimately, will be a negation of choice.

A peace of sorts is achieved in the closing chapters. She sinks into "salvation" as one sinks into sleep (Larsen notes, "And in that moment she was lost—or saved") after wandering into the storefront church out of the storm. Emotionally and physically weary, she is open to the influence of the crowd, the ritual, the emotion: "A curious influence penetrated her. . . . she felt herself possessed . . . felt a brutal desire to shout and to sling herself about . . . the strength of the obsession . . . weakness and nausea. . . . Maddened, she grasped at the railing, and with no previous intention began to yell like one insane, drowning every other clamor" (188, 189). She sinks into "salvation," into self, into race, which represents a stilling of the voices, an end to ambiguity, an end to choice, but also, and finally, a sinking into that quicksand suggested, and threatened, by the title.[21]

Passing, published only one year after *Quicksand*, reveals how deeply the themes of *Quicksand* preoccupied Nella Larsen. In *Passing* Larsen again creates a character who has the "dreadful freedom" of racial choice; in fact, *Passing* is so like *Quicksand* that it could almost be titled *Quicksand*, volume 2. It is no longer a question, as it was in *Quicksand*, of going to Denmark; in *Passing* Clare Kendry can pass for white in America and in fact is married to a white man who is ignorant of her "color." But should she go back?—that is, rejoin her black world? In *Quicksand* the conflicts raged within Helga Crane; in *Passing* Helga Crane's qualities are divided between Irene Redfield and Clare Kendry. The control so vital to Helga Crane is reflected by Irene Redfield's preoccupation with security and propriety; Helga Crane's attraction to black life is expressed by the passionate yearning of Clare Kendry. It is as though the troubled Helga Crane of *Quicksand* has undergone analysis only to become the split Irene Redfield/Clare Kendry of *Passing*.

To Irene Redfield, security is the most precious quality: "Security. Was it just a word? If not, then was it only by the sacrifice of other things, happiness, love, or some wild ecstasy that she had never known, that it could be obtained? . . . security was the most important and desired thing in life. Not for any of the others, or for all of them, would she exchange it. She wanted only to be tranquil. Only, unmolested, to be allowed to direct for their own best good the lives of her sons and her husband."[22] For the sake of security and control, life with her husband becomes a series of routinized gestures, interaction becomes staging, talk becomes dialogue, and relations become the public performing of the privately rehearsed. In such an economy of interchange, emotions are threatening and are controlled, as in her response to fears about a possible relationship between her husband and Clare Kendry: "She must not work herself up. She must not! Where were all the self-control, the common sense, that she was so proud of?" (174). Order, balance, control are achieved, in part, by the exclusion of unpleasant, potentially disruptive topics. The "race problem," for example, is not to be discussed with her two sons, since, as she declared to her husband, "'I want their childhood to be happy and as free from the knowledge of such things as it possibly can be'" (172). Her attitude toward sex is similar, recalling Helga Crane's practice of denial; her fastidiousness regarding her son Junior's exposure to sexual knowledge is significantly responded to by her husband: "'The sooner and the more he learns about sex, the better for him. And most certainly if he learns that it's a grand joke, the greatest in the world. It'll keep him from lots of disappointments later on'" (105). Even with regard to her husband's affair with Clare Kendry, it is less the affair itself than the knowledge that others might have of it that is potentially most disruptive: "In that second she saw that she could bear anything, but only if no one knew that she had anything to bear. It hurt. It frightened her, but she could bear it. . . . It hurt. It hurt like hell. But it didn't matter, if no one knew" (157, 159).

In contrast to Irene Redfield, Clare Kendry embodies desire, the sexual, the barely checked impulse. It was said of her, from early youth, "'Clare always had a—a—having way with her'" (46). At times she seems more a personification of the id than a character, as in her declaration to Irene Redfield, "'It's just that I haven't any proper morals or sense of duty, as you have, that makes me act as I do. . . . Can't you realize that I'm not like you a bit? Why, to get the things I want badly enough, I'd do anything, hurt anybody, throw anything away. Really, 'Rene, I'm not safe'" (139). What she wants, above all, is to be back among Negroes—"'For I am lonely, so lonely,'" she writes to Clare. She employs the adjective "pale," which recurs in Helga Crane's description of her Copenhagen milieu, to describe the white world in which she is passing: "'You can't know how in this pale life of mine I am all the time seeing the bright pictures of that other past I once thought I was glad to be free of. . . . It's like an ache, a pain that never ceases'" (33).[23] She yearns to be with "my own people" (92): " 'I've been so lonely since! You can't know. Not close to a single soul. Never anyone to really talk to. . . . You don't know, you can't realize how I want to see Negroes, to be with them again, to talk with them, to hear them laugh' " (116, 123).[24]

But being back among Negroes, which would follow upon her husband's learning the truth, would also threaten Irene Redfield's marriage, since Clare Kendry would no longer be constrained to save her own. Gone would be Irene Redfield's marriage, her security, her control. Such a conflict within a single character—as in the case of Helga Crane in *Quicksand*—could be dealt with by repression of the troubling/threatening desire/impulse. On the enlarged stage of *Passing*, Larsen turns to the dramatic equivalent: When Clare Kendry's racist husband bursts into the party to confront Clare Kendry and her black friends, and Clare Kendry smiles as in acknowledgment of the end of her masquerade, Irene Redfield's reaching out to her becomes the unseen shove that pushes her through the window to her death. Thus the violence done to the self in *Quicksand* becomes the violence done to the other in *Passing*, and Helga Crane's sinking into quicksand becomes Clare Kendry's fall to her death. The wrenchings of racial ambivalence and desire are violently stilled.

Stilled, too, was Nella Larsen's voice after the publication of *Passing*. She never completed a projected third novel and died "in relative obscurity in Brooklyn in 1963."[25] She is described by Adelaide Cromwell Hill, in her introduction to the American Library edition of *Quicksand*, as an "outwardly abrupt, inwardly insecure and sensitive woman, always wishing to seem apart from her race, to be accepted as a writer, not as a Negro" (16). The "facts" of her life are, basically, those of her character Helga Crane: "Born in Chicago in 1893, of a West Indian father and a Danish mother, Nella Larsen grew up in that city with her mother first widowed and then remarried to 'one of her own kind,' who did not look with favor on Nella—a reminder of his wife's earlier life. Miss Larsen received her high school education in Chicago and went for one year to Fisk University in Nashville, Tennessee. Upon leaving Fisk she spent two years in Denmark auditing classes at the University of Copenhagen" (13). Her movement from career to career (librarian, writer, nurse); her marriage to a black professional and her later divorce; her travels to Denmark, Europe, New York—all suggest the unsettled movement of her character Helga Crane. And perhaps her silence, too, is foreshadowed in the stilling of Helga Crane: "Miss Larsen disappeared from public life, never published again, and apparently worked as a supervising nurse at Bethel Hospital in Brooklyn until she retired" (15).

CHAPTER FOURTEEN

Jean Toomer

MOVING FROM BIOGRAPHY to art is always potentially presumptuous, but in the case of Jean Toomer one is encouraged in such presumption by Toomer's own writings. Arna Bontemps has remarked that a biography Toomer sent friends at the *Liberator* in 1922 "foreshadowed a wild search for identity that was to drive Toomer through all the years that followed till his death in 1967."[1] Toomer's comments on his life represent a more ordered approach to the disorder and ambivalence experienced by so many of his characters:

> Racially, I seem to have (who knows for sure) seven blood mixtures: French, Dutch, Welsh, Negro, German, Jewish, and Indian. Because of these, my position in America has been a curious one. I have lived equally amid the two race groups. Now white, now colored. From my own point of view I am naturally and inevitably an American. I have strived for a spiritual fusion analogous to the fact of racial intermingling. Without denying a single element in me, with no desire to subdue one to the other, I have sought to let them function as complements. I have tried to let them live in harmony. Within the last two or three years, however, my growing need for artistic expression has pulled me deeper and deeper into the Negro group. And as my powers of receptivity increased, I found myself loving it in a way that I could never love the other. It has stimulated and fertilized whatever creative talent I may contain within me. A visit to Georgia last fall was the starting point of almost everything of worth that I have done. I heard folk-songs come from the lips of Negro peasants. I saw the rich dusk beauty that I had heard many false accents about, and of which till then, I was somewhat skeptical. And a deep part of my nature, a part that I had repressed, sprang suddenly to life and responded to them. Now, I cannot conceive of myself as aloof and separated. My point of view has not changed; it

has deepened, it has widened. Personally, my life has been torturous and dispersed. (viii–ix)

The life that is torturous and dispersed, the ambivalence of a Dan, a Paul, a Kabnis, is calmed by the experience of Georgia, by the artifice of art. But only one year after the publication of *Cane* (1923) he was, according to Bontemps, "explaining to his friends, 'I am. What I am and what I may become I am trying to find out'" (xiii). What he ultimately found personally is perhaps expressed in the notes for an autobiography included in Bontemps's introduction to the Harper Perennial Classic edition of *Cane*:

> [Upon setting out for the University of Wisconsin] I would again be entering a white world; and, though I personally had experienced no prejudice or exclusion either from the whites or the colored people, I had seen enough to know that America viewed life as if it were divided into white and black. Having lived with colored people for the past five years, at Wisconsin the question might come up. What was I? I thought about it independently, and, on the basis of fact, concluded that I was neither white nor black, but simply an American. I held this view and decided to live according to it. I would tell others if the occasion demanded it. (xv)

What he found artistically was silence, writings for the *Friends Intelligencer*, notes for an undeveloped autobiography.

But there was no silence in *Cane*. Its many voices—drawling and urgent, channeled through the narrator and expressed directly—spoke of black life, South and North, in ways new and marvelous. And its influence, according to Bontemps, was felt by such 1920s contemporaries as Langston Hughes, Countee Cullen, Eric Walrond, Zora Neale Hurston, Wallace Thurman, and Rudolph Fisher, as well as by subsequent writers in America, Africa, and the West Indies (x).

Cane is, in fact, many books. It is a young man's book, whose women—Karintha, Fern, Louisa—are dream-visions: "Men had always wanted her, this Karintha, even as a child, Karintha carrying beauty, perfect as dusk when the sun goes down" (1). It is a love song to black women, but to black women as a young man imagines them. Relatively uncomplicated, they are largely one-dimensional embodiments of the desirable: of the sensual and the sexual, and of something larger that seems to suggest roots, the maternal and the earth, the earth-mother. His women embody a certitude that reflects both their closeness to natural process and their rootedness in the land and soil. Toomer, preoccupied with place, sees Fern, for example, through metaphors of space. She becomes the hub of the wheeled universe: "If you walked up the Dixie Pike most any time of day, you'd be most like to see her. . . . the whole countryside seemed to flow into her eyes" (26, 27). Toomer's women require only surrender—to that nature that in their being they complete; but Toomer's men are talkers, and only in the concluding paragraphs are they (is Kabnis) able to still the voices in their heads and their own tongues. And this stilling is achieved through the love of a woman.[2]

Cane is a philippic against the city. The city is the place of locks, bolts, houses, grime, straight lines, the look of the other, unnatural relationships. It is the place of conventional attitudes, the dictatorship of the expected, and in this respect *Cane* is an indictment of middle-class respectability and dullness.[3] It is the place, as in "Box Seat," which is waiting for its savior, waiting for its Moses, however ironically, however vainly.[4] A Fern, transplanted to Harlem, represents a kind of violation: "Picture if you can, this cream-colored solitary girl sitting at a tenement window looking down on the indifferent throngs of Harlem. Better that she listen to folk-songs at dusk in Georgia, you would say, and so would I" (28). The soul of the woman in "Calling Jesus"—a woman transplanted from cane to asphalt—cannot pass the iron hinges, the storm doors, but, like a "little thrust-tailed dog," sits all night in the vestibule whimpering, shivering. And when you meet the woman on the street, it is only when she forgets the urban present that the soul, steeped in the natural and the rural, can start forth: "When you meet her in the daytime on the streets, the little dog keeps coming. Nothing happens at first, and then, when she has forgotten the streets and alleys, and the large house where she goes to bed at nights, a soft thing like fur begins to rub your limbs, and you hear a low, scared voice, lonely, calling, and you know that a cool something nozzles moisture in your palms. Sensitive things like nostrils, quiver. Her breath comes sweet as honeysuckle whose pistils bear the life of coming song.

And her eyes carry to where builders find no need for vestibules, for swinging on iron hinges, storm doors" (102–103). Through forgetting, and through dreams: "Some one . . . echo Jesus . . . soft as the bare feet of Christ moving across bales of southern cotton, will steal in and cover it [her soul] that it need not shiver, and carry it to her when she sleeps: cradled in dream-fluted cane" (103).

Cane is an evocation of roots, of place, of home. The place is typically rural Georgia, though at times it is simply the South, as in "Avey": "And when the wind is from the South, soil of *my* homeland falls like a *fertile* shower upon the *lean* streets of *the* city" (85; emphasis added). (The city, here as elsewhere, is the locus of infertility and displacement.) The "I" persona speaks more intimately and personally in "Song of the Son":

> O land and soil, red soil and sweet-gum tree,
> So scant of grass, so profligate of pines,
> Now just before an epoch's sun declines
> Thy son, in time, I have returned to thee,
> Thy son, I have in time returned to thee.

He returns to become/to be the seed, the tongue, the song, the song singer, the son of the cross/tree:

> O Negro slaves, dark purple ripened plums,
> Squeezed, and bursting in the pine-wood air,
> Passing, before they stripped the old tree bare
> One plum was saved for me, one seed becomes
> An everlasting song, a singing tree,
> Caroling softly souls of slavery,
> What they were, and what they are to me.
> Caroling softly souls of slavery. (21)

"When one is on the soil of one's ancestors, most anything can come to one," declares the persona in "Fern," as did the vision that came to the black woman in Georgia ("People have them in Georgia more often than you would suppose"), who "once saw the mother of Christ and drew her in charcoal on the courthouse wall" (31). Toomer—out of the soil of Georgia, the soil of his ancestors—becomes a bearer of visions, a "singing tree / Caroling softly souls of slavery."[5]

Cane is an experimental work. In fact, for a period noted for experimentation, Cane is an outstanding example. Within Cane, Toomer experimented with the forms of poetry, drama, and fiction. Stylistically, Toomer's prose includes expressionism ("Her mind is a pink mesh-bag filled with baby toes" [45]); interior monologue ("This loneliness, dumbness, awful, intangible oppression is enough to drive a man insane. Miles from nowhere. A speck on a Georgia hillside" [162]); borrowings from the visual arts (John, in "Theater," is a cubist still life—"Light streaks down upon him from a window high above. One half his face is orange in it. One half his face is in shadow" [91]—the division paralleling other divisions: body/mind, reality/dream); symbolism ("Her soul is like a little thrust-tailed dog that follows her, whimpering" [102]); folk spirituals ("Let's open our throats, brother, and sing 'Deep River' when he goes down" [75]); poetry ("Up from the skeleton stone walls, up from the rotting floor boards and the solid hand-hewn beams of oak of the pre-war cotton factory, dusk came. Up from the dusk the full moon came. Glowing like a fired pine-knot, it illumined the great door and soft showered the Negro shanties aligned along the single street of factory town" [51]). Much writing in the twenties was energized by the new psychology, and Toomer moved skillfully into the internal worlds of his characters. In addition, the tripartite division of Cane mirrors the psychological split (between sections, within characters) between the urban North and rural Georgia and the disassociation of sensibility induced by uprootedness.

Three of the major experimental writers of the period—Sherwood Anderson, T. S. Eliot, and Eugene O'Neill—seem to have influenced Toomer's writing. The presence of Anderson (Eliot and O'Neill will be considered later) seems most clear in the similarities between the recurring "I" narrator in the first two sections of Cane and George Willard, the narrator in Winesburg, Ohio. The narrator's comment to the policeman in "Avey"—"I tell him I come there to find that truth that people bury in their hearts" [85–86]—recalls the comments on truth in "The Book of the Grotesque" from Winesburg, Ohio.[6] The pieces in Cane, as in Winesburg, Ohio, are often a mix of the mood piece and character sketch: both probe the psychology of their characters; both evoke the strong influence of place in the lives, however twisted, of their characters.[7]

And, perhaps more central than any other quality, *Cane* is a study in ambivalence. Characters are divided against themselves, which blurs for them the perceiving of their own lives. Affected, as a consequence, are self-knowledge, intimacy, place, and history. Ambivalence particularly characterizes Dan and Muriel in "Box Seat," John in "Theater," Bona and Paul in "Bona and Paul," and Kabnis in the closing section.

The prose poem "Seventh Street," which is the first piece in the second section, introduces the reader to the rough energy and vitality of newly migrated blacks in the city:

> A crude-boned, soft-skinned wedge of nigger life breathing its loafer air, jazz songs and love, thrusting unconscious rhythms, black reddish blood into the white and whitewashed wood of Washington. Wedges rust in soggy wood . . . Split it! In two! Again! Shred it! . . . the sun. Wedges are brilliant in the sun; ribbons of wet wood dry and blow away. Black reddish blood. Pouring for crude-boned soft-skinned life, who set you flowing? Blood suckers of the War would spin in a frenzy of dizziness if they drank your blood. Prohibition would put a stop to it. Who set you flowing? White and white-wash disappear in blood. Who set you flowing? Flowing down the smooth asphalt of Seventh Street, in shanties, brick office buildings, theaters, drug stores, restaurants, and cabarets? (71–72)

Their energy and vitality, their flowing blood, is placed in opposition to the white world of Washington, a fixed world of place, of old structures and old possessions.

But already in the next piece, "Rhobert," black life has been transformed by the city. Rhobert is both person, symbol, and automaton. He is a person who owns a house, but the house owns him (as in Emerson's "things are in the saddle / And ride mankind" and Thoreau's "it turns out that men are not so much the keepers of cattle as cattle are the keepers of men," such men as those of Thoreau who daily push a barn fifty feet long down the road). He has become the house—Rhobert the robot. He wears it like a diver's helmet: "Rods of the house like antennae of a dead thing, stuffed, propped up in the air. He is way down. He is sinking. His house is a dead thing that weights him down" (73). And for this "dead thing" he will sacrifice the living: "Like most men who wear monstrous helmets, the pressure it exerts is enough to convince him of its practical infinity. And he cares not two straws as to whether or not he will ever see his wife and child again. Many a time he's seen them drown in his dreams and has kicked about joyously in the mud for days after" (74). Ironically, water, which should be life-giving/sustaining, will crush him if he pulls off his helmet. The water is also, again ironically, the water of the spiritual "Deep River" ("Deep river, Lord / My home is over Jordan"), but "home," which figures so profoundly in the black experience (consider the multiple significances of the spiritual refrain: "I got a home ina dat rock, don't you see? / I got a home ina dat rock, don't you see? / Between earth and sky / I heard my savior cry / 'You got a home ina dat rock / Don't you see?'"), becomes a house, which is an early instance of its use by Toomer as a symbol for constraint, for spiritual and physical death.

Karintha was unchanged—by time, by experience. At the end of her piece in the first section of *Cane* she is "perfect as dusk when the sun goes down," an echo of the opening line. By contrast, at the conclusion to "Avey," "Avey's face was pale, and her eyes were heavy. She did not have the gray crimson-splashed beauty of the dawn." She was an "orphan woman" (88). Urban time is too much with Avey. "'You look older,'" was how she greeted the protagonist, and she leaves the man she is with to go walking with him and to sit on the grass of the hill at Soldiers' Home. There he tells her of his dreams, and the telling is perhaps the most youthful and romantic section of the book:

> I traced my development from the early days up to the present time, the phase in which I could understand her. I described her own nature and temperament. Told how they needed a larger life for their expression. How incapable Washington was of understanding that need. How it could not meet it. I pointed out that in lieu of proper channels, her emotions had overflowed into paths that dissipated them. I talked, beautifully I thought, about an art that would be born, an art that would open the way for women the likes of her. I asked her to hope, and build up an

inner life against the coming of that day. I recited some of my own things to her. I sang, with a strange quiver in my voice, a promise-song. (86–87)

He grows passionate, only to find that she has been sleeping. She has slipped out of time: "Then I looked at Avey. Her heavy eyes were closed. Her breathing was as faint and regular as a child's in slumber. My passion died" (87). *In* time, for Avey, is the world of barter, and her store for barter has been her self.[8]

In "Avey," even the trees of Washington, D.C. are unnaturally constrained: "The young trees had not outgrown their boxes then. V Street was lined with them. When our legs were cramped and stiff from the cold of the stone, we'd stand around a box and whittle it. I like to think now that there was a hidden purpose in the way we hacked them with our knives. I like to feel that something deep in me responded to the trees, the young trees that whinnied like colts impatient to be let free" (76). In "Box Seat," which even in its title suggests the recurring theme of constraint, the young woman Muriel is boxed into houses and into the social conventions the houses both foster and reflect; but Dan, her lover, is no Moses—though able to understand, he is unable to act.

An opposition is established in the first two paragraphs of "Box Seat":

> Houses are shy girls whose eyes shine reticently upon the dusk body of the street. Upon the gleaming limbs and asphalt torso of a dreaming nigger. Open your liver lips to the lean, white spring. Stir the root-life of a withered people. Call them from their houses, and teach them to dream.
>
> Dark swaying forms of Negroes are street songs that woo virginal houses. (104)

The energy and vitality suggested in "Seventh Street" are transmuted in these paragraphs into sexual energy. House and street would seem psychosexually to suggest uterus and penis, an implication extended in the lines, "The eyes of houses faintly touch him [Dan] as he passes them. . . . Floating away, they dally wistfully over the dark body of the street" (104).

Dan is coming to see Muriel in one of the houses. The houses are like prisons. Toomer here, as in the section "Calling Jesus," draws attention to gates, to the iron gate. When he can't immediately find the bell, Dan exhibits a self-consciousness bred of racism: "Mounts the steps, and searches for the bell. Funny, he can't find it. He fumbles around. The thought comes to him that some one passing by might see him, and not understand. Might think that he is trying to sneak, to break in" (105). Dan responds internally with the anger that is never publicly expressed: "Dan: Break in. Get an ax and smash in. Smash in their faces. I'll show em. Break into an engine-house, steal a thousand horse-power fire truck. Smash in with the truck. I'll show em. Grab an ax and brain em. Cut em up. Jack the Ripper. Baboon from the zoo. And then the cops come. No, I aint a baboon. I aint Jack the Ripper. I'm a poor man out of work. Take your hands off me, you bull-necked bears. Look into my eyes. I am Dan Moore. I was born in a canefield. The hands of Jesus touched me" (105–106). His response is an impulse to violence and power and their expression; a consciousness of the violence (physical, psychological) of the white other; an assertion of roots and of one's brotherhood in the eyes/hands of God (the hands of the "bull-necked bears" become the hands of Jesus).

The Mrs. Pribby (with her name connoting primness) who opens (unlocks) the door is more warder than landlady. She is the metallic expression of her metal house:

> Her eyes are weak. They are bluish and watery from reading newspapers. The blue is steel. It gimlets Dan while her mouth flaps amiably to him. . . .
>
> Mrs. Pribby retreats to the rear of the house. She takes up a newspaper. There is a sharp click as she fits into her chair and draws it to the table. The click is metallic like the sound of a bolt being shot into place. Dan's eyes sting. Sinking into a soft couch, he closes them. The house contracts about him. It is a sharp-edged, massed, metallic house. Bolted. About Mrs. Pribby. Bolted to the endless rows of metal houses. Mrs. Pribby's house. The rows of houses belong to other Mrs. Pribbys. No wonder he couldn't sing to them. (107)

Muriel has taken on the coloration of her container: she "thuds" down the stairs, "clicks" into her chair.

As the mannered play of the afternoon encounter between Dan

and Muriel is acted out, Eliot's "The Love Song of J. Alfred Prufrock" and *The Waste Land* seem to hover over this world. Dan, as Prufrock, makes his visit, but he is, as Muriel tells herself, a "timid lover, brave talker" (110). (She tells him he "'ought to work more and think less'" [111].) Eliot's "a hundred visions and revisions" become Toomer's "a hundred platitudes" (111). Just as Prufrock, Dan is unable to force the moment to its crisis:

> A sharp rap on the newspaper in the rear room cuts between them. The rap is like cool thick glass between them. Dan is hot on one side. Muriel, hot on the other. They straighten. Gaze fearfully at one another. Neither moves. ["It's time," in both Eliot's world and Toomer's.] A clock in the rear room, in the rear room, the rear room, strikes eight. Eight slow, cool sounds. Bernice. [The encounter concluded, Muriel's actions recall the postassignation actions of *The Waste Land*.] Muriel fastens on her image. She smoothes her dress. She adjusts her skirt. (115)

In *The Waste Land*, one waits for the redemptive rain to bring life to the dull roots; in the opening lines of "Box Seat," it is the spring that might "stir the root-life of a withered people" (104). The symbolic implications of roots evolve through "Box Seat," becoming both one's cultural/spiritual roots and an ironic commentary on the uprooted waste land of the city. The implications are developed as Dan waits for Muriel: "Dan goes to the wall and places his ear against it. A passing street car and something vibrant from the earth sends a rumble to him. That rumble comes from the earth's deep core. It is the matter of powerful underground races. Dan has a picture of all the people rushing to put their ears against walls, to listen to it. The next world-savior is coming up that way" (108). As the multitudes in Hart Crane's "Proem: To Brooklyn Bridge" (*The Bridge* was Crane's response to *The Waste Land*) sit in the theater gazing upon the shadow of the shadow of an image, recalling Plato's gazers, so Toomer's multitude presses ears to walls, to hear only the subway. Dan's ironic, questioning mind undercuts this "salvation": "coming up. A continent sinks down. The new-world Christ will need consummate skill to walk upon the waters where huge bubbles burst" (108). Christ, who could walk upon water, will need to walk upon the gaseous bubbles of a chemical river, as bereft of possibility as Eliot's "sweet Thames." Nor will a Moses lead a people out of bondage: "Suppose the Lord should ask, where was Moses when the light went out? . . . Oh, come along, Moses, you'll get lost" (117, 125). Roots, underground, and salvation combine later in the theater:

> He shrivels close beside a portly Negress whose huge rolls of flesh meet about the bones of seat-arms. A soil-soaked fragrance comes from her. Through the cement floor her strong roots sink down. They spread under the asphalt streets. Dreaming, the streets roll over on their bellies, and suck their glossy health from them. Her strong roots sink down and spread under the river and disappear in blood-lines that waver south. Her roots shoot down. Dan's hands follow them. Roots throb. Dan's heart beats violently. He places his palms upon the earth to cool them. Earth throbs. Dan's heart beats violently. He sees all the people in the house rush to the walls to listen to the rumble. A new-world Christ is coming up. Dan comes up. He is startled. The eyes of the woman dont belong to her. They look at him unpleasantly. From either aisle, bolted masses press in. He doesn't fit. (118–119)

There is no rain, no salvation in Toomer's waste land. Nor will the mermaids sing to him; rather, he is sung to by the bloodied dwarf, who has himself just engaged, with another dwarf, in a perverse parody of the battle royal. The dwarf interrupts Dan's vaunting meditations. Prufrock had pondered, "Do I dare disturb the universe?" Dan meditates, "I am going to reach up and grab the girders of this building and pull them down. The crash will be a signal. Hid by the smoke and dust Dan Moore will arise. In his right hand will be a dynamo. In his left, a god's face that will flash white light from ebony. I'll grab a girder and swing it like a walking-stick. Lightning will flash. I'll grab its black knob and swing it like a crippled cane. Lightning . . . Some one's flashing . . . some one's flashing . . . Who in hell is flashing that mirror? Take it off me, godam you" (126–127).

The theater furnishes no larger arena, no space for the spirit to grow. It is the house writ large: "People come in slowly . . . and fill vacant seats of Lincoln Theater. Each one is a bolt that shoots into a slot, and is locked there. Suppose the Lord should ask, where was Moses when the light went out? I suppose Gabriel should blow his trumpet! The seats are slots. The seats are bolted houses" (117). In the theater, the warder is internalized. In the house Muriel thinks, "Dan, I could love you if I tried. . . . I wont let myself. I? Mrs. Pribby who reads newspapers all night wont. What has she got to do with me? She *is* me, somehow. No she's not. Yes she is. She is the town, and the town wont let me love you, Dan" (110). The Mrs. Pribbys accompany her into the theater: "Muriel has on an orange dress. Its color would clash with the crimson box-draperies. Its color would contradict the sweet rose smile her face is bathed in, should she take her coat off. She'll keep it on. Pale purple shadows rest on the planes of her cheeks. Deep purple comes from her thick-shocked hair. Orange of the dress goes well with these. Muriel presses her coat down from around her shoulders. Teachers are not supposed to have bobbed hair. She'll keep her hat on" (116). The rain does not fall on *The Waste Land*; Christ does not ascend the subway stairs in *Cane*.

Ambivalence characterizes many of the urban characters in *Cane*: Dan and Muriel in "Box Seat," John in "Theater," Bona and Paul in "Bona and Paul." Unlike the black characters in the Georgia sections (with the exception of Ralph Kabnis), their mental life tends to be a play of contradictory impulses. To reflect this quality, Toomer employs internal monologue, which, in the divided consciousness of his characters, becomes very much a dialogue—it is as though the various areas of the unconscious were engaged in debate. We overhear these voices when, for example, Bona ponders Paul's nature. This rhetorical ambivalence is paralleled by Paul's ambivalence regarding his identity. He is living as a white man, as a young student in Chicago with a white Norwegian roommate. He stands before his South Side window, thrown into "swift shadow" by the "hurtling Loop-jammed L Trains," but he is carried in imagination to Georgia:

> Gray slanting roofs of houses are tinted lavender in the setting sun. Paul follows the sun, over the stockyards where a fresh stench is just arising, across wheat lands that are still waving above their stubble, into the sun. Paul follows the sun to a pine-matted hillock in Georgia. He sees the slanting roofs of gray unpainted cabins tinted lavender. A Negress chants a lullaby beneath the mate-eyes of a Southern planter. Her

breasts are ample for the suckling of a song. She weans it, and sends it, curiously weaving, among lush melodies of cane and corn. Paul follows the sun into himself in Chicago. (137–138)

The division in Paul's soul—black/white, Georgia/Chicago—is, at least for a while, bridged when he and Bona and his roommate and his girl go out for an evening at the Crimson Gardens. As the four enter the nightclub, the other patrons "leaned towards each other over ash-smeared tablecloths and highballs and whispered: What is he, a Spaniard, an Indian, an Italian, a Mexican, a Hindu, or a Japanese?" (145). Their stare, that look of the other in its assertion of difference, stills his own ambivalence, quiets the voices in a world overrich in possibility:

> A strange thing happened to Paul. Suddenly he knew that he was apart from the people around him. Apart from the pain which they had unconsciously caused. Suddenly he knew that people saw, not attractiveness in his dark skin, but difference. Their stares, giving him to himself, filled something long empty within him, and were like green blades sprouting in his consciousness. There was fullness, and strength and peace about it all. He saw himself, cloudy, but real. He saw the faces of the people at the tables round him. White lights, or as now, the pink lights of the Crimson Gardens gave a glow and immediacy to white faces. The pleasure of it, equal to that of love or dream, of seeing this. Art and Bona and Helen? He'd look. They [Bona, his roommate, Art, and his girl, Helen] were wonderfully flushed and beautiful. Not for himself; because they were. (145–146)

What will become of Paul in urban Chicago is not entirely clear at the end of "Bona and Paul." Paul and Bona leave the Crimson Gardens, apparently to consummate the passion aroused by their dancing. But Paul returns to assert to the Negro doorman that his "knowing" look doesn't *know*, that something other, more significant, is about to occur, but when he returns to Bona she is gone. Whether his awareness, too, will take flight in the shadow of the L is unclear. However, Paul's divided consciousness embodies the divisions central to *Cane* and thus serves as a bridge between the urban pieces from the second section and the "Kabnis" section set in rural Georgia.

Ralph Kabnis is not a "man without qualities,"⁹ but he is a man unable to cohere. Drawn by the loveliness, the spirit of the place, his will ("Night winds in Georgia are vagrant poets, whispering. Kabnis, against his will, lets his book slip down, and listens to them" [157]) rages against it:

> Kabnis is about to shake his fists heavenward. He looks up, and the night's beauty strikes him dumb. He falls to his knees. Sharp stones cut through his thin pajamas. The shock sends a shiver over him. He quivers. Tears mist his eyes. He writhes.
>
> "God Almighty, dear God, dear Jesus, do not torture me with beauty. Take it away. Give me an ugly world. Ha, ugly. Stinking like unwashed niggers. Dear Jesus, do not chain me to myself and set these hills and valleys, heaving with folk-songs, so close to me that I cannot reach them. There is a radiant beauty in the night that touches and . . . tortures me. Ugh. Hell. Get up, you damn fool. Look around. What's beautiful there? Hog pens and chicken yards. Dirty red mud. Stinking outhouse." (161–162)

He feels his insubstantiality: "Ralph Kabnis is a dream" (158). He feels the "hostility" of the place: "'Hell of a mess I've got in: even the poultry is hostile'" (159). He yearns to be where he isn't: "Somewhere, far off in the straight line of his sight, is Augusta. Christ, how cut off from everything he is. And hours, hours north, why not say a lifetime north? Washington sleeps. Its still peaceful streets, how desirable they are. Its people whom he had always halfway despised. New York? Impossible. It was a fiction. He had dreamed it. An impotent nostalgia grips him" (163). He is oppressed by the strangeness, the oppression of whites, the difference: "The stillness of it: where they burn and hang men, you cant smoke. Cant take a swig of licker" (164).

In order to externalize Kabnis's internal struggle, Toomer turns to the theater, a theater whose psychological probing recalls the theater of Eugene O'Neill. Much of the "Kabnis" section is written in dialogue; but the theatrical machinery also includes stage settings, especially at the beginning of part 5, and parenthetical descriptions of stage "business." O'Neill's personification of psychological processes is most clearly reflected in Toomer's use of the doppelgänger figure,[10] in the character of Lewis, to reveal both repressed and potential aspects of Kabnis's character:

> Lewis enters. He is the queer fellow who has been referred to. A tall wiry copper-colored man, thirty perhaps. His mouth and eyes suggest purpose guided by an adequate intelligence. He is what a stronger Kabnis might have been, and in an odd faint way resembles him. As he steps towards the others, he seems to be issuing sharply from a vivid dream. (189–190)

> His [Lewis's] eyes turn to Kabnis. In the instant of their shifting, a vision of the life they are to meet. Kabnis, a promise of a soil-soaked beauty; uprooted, thinning out. Suspended a few feet above the soil whose touch would resurrect him. Arm's length removed from him whose will to help. . . . There is a swift intuitive interchange of consciousness. Kabnis has a sudden need to rush into the arms of this man. His eyes call, "Brother." And then a savage, cynical twist-about within him mocks his impulse and strengthens him to repulse Lewis. (191–192)

> Lewis: Life has already told him [Kabnis] more than he is capable of knowing. It has given him in excess of what he can receive. I have been offered. Stuff in his stomach curdled, and he vomited me. (200)

The truths that his "other," Lewis, utters Kabnis does not want to hear. Primarily, he wishes to separate himself from the commonality of blacks and from the black past. Stokely Carmichael, in the sixties, suggested the impossibility of such a separation through his rhetorical question, "What do they call a black Ph.D. in the South? Nigger." In his ignorance, Kabnis suggests that class might make a difference:

> Kabnis: But they wouldnt touch a gentleman—fellows, men like us three here—
> Layman: Nigger's a nigger down this away, Professor. An only two dividins: good and bad. An even they aint permanent categories. They sometimes mixes um up when it comes t lynchin. (171–172)

Later, Lewis identifies Father John as "symbol, flesh, and spirit of the past." Kabnis resists Lewis's implications:

> Kabnis: . . . he aint my past. My ancestors were Southern blue-bloods—
> Lewis: And black.

Kabnis: Aint much difference between blue an black.
Lewis: Enough to draw a denial from you. Cant hold them, can you?
Master; slave. Soil; and the overarching heavens. Dusk; dawn. They
fight and bastardize you. The sun tint of your cheeks, flame of the great
season's multi-colored leaves, tarnished, burned. (217–218)

Lewis, unlike Kabnis, is able to contain the contradictions, the
"pain and beauty of the South": "Lewis, seated now so that his eyes
rest upon the old man, merges with his source and lets the pain and
beauty of the South meet him there. White faces, pain-pollen, settle downward through a cane-sweet mist and touch the ovaries of
yellow flowers. Cotton-bolls bloom, droop. Black roots twist in a
parched red soil beneath a blazing sky. Magnolias, fragrant, a trifle
futile, lovely, far off" (214–215).

Kabnis's contradictions, ambivalence, rage are drawn out of him
by the touch of Carrie, Fred Halsey's daughter, the morning after the
night's drinking: "She turns him to her and takes his hot cheeks in
her firm cool hands. Her palms draw the fever out. With its passing,
Kabnis crumples. He sinks to his knees before her, ashamed, ex-
hausted" (238). His condition is a sickness, and a black southern
woman, close to and rooted in the soil, is redemptive; she thus
embodies the three recurring threads: the song of praise to black
women, the criticism of the city, and the evocation of roots. Earlier,
Toomer had combined, in Carrie's interaction with Lewis, the symbolic associations of Mary, Jesus, and the sun: "The sun-burst from
her eyes floods up and haloes him [Lewis]. Christ-eyes, his eyes look
to her" (205). In the concluding paragraphs of *Cane*, Toomer again
turns to this set of symbols:

And then, seeing Carrie's eyes upon him, he [Kabnis] swings the pail
carelessly and with eyes downcast and swollen trudges upstairs to the
work-shop. Carrie's gaze follows him till he is gone. Then she goes to
the old man and slips to her knees before him. Her lips murmur, "Jesus,
come."
     Light streaks through the iron-barred cellar window. Within its soft
circle, the figures of Carrie and Father John.
     Outside, the sun arises from its cradle in the tree-tops of the forest.
Shadows of pines are dreams the sun shakes from its eyes. The sun

arises. Gold-glowing child, it steps into the sky and sends a birth-song slanting down gray dust streets and sleepy windows of the southern town. (239)

The scene is one of nativity, where Carrie and Father John merge with Mary and Joseph and the love of Carrie and Kabnis becomes the child Jesus, becomes the sun that sets in "Bona and Paul" and rises in the closing lines to suggest a new world, a new dispensation. In the opening paragraphs Ralph Kabnis had seen himself as a dream, and "dreams are faces with large eyes and weak chins and broad brows that get smashed by the fists of square faces." The violence of this beginning becomes the natural mixing of dreams and pines and sun in the closing paragraphs. The "Kabnis" section, which begins in darkness, ends in light.

CHAPTER FIFTEEN

Conclusion

In *Loss of the Self in Modern Literature and Art,* Wylie Sypher traces the self's diminished splendor: "The heroic figure of free man—a dream of the enlightenment, the Promethean self pinnacled in the steady bright light of the eternal, beyond time and history—is plunged into the institutional lower world where the law of large numbers closes in and the average is a prison where the self loses identity."[1] Submergence in numbers is only one of the conditions Sypher cites. Another is the rise of the functionary, and though he never cites Max Weber's work on bureaucracy, Weber's bureaucratic man-made-flesh is present in his examples: Robert Musil's *The Man without Qualities,* C. P. Snow's bureaucrats from the bureaucracies of applied science, William Whyte's "organization man." Such figures illustrate the "individual vanishing behind the functionary" (14), the "self [that] is neutralized" (15), for whom the real question becomes the "problem of authenticity—in what sense we have an existence that is really 'ours'" (28). Other conditions of this existence, or inexistence, include no longer being in a position to make decisions that are effective ("His determinations are not, in the older sense of the word, his own" [13]); no longer being at the center of the universe (Robbe-Grillet's observation, cited by Sypher, that "things are things, and man is only man" [111]); no longer being able to trust language, like a high wire, to carry us across the nothing to something. The paternity of such a world includes Camus's Meursault, slouching through indifference toward a death; Kafka's Joseph K., "nameless victim of bureaucracy and lineal descendant of the underground man" (136); and the identityless characters of Ionesco, who "easily become the opposites of themselves" (96).

What is particularly intriguing, for my purposes, in Sypher's study is how little it pertains to the black experience in America and to the shape of modern black literature.[2] Three factors contribute to this difference: (1) Those qualities in the world at large that have tended to diminish the self, either enlightenment or romantic, have been mediated, and transformed, for blacks through the peculiar relationship of black and white. For this reason, the black experience includes no counterpart to the growing experience of powerlessness Sypher identifies: "Before the trampling march of unconscious power—as Bertrand Russell put it—it was possible to take a certain defiant attitude that looked something like nobility" (13). Slavery and racism have fostered an awful stability: slaves and blacks have always experienced powerlessness. But for this reason, also, their experience of powerlessness is more immediate and personal; in the black experience power is not perceived as something amorphous and abstract. Rather, it is "the man," squeezing black lives. (2) The black experience has not favored the development of romantic notions of the self, of a self separate from, and ultimately superior to, the selves of others; rather, both the African tribal experience and the experience of slavery and racism have encouraged a collective view, in which one's fate is common, not singular. (3) The expressiveness available to selves—enlightenment, romantic, whatever—has simply not been available to blacks. The congruence assumed by Puritans (other than those influenced by such as Anne Hutchinson) between inner man and outer expression is reflected, in the nineteenth century, in Emerson's sublime faith in the correspondence between the hidden and the exposed, between mundane act and divine plan. This is the innocence that led Henry James, Sr., to speak of his friend's "as yet unfallen state." Blacks, as I have discussed at some length, were not permitted to express the inner man. In fact, this dimension of the black experience is more accurately expressed by some lines from a nonsense verse than by all the sense of Emerson's imagining: "As I was going up the stair / I met a man who wasn't there. / He wasn't there again to-day. / I wish, I wish he'd stay away."[3] We call such rhymes nonsense rhymes. They place our world temporarily out of focus; it is the play with reality of children: the world seen dizzily from spinning, the spatial disorder from tumbling head over heels down the hill. But this is the world of black/white interaction, the sense of institutionalized non-sense.

The language of Chief Justice Roger B. Taney, writing the majority opinion in the 1857 Dred Scott decision, conceptualizes this non-sense perception of the self: that blacks (Taney speaks of the "negro" and the "African race") "had no rights or privileges but such as those who held the power and the Government might choose to give them" and that "they had no rights which the white man was bound to respect."[4] In effect, those borders of the self that we all instinctively sense and that we learn from the ethologists are clearly cultural simply do not exist for the black in the presence of whites. They may be breached by word, gesture, act, violence. And in interaction, expressiveness flows from white to black, as does meaning.

The fruit of such a world is the treatment of the self by the writers I have been considering, who began to publish in the decades following the emancipation and who represent the beginnings of modern black literature. Their characters are terribly conscious of the "look" of the white other, and they express this consciousness through masking, self-hatred, racial ambivalence, and passing.[5] But this fruit, this bitter fruit, should not be seen as a single harvest. As perceptive a critic as W. E. B. Du Bois could write of *Passing*, "It is all a petty, silly matter of no real importance which another generation will comprehend with great difficulty."[6] Du Bois's 1929 review statement, quoted approvingly by Hoyt Fuller in his introduction to the 1971 reissue of *Passing*, accords with the later problack consciousness of the 1960s and early 1970s, when it was "cool" to deride the notion of passing for white. But one can partake of this consciousness without ignoring the deep social-psychological pressures revealed by Nella Larsen's writing, where art seems almost exorcism. In fact, all the writers I have been discussing are responding, some with more seeming detachment than others, to deep, pervasive attitudes. And though other portrayals of the self will appear in the literature, the preoccupations of these earlier writers help to clarify character and scene in many modern and contemporary works in black literature.[7]

But theories which generalize about the disappearance of the self in modern literature must also take into account the increasing assertiveness of the self in both black literature and black culture, an assertiveness which found early expression in such various voices as Washington's Atlanta Exposition address;[8] statements from the Niagara movement; the rhetorical and often passionate *The Souls of Black Folk* and Du Bois's editorials in the *Crisis*; Marcus Garvey's sensitive articulation of the psychology of the oppressed; and the writings and statements of such writers as Hughes, Hurston, and McKay, who found their models among the masses rather than among the black bourgeoisie. This assertiveness, which was most forcefully expressed by the Black Arts and Black Power movements of the 1960s and 1970s, points to the increasing complexity in the view of the black self, a topic which can only be touched on in these concluding comments.[9] But consider the following assertions of self: Bigger Thomas's "'But what I killed for, I *am*!'" in Wright's *Native Son* (1940); the protagonist's "'I yam what I am'" in Ellison's *Invisible Man* (1952); and Max Reddick's "*All you ever want to do is remind me that I am black. But, goddamn it, I also am*" in Williams's *The Man Who Cried I Am* (1967). These surely are not disappearing selves. Rather, they are more like disappeared selves, striving to reappear. They are Ellison's protagonist, waiting for spring. Their consciousness is reflected in numerous titles: *Nobody Knows My Name, No Name in the Street, Invisible Man, Native Son, Manchild in the Promised Land, Notes of a Native Son, The Man Who Cried I Am*. They recall that earlier voice, Frederick Douglass's in his 1845 slave narrative: "You have seen how a man was made a slave; you shall see how a slave was made a man." And they express that terrible awareness of Richard Wright's in *Black Boy* one hundred years later: "I had learned there were men against whom I was powerless, men who could violate my life at will." They suggest the rediscovery in the sixties—through Black Consciousness, Black Power, Black Arts—of Marcus Garvey's "Black is beautiful." And they move toward the possibilities, grounded in self-knowledge, expressed by Toni Morrison's Pilate Dead in *Song of Solomon*: "'If I'd uh knowed more I coulda loved more.'"

But always, within the consciousness of the black writer, is the knowledge of the disappeared and the disappearing. Mixed with the "I am" is the "You're not" in that eye in which, as Baldwin describes it in *If Beale Street Could Talk*, you do not exist.[10] This conflict, these strange fruits, this peculiar progeny are a part of the heritage of America's black writers—and they have been the preoccupation of the writers I have been considering in the second part of this study—and must be contained within the literature, as that "double consciousness" which Du Bois spoke of in 1903 must be contained "in one dark body, whose dogged strength alone keeps it from being torn asunder" (17).

NOTES

One. Introduction

1. Douglass's comment that "slavery was a poor school for the human intellect and heart" would seem only too obvious. However, historian Ulrich B. Phillips, whose writings strongly influenced subsequent historiography, characterized plantation slavery quite differently: "On the whole the plantations were the best schools yet invented for the mass training of that sort of inert and backward people which the bulk of the American negroes represented." The "plantation of the standard Southern type was . . . a school constantly training and controlling pupils." Phillips does acknowledge a "cardinal shortcoming": the "lack of any regular provision for the discharge of pupils upon completion of their training." Ulrich Bonner Phillips, *American Negro Slavery* (New York: D. Appleton and Company, 1918), pp. 342, 343. Douglass's quote is taken from William Lloyd Garrison, Preface to Frederick Douglass, *Narrative of the Life of Frederick Douglass* (1845; repr. Garden City: Doubleday and Company, Dolphin Books, 1963), pp. x–xi. Even earlier Hegel had described Western slavery as "a phase of *education*—a mode of becoming participant in a higher morality and the culture connected with it." Quoted in Henry Louis Gates, Jr., *Figures in Black: Words, Signs, and the "Racial" Self* (New York: Oxford University Press, 1987), p. 20.
2. John Hope Franklin, *From Slavery to Freedom: A History of Negro America*, 3rd ed. (New York: Random House–Vintage Books, 1969), p. 246.
3. By 1849 it had gone through seven printings and was out of print.
4. The questions were posed to Franklin on his travels after leaving home at the age of seventeen: "I cut so miserable a Figure too, that I found by the Questions ask'd me I was suspected to be some runaway Servant, and in danger of being taken up on that Suspicion. . . . Here I got a Dinner. And while I was eating it, several sly Questions were ask'd me, as it seem'd to be suspected from my youth and Appearance, that I might

be some Runaway." Benjamin Franklin, *The Autobiography*, in George McMichael, ed., *Anthology of American Literature*, vol. 1 (New York: Macmillan Publishing Company, 1980), p. 25. When Huck Finn posed as a girl named Sarah Williams, Mrs. Judith Loftus found him out and expressed an attitude regarding the nature of the apprentice's life: "'You just tell me your secret, and trust me. I'll keep it; and, what's more, I'll help you. So'll my old man if you want him to. You see, you're a runaway 'prentice, that's all. It ain't anything. There ain't no harm in it. You've been treated bad, and you made up your mind to cut. Bless you, child, I wouldn't tell on you.'" Samuel Langhorne Clemens, *Adventures of Huckleberry Finn* (1884; repr. New York: W. W. Norton and Company, 1961), p. 52. Melville's protagonist describes the paper mill: "Not a syllable was breathed. Nothing was heard but the low, steady overruling hum of the iron animals. The human voice was banished from the spot. Machinery—that vaunted slave of humanity—here stood menially served by human beings, who served mutely and cringingly as the slave serves the Sultan. The girls did not so much seem accessory wheels to the general machinery as mere cogs to the wheels." The machinery metaphor mechanizes his first impression of the "maids" developed upon entering the mill: "At rows of blank-looking counters sat rows of blank-looking girls, with blank, white folders in their blank hands, all blankly folding blank paper." Herman Melville, "The Tartarus of Maids," in Jay Leyda, ed., *The Complete Stories of Herman Melville* (New York: Random House, 1949), pp. 202, 201.

5. Clement Eaton, *The Growth of Southern Civilization* (New York: Harper, 1961), see esp. pp. 311–313.

6. Chapter 30 of southern sociologist George Fitzhugh's *Cannibals All! Or, Slaves Without Masters* (1857; repr. Cambridge: Harvard University Press, 1960) is titled "The Philosophy of the Isms—Showing Why They Abound at the North, and Are Unknown in the South." This is due, Fitzhugh explains, to the fact that "the exploitation, or unjust exactions of skill and capital in free society, excite the learned and philanthropic to devise schemes of escape, and impel the laborers to adopt those schemes, however chimerical, because they feel that their situation cannot be worsted. They are already slaves without masters." Ibid., p. 228.

7. Cited in Carl N. Degler, *Out of Our Past: The Forces that Shaped Modern America*, 3rd ed. (New York: Harper and Row, 1970), pp. 177–178. During the civil rights movement, "the fell spirit of abolition" became the "outside agitator."

8. Fitzhugh, *Cannibals All*, p. 18. That a Fitzhugh and a Marx might use

the same data is an interesting commentary on the uses of evidence. Fitzhugh will determine, on the basis of his evidence, that workers should volunteer to be enslaved. Leon F. Litwack has observed, in his consideration of the position of free Negroes in the South during the Civil War, that others came to similar conclusions: "The ultimate so-lution, adopted by several states, was to encourage free blacks to select a master and voluntarily enter into slavery. After all, a Savannah news-paper observed, 'every day we hear our slaves pronounced the happiest people in the world. Why then this lamentation over putting the free negro in his only proper . . . condition?' " (ellipses in Litwack). Leon F. Litwack, *Been in the Storm So Long: The Aftermath of Slavery* (1979; repr. New York: Random House–Vintage Books, 1980), p. 29.

9. Consider, for example, Currier & Ives's *"Low Water" on the Missis-sippi*. The focus of the lithograph is the slave family at their cabin on a bank of the Mississippi. A black male is playing what appears to be a banjo. A boy and girl, who are like small adults, are caught in what appears to be a movement from a quadrille. A woman stands in the door of the cabin. Four other children are frozen in various postures of danc-ing. A "granny" sits on a log. In the background is the "big house," complete with columns and lady in hoop skirt. In the river float two steamboats, one raft. The lithograph, dated 1868, is included as plate 26 in Colin Simkin, ed., *Currier and Ives' America* (New York: Crown Publishers, 1952).

10. Quoted in Tremaine McDowell, "The Negro in the Southern Novel prior to 1850," in Seymour L. Gross and John Edward Hardy, eds., *Images of the Negro in American Literature* (Chicago: University of Chicago Press, 1966), pp. 58, 57, 59. The Reverend Atticus G. Haygood declared in 1881: "Negroes got all the good of slavery." Quoted in George M. Frederickson, *The Black Image in the White Mind* (1971; repr. New York: Harper and Row, Harper Torchbooks, 1972), p. 205.

11. Litwack, *Been in the Storm So Long*, pp. 42–44.

12. Slave narratives are autobiographical accounts of former slaves. Gilbert Osofsky notes that thousands of brief narratives appeared in the aboli-tionist press and in documentary accounts, and that "four-score full-length autobiographies of slaves" were published before the Civil War. Gilbert Osofsky, *Puttin' on Ole Massa* (New York: Harper and Row, Harper Torchbooks, 1969), pp. 9–10.

13. Larry Gara, "The Professional Fugitive in the Abolition Movement," *Wisconsin Magazine of History* 48 (1965): 196.

14. Quoted in ibid., p. 198.

15. Ibid., pp. 200, 201.

16. Charles H. Nichols, "Who Read the Slave Narratives?" *Phylon Quarterly* 20 (1959): 149–150.

17. Quoted in Gara, "Professional Fugitive," p. 197. Gates's stress on the formal rather than the historical can be seen in his turning to formal rather than sociohistorical influences in the development of the slave narrative: "The slave narrative, I suggest, is a countergenre, a mediation between the novel of sentiment and the picaresque, oscillating somewhere between the two in a bipolar moment, set in motion by the mode of the confession." It would seem to be Gates's formal approach that leads him to assign temporal priority to the slave narrative: "Indeed, as we shall see, the slave narrative spawned its formal negation, the plantation novel." However, a good argument can be made for reversing the order or priority, or for assigning no priority at all, since the most popular proslavery plantation romances of George Tucker, William Gilmore Simms, James Kirke Paulding, John Pendleton Kennedy, and Nathaniel Beverly Tucker appeared primarily in the 1820s and 1830s, with the majority appearing in the 1830s; whereas many of the most popular slave narratives—including those of Charles Ball, Henry Bibb, Henry Box Brown, William Wells Brown, William and Ellen Craft, Frederick Douglass, Josiah Henson, and Solomon Northup—did not appear until after 1840. The formal approach must be supplemented by the historical, by an attention to the growing sectional strife in the early 1830s, and to the demands of curiosity and propaganda. But Gates is aware that his position is extreme; in his introduction he notes: "I argued for a formalism that even then seemed somewhat excessive and too polemical to be a productive theory of criticism. Rather, I meant for it to be *corrective* and polemical, to raise as much heat as light." Gates, *Figures in Black*, pp. 81, xxviii.

18. "The slave narrator's political role requires the use of description, detail, and concrete language. He is called upon, as part of his activity in the antislavery movement, to supply first-hand information about slavery from the victim's point of view. What it was like to pick cotton and tobacco, how often and for what offenses the slaves were shipped, their standard of living, the duties expected of them, what took place during a slave auction." Stephen Butterfield, *Black Autobiography in America* (Amherst: University of Massachusetts Press, 1974), p. 34.

19. Included with Douglass, *Narrative*, p. xxi.

20. Osofsky, *Puttin' on Ole Massa*, p. 12.

21. Ibid. The question of verifiability was not limited to the narratives. Henry Louis Gates, Jr., writing on *Poems on Various Subjects, Reli-*

gious and Moral, by Phillis Wheatley, Negro Servant to Mr. Wheatley of Boston, notes that "no fewer than eighteen certificates of authenticity" that preface the book, "including one by John Hancock and another by the Governor of Massachusetts, Thomas Hutchinson, meant to 'leave no doubt, that she is its author.' " Henry Louis Gates, Jr., "Preface to Blackness: Text and Pretext," in Dexter Fisher and Robert B. Septo, eds., *Afro-American Literature: The Reconstruction of Instruction* (New York: Modern Language Association of America, 1979), p. 46.

22. Frederick Douglass, *Life and Times of Frederick Douglass* (1892; repr. New York: Crowell-Collier Publishing Company, 1962), p. 146.

Two. Some Motes in the Nineteenth-Century Eye

1. William Charvat, *The Origins of American Critical Thought 1810–1835* (1936; repr. New York: A. S. Barnes and Company, Inc., 1961), pp. 9, 7, 9, 12, 18, 20.

2. Russel Blaine Nye, *Society and Culture in America, 1830–1860* (New York: Harper and Row, 1974), p. 72.

3. Ibid., p. 83.

4. Henry Wadsworth Longfellow, in Richard Ruland, ed., *The Native Muse: Theories of American Literature*, vol. 1 (1972; repr. New York: E. P. Dutton and Company, 1976), p. 246.

5. Capt. John Smith, "A Description of New England," in McMichael, *Anthology*, pp. 27–28.

6. Hector St. John de Crèvecoeur, *Letters from an American Farmer* (1782; repr. London: J. M. Dent and Sons, Everyman's Library, 1945), pp. 40, 41.

7. Ibid., p. 41.

8. Quoted in George E. Probst, *The Happy Republic: A Reader in Tocqueville's America* (New York: Harper and Brothers, 1962), p. xi.

9. William Dean Howells, *Criticism and Fiction* (New York: Harper and Brothers, 1891), pp. 129, 128.

10. Daniel J. Boorstin, *The Americans: The National Experience* (1965; repr. New York: Random House–Vintage Books, 1967), p. 308. See also pp. 307–324.

11. Nye, *Society and Culture*, p. 137. See also pp. 137–141.

12. Harry Levin, *The Power of Blackness* (New York: Random House–Vintage Books, 1958), p. 7. Even while the antislavery orator was stressing difference, he was appealing to higher values, religious and democratic, communally held. In keeping with the prevailing modes of the nineteenth century, both Douglass and Washington will emphasize the

importance of oratory. It is his reading *The Columbian Orator*, which included a dialogue between a master and a slave and one of Sheridan's speeches on behalf of Catholic emancipation, that is central in the twelve-year-old Douglass's development: "The reading of those documents enabled me to utter my thoughts, and to meet the arguments brought forward to sustain slavery." Douglass, *Narrative*, p. 42. Gates argues that Douglass "seems to have given a priority to the spoken word over the written word." Gates elaborates: "As he wrote in 1849, 'Speech! Speech! The live, calm, grave, clear, pointed, warm, sweet, melodious, and powerful human voice is [the] chosen instrumentality' of social reform. While writing served its purpose, some matters were of such urgency that the spoken word was demanded. 'Humanity, justice and liberty,' wrote Douglass, 'demand the service of the living human voice.'" Gates, *Figures in Black*, p. 106. Baker notes that in Washington's *Up from Slavery* "more than forty of two hundred total pages are devoted to oratorical concerns." Houston A. Baker, Jr., *Modernism and the Harlem Renaissance* (Chicago: University of Chicago Press, 1987), p. 31. Everyone recalls Washington's chapter on the Atlanta Exposition address, but many may not remember two other chapter titles: "Two Thousand Miles for a Five-Minute Speech" and "The Secret of Success in Public Speaking."

13. Robert E. Lee, letter in Henry Steele Commager and Allan Nevins, eds., *The Heritage of America: Readings in American History*, rev. ed. (Boston: D. C. Heath and Company, 1949), p. 795.

14. Degler, *Out of Our Past*, p. 212.

15. "Revived in the '80s, the songs of Stephen Foster, with their romantic pictures of happy plantation life, and Harris's tales of Uncle Remus—rather than the suffering figure of Stowe's Uncle Tom—gave Americans their sense of the lost South. Publishers of history textbooks who sought national adoptions were wise, in the light of this spirit of tolerance, to present the war as 'a careful balance of right on both sides.'" Jay Martin, *Harvests of Change: American Literature 1865–1914* (Englewood Cliffs: Prentice-Hall, 1967), pp. 27–28.

16. This mutuality did not of course apply to the "new issue" Negro, "spawn" of northern victory and Reconstruction, but only to the "real," the "old timey" Negro (generally of lowercase *n*) of plantation days. This mythic figure is evoked in an 1887 address by Henry W. Grady: "I want no truer soul than that which moved the trusty slave, who for four years while my father fought with the armies that barred his freedom, slept every night at my mother's chamber door, holding her and her

children as safe as if her husband stood guard, and ready to lay down his humble life on her threshold. History has no parallel to the faith kept by the negro in the South during the war." Quoted in Frederickson, *The Black Image*, p. 207. In using the term *mythic* I do not mean to impugn the report but to suggest the ideological uses made of such isolated instances.

17. William Bradford, concluding one of those lists of lacks—"no friends to welcome them ... nor inns ... no houses or much less towns"— which subsequent writers will compile, characterized the land as a "hideous and desolate wilderness, full of wild beasts and wild men," separated by a mighty ocean "from all the civil parts of the world." William Bradford, *Of Plymouth Plantation*, in McMichael, *Anthology*, p. 38.

18. Edward Pessen, *Riches, Class, and Power before the Civil War* (Lexington: D. C. Heath and Company, 1973), pp. 41–42, 31. Pessen has summarized his findings for the three areas. For New York City: "If one half of corporate capital of 1828 is attributed to outsiders—which is probably overgenerous—and the rest to elite taxpayers, the share of New York City wealth owned by the upper 4 per cent (exclusive of the city's wealth owned by rich non-residents) would be 63 per cent of the actual wealth; the top 1 per cent alone would account for 40 per cent of the total. By 1845, under this formula, the richest 1 per cent of the population owned 50 per cent and the upper 4 per cent slightly more than 80 per cent of the city's actual wealth." For Brooklyn: "By 1841, the poorest 66 per cent of Brooklyn's population owned less than 1 per cent of its wealth, with only about one out of five families (exclusive of non-resident taxpayers) taxed on any property at all. . . . Brooklyn's richest 1 per cent of wealth-holders, like their New York City counterparts, emerge with one half of their city's wealth." For Boston: "By 1848, the wealthiest 4 per cent in the population had amassed close to the two-thirds of their city's wealth owned by their New York City counterparts. Perhaps the most striking single change between 1833 and 1848 was the decline in the share of assessed wealth held by Boston's poorest taxpayers. By the later year, the poorest 81 per cent of the population owned less than 5 per cent of the city's assessed wealth. They undoubtedly held an even smaller proportion of its actual wealth." Ibid., pp. 35, 38, 39.

In the text I speak of the "various myths of classlessness." One of these is the variant myth that argues that those at the top had humble beginnings—the Horatio Alger or rags-to-riches myth. Pessen finds this myth (alive and well in the remarks of such figures as Henry Clay and

Tocqueville) to be untenable for the antebellum period. Ibid., pp. 77–91. Others, of course, have found the myth untenable for subsequent periods. It is in fact somewhat ironic that Benjamin Franklin himself provided the key to its untenability when he observed that "money is of a prolific and generating nature," that "money begets money."

19. Ibid., pp. 31, 42.

20. Edward Pessen, *Most Uncommon Jacksonians: The Radical Leaders of the Early Labor Movement* (Albany: State University of New York Press, 1967), p. 112.

21. Southern practice was, of necessity, contradictory, faced with the ineluctable fact of humanity in the person of a possession. These contradictions surface, for example, in the sermons enjoining slaves to act "responsible" toward their masters, while at the same time citing their difference as a justification for enslavement. They surface, too, both in the bonds of affection that sometimes existed and in the bonds of hatred that also existed. In fact, the entire range of human emotions was played out in the relationship of master and slave, however distorted by the fact of, and the justifications for, ownership.

22. Fitzhugh, *Cannibals All*, p. 205.

23. Frederickson, *The Black Image*, p. 56.

24. Thomas Wentworth Higginson, *Army Life in a Black Regiment* (New York: Crowell-Collier Publishing Company–Collier Books, 1969), pp. 40–41, 51, 62, 134. I would, however, qualify Frederickson's evaluation: "Further association did not change Higginson's opinion that his charges were 'the world's perpetual children, docile, gay, and loveable.'" Frederickson, *The Black Image*, p. 170. Higginson's view is more complex. A revealing observation is his journal comment that "As one grows more acquainted with the men, their individualities emerge; and I find, first their faces, then their characters, to be as distinct as those of whites." *Army Life*, p. 53. Higginson was open to complexity and, as a good officer, wanted to know the nature of his men. At another and earlier point in the journal he describes his overhearing an old slave, Cato, regaling a circle of thirty or forty black soldiers with the ingenuities of his escape. Higginson notes "a succession of tricks beyond Moliere, of acts of caution, foresight, patient cunning," and sums up: "Yet to-morrow strangers will remark on the hopeless, impenetrable stupidity in the daylight faces of many of these very men, the solid mask under which Nature has concealed all this wealth of mother-wit." Ibid., p. 38. "Further association" led Higginson to praise their "capacity of honor and fidelity," among other qualities. Ibid., p. 66.

25. Cited in Frederickson, *The Black Image*, p. 209.
26. In *The Clansman* Thomas Dixon, Jr., describes the Negro as "half child, half animal."
27. Frederickson, *The Black Image*, pp. 53–54, 55.
28. Ibid., p. 54.
29. Ibid., p. 274.
30. Ibid., p. 277.
31. Ibid., p. 280.
32. Thomas Dixon, Jr., *The Clansman: A Historical Romance of the Ku Klux Klan* (New York: Doubleday, Page and Company, 1905), p. 304.
33. Thomas Nelson Page, *Red Rock: A Chronicle of Reconstruction* (1898; repr. New York: Charles Scribners' Sons, 1946), p. 360.

Three. Differences in Perception

1. Nathan Irvin Huggins, *Black Odyssey* (New York: Vintage Books, 1977), pp. 5, 12.
2. P. C. Lloyd, *Africa in Social Change* (Harmondsworth: Penguin Books, 1969), p. 33.
3. Elizabeth Colson, "Native Cultural and Social Patterns in Contemporary Africa," in C. Grove Haines, ed., *Africa Today* (Baltimore: Johns Hopkins Press, 1955), p. 70.
4. Perry Miller and Thomas H. Johnson, *The Puritans*, vol. 1 (New York: Harper and Row, 1963), pp. 182, 14.
5. Harvey Wish, *Society and Thought in Early America* (New York: Longmans, Green and Company, 1950), p. 9.
6. Winthrop D. Jordan, *White over Black* (Baltimore: Pelican Books, 1969), pp. 71–82; Kenneth Stampp, *The Peculiar Institution* (New York: Vintage Books, 1956), pp. 21–23.
7. Franklin, *From Slavery to Freedom*, p. 31.
8. Daniel J. Boorstin, *The Americans: The Colonial Experience* (New York: Vintage Books, 1958), pp. 155–156; Nye, *Society and Culture*, pp. 24–31.
9. Benvenuto Cellini's autobiography begins: "All men of whatsoever quality they be, who have done anything of excellence, or which may properly resemble excellence, ought, if they are persons of truth and honesty, to describe their life with their own hand." *The Autobiography of Benvenuto Cellini* (New York: Garden City Publishing Company, 1927), p. 5. Jean-Jacques Rousseau's autobiography begins: "1712–1719: I have resolved on an enterprise which has no precedent, and which,

once complete, will have no imitator. My purpose is to display to my kind a portrait in every way true to nature, and the man I shall portray will be myself. . . . Simply myself. I know my own heart and understand my fellow man. But I am made unlike any one I have ever met; I will even venture to say that I am like no one in the whole world. I may be no better, but at least I am different." Jean-Jacques Rousseau, *The Confessions* (1781; repr. Harmondsworth: Penguin Books, 1965), p. 17.

10. Henry David Thoreau, *Walden* (1854; repr. New York: Washington Square Press, 1966), p. 1.
11. Douglass, *Narrative*, p. 1.
12. Ibid., pp. 114–115.
13. Thoreau, *Walden*, p. 127.
14. Ibid., p. 39.
15. Ibid., p. 105.
16. Douglass, *Narrative*, pp. 82, 83.
17. Ralph Ellison, *Invisible Man* (New York: Random House, 1952), p. 113.
18. Langston Hughes, *The Best of Simple* (New York: Hill and Wang, 1961), p. 20.
19. Ellison, *Invisible Man*, pp. 376, 377.
20. Ibid., p. 133.
21. Ibid., p. 134.
22. Ibid., pp. 183–184.
23. Ibid., p. 196.
24. Ibid., p. 194.
25. Ibid., pp. 198–199.
26. Ibid., pp. 199–202.
27. Ibid., p. 207.
28. Eliot echoes at other points too. His waiting for rain, or water, becomes Ellison's protagonist's "long[ing] for water" and his testicles "*dripping down through the sunlight into the dark red water.*" Eliot's "London Bridge is falling down falling down falling down" becomes the iron bridge from which the protagonist's testicles dangle. Eliot's mixing of April and death in the opening lines echoes in Ellison's closing paragraphs: "There's a stench in the air . . . the smell either of death or of spring . . . there *is* death in the smell of spring." Ibid., pp. 10, 430, 438.
29. Ibid., pp. 7–9.
30. Ibid., p. 222.
31. Ibid., p. 333.
32. Ibid., p. 335.
33. Ibid., p. 384.

34. Ibid., p. 438.

35. Ibid., p. 439.

36. Baker, too, has argued in his criticism for the importance of a "collectivistic ethos" in the black experience. Houston A. Baker, Jr., *Long Black Song: Essays in American Literature and Culture* (Charlottesville: University Press of Virginia, 1972), p. 16.

Four. The "Probable and Ordinary Course of Man's Experience"

1. The distinction is identified in contemporary criticism with such studies as Richard Chase's *The American Novel and Its Tradition*, which extends into the twentieth century the implications of Hawthorne's preface to *The House of the Seven Gables*, and Lionel Trilling's *The Liberal Imagination*. Recent studies criticizing the approach include David H. Hirsch's *Reality and Idea in the Early American Novel*, Nicholaus Mills's *American and English Fiction in the Nineteenth Century: An Antigenre Critique and Comparison*, and Nina Baym's *Novels, Readers, and Reviewers: Responses to Fiction in Antebellum America*. It is not my intention to consider the argument but only to appropriate the distinction for my own purposes.

2. Nathaniel Hawthorne, *The House of the Seven Gables* (1851; repr. New York: Penguin Books, 1981), p. 1. The distinction was earlier asserted by William Gilmore Simms for his own practice in *The Yemassee* (1835). Anthony Trollope, commenting on Hawthorne's *The Marble Faun*, presents a British view: "The creations of American literature generally are no doubt more given to the speculative,—less given to the realistic,— than are those of English literature. On our side of the water we deal more with beef and ale, and less with dreams." Included in Ruland, *Native Muse*, p. 388.

3. This mix can be found in many of the short stories: "Young Goodman Brown," "The Minister's Black Veil," "Rappaccini's Daughter," "Ethan Brand," and "The Artist of the Beautiful," among others.

4. Douglass, *Narrative*, p. 72.

5. Ibid.

6. The maker—possibly at odds with the ordinary, workaday world, straining that world through his consciousness—was stressed as early as 1816 by Edward Tyrell Channing, Boylston Professor of Rhetoric and Oratory at Harvard, in an article in the *North American Review*: "There is, too, a great middling crowd of readers whose vocabulary of criticism extends little further than to '*unnatural, out-of-life*,' etc.; and words of this sort

they are sure to level against every man who ventures upon the marvellous, wild and unreal. These are the practical men who judge everything by what they call common sense. They laugh at the folly of encouraging men in the indolent luxuries and unprofitable excesses of
imagination and feeling when we were sent here to work, to be useful,
to conquer the vices, and bring home the wanderings of the mind."
Cited in Ruland, *Native Muse*, pp. 85–86.

7. Richard Poirier, *A World Elsewhere* (1966; repr. London: Oxford University Press, 1973), pp. 10, 3, 4.

8. It is interesting to note that Emerson's apothegms often graced the of-
fices of the captains of industry in the nineteenth century.

9. I am obviously considering broad tendencies within the literature. At
the same time, the preoccupation of such a critic as Henry Louis Gates,
Jr., with the more formal properties—with the "repetition of formal
structures, and their difference"—can easily fit within the approach
I am taking in this study. The play of language—the parodic, the
signifying—is often a linguistic adjustment to the play of social forces.
It is language masking and will be considered in my discussion of the
use of moral statement in black literature. Henry Louis Gates, Jr., "The
blackness of blackness: a critique of the sign and the Signifying Monkey," in his *Black Literature and Theory* (New York: Methuen, 1984),
pp. 285–286.

It should be added that Gates has criticized what he terms the critical
bias toward referentiality in *Figures in Black*: "Black literacy, then, became far more preoccupied with the literal representation of social content than with literary form, with ethics and thematics rather than poetics and aesthetics. Art, therefore, was argued implicitly and explicitly to
be essentially referential. This theory assumed, first of all, that there existed a common, phenomenal world, which could be reliably described
by the methods of empirical historiography or else by those of empirical
social science. It assumed, second, that the function of the black writer
was to testify to the private world of black pain and degradation, determined by a pervasive white and unblinking racism. Not only would
creative writing at last make visible the face of the victimized and invisible black person, but it would also serve notice to the white world
that individual black people had the requisite imagination to create
great art and therefore to be 'equal.' " Gates, *Figures in Black*, p. 45.

10. Ann Petry, *The Street* (1946; repr. New York: Pyramid Books, 1971),
p. 32.

11. Ibid., p. 44.

12. Ellison, *Invisible Man*, p. 165.

13. Richard Wright, *The Long Dream* (1958; repr. New York: Ace Publishing Corporation, 1958), p. 348.

14. The most significant of Du Bois's publications was *The Souls of Black Folk*, published in 1903. A number of Claude McKay's poems, especially his 1919 "If We Must Die," drew attention to a new, artistically effective militancy. Arna Bontemps states that the young Negro writers' reaction to the 1923 publication of Jean Toomer's *Cane* "marked an awakening that soon thereafter began to be called a Negro Renaissance." Arna Bontemps, Introduction to Jean Toomer, *Cane* (1923; repr. New York: Harper and Row, 1969), p. x. In 1926, Langston Hughes, writing in the *Nation*, declared, "We younger Negro artists who create now intend to express our individual dark-skinned selves without fear or shame. If white people are pleased we are glad. If they're not, it doesn't matter. We know we are beautiful. And ugly too. The tom-tom cries and the tom-tom laughs. If colored people are pleased we are glad. If they are not, their displeasure doesn't matter either. We build our temples for tomorrow, strong as we know how, and we stand on top of the mountain, free within ourselves." Langston Hughes, "The Negro Artist and the Racial Mountain," in Michael W. Peplow and Arthur P. Davis, eds., *The New Negro Renaissance: An Anthology* (New York: Holt, Rinehart and Winston, 1975), p. 476.

15. After using a white man's library card in order to check books out of the Memphis Public Library, Wright was startled by H. L. Mencken's iconoclasm in his *A Book of Prefaces*: "Yes, this man was fighting, fighting with words. He was using words as a weapon, using them as one would use a club. Could words be weapons? Well, yes, for here they were. Then, maybe, perhaps, I could use them as a weapon? No. It frightened me. I read on and what amazed me was not what he said, but how on earth anybody had the courage to say it." Richard Wright, *Black Boy* (1945; repr. New York: Harper and Row, 1966), p. 272.

16. Cited in Stephen Henderson, *Understanding the New Black Poetry: Black Speech and Black Music as Poetic References* (New York: William Morrow and Company, 1973), pp. 17–18.

17. Ellison, *Invisible Man*, pp. 205–206.

18. Ernest J. Gaines, *Of Love and Dust* (1967; repr. New York: Bantam Books, 1969), pp. 9–10.

19. Richard Wright, *Lawd Today* (1963; repr. New York: Avon Books, 1969), pp. 183–184.

20. John A. Williams, *The Man Who Cried I Am* (New York: Signet Books, 1968), pp. 85–86.

Five. The Experience of Power and Powerlessness

1. Litwack, *Been in the Storm So Long*, pp. 9, 10.
2. The Sambo image was lent a certain legitimacy in contemporary historiography by the publication of Stanley M. Elkins's *Slavery: A Problem in American Institutional and Intellectual Life* (Chicago: University of Chicago Press, 1959). Elkins argues that the qualities associated with the image—helpless and total dependency, infantilism (the "perpetual child"), irresponsibility, etc.—reflect, as slave owners claimed, the dominant plantation type, but that these qualities were not due to race, as the owners argued, but, rather, were due to the "closed system" of plantation slavery. See esp. pp. 88, 98, 102, 130. Elkins's approach has drawn considerable criticism, particularly on the grounds of his having confused the mask with the man. For a range of this criticism, see Ann J. Lane, ed., *The Debate over Slavery: Stanley Elkins and His Critics* (Urbana: University of Illinois Press, 1971).
3. Douglass, *Narrative*, p. 5.
4. Ibid., p. 74.
5. Ibid., p. 12.
6. Ibid., p. 6.
7. Harriet Martineau, traveling through the South in the nineteenth century, viewed the exploitation of blacks with pity (extended also to the plantation wives) and their masters with scorn: "What security for domestic purity and peace there can be where every man has had two connexions, one of which must be concealed; and two families, whose existence must not be known to each other; where the conjugal relation begins in treachery, and must be carried on with a heavy secret in the husband's breast, no words are needed to explain. . . . There is no occasion to explain the management of the female slaves on estates where the object is to rear as many as possible, like stock, for the southern market; nor to point out the boundless licentiousness caused by the practice: a practice which wrung from the wife of a planter, in the bitterness of her heart, the declaration that a planter's wife was only 'the chief slave of the harem.'" Harriet Martineau, *Society in America*, vol. 2 (London: Saunders and Otley, 1837), pp. 327–328.
8. Wright, *Black Boy*, pp. 84, 83.

Six. "The Day Had Passed Forever When I Could Be a Slave in Fact"

1. Douglass, *Narrative*, p. 33.
2. Ibid., p. 36.
3. Ibid., pp. 42, 43.
4. Ibid., p. 44.
5. Gates attributes the popularity of Douglass's *Narrative* and of slave narratives to the interest in autobiographies, as well as to its similarities to the European picaresque and the sentimental novels. Gates, *Black Literature and Theory*, pp. 213–215. Unexplored is the possible insight these windows to the South could provide on the nature of work and workers in an era of increasing class division and worker agitation.
6. Robert K. Merton, *Social Theory and Social Structure* (1957; repr. Glencoe: The Free Press, 1958), p. 234.
7. Douglass, *Narrative*, p. 1.
8. Ibid., pp. 30, 47–48, 50, 65.
9. Edward T. Hall, *The Hidden Dimension* (1966; repr. Garden City: Doubleday and Company, Anchor Books, 1969), p. 8.
10. Bertram Doyle, *The Etiquette of Race Relations* (1937; repr. New York: Shocken Books, 1971), p. 14.
11. Henry Bibb, "Narrative of the Life and Adventures of Henry Bibb, an African Slave," in Osofsky, *Puttin' on Ole Massa*, pp. 77–78.
12. Gilbert Osofsky, *The Burden of Race: A Documentary History of Negro-White Relations in America* (1967; repr. New York: Harper and Row, Harper Torchbook, 1968), p. 18.
13. Gaston Bachelard, *The Poetics of Space* (1958; repr. Boston: Beacon Press, 1969), p. 7.
14. Bibb, "Narrative," p. 120.
15. Gustavus Vassa, "The Life of Olaudah Equino or Gustavus Vassa, the African," in Arna Bontemps, ed., *Great Slave Narratives* (Boston: Beacon Press, 1969), p. 27.
16. Solomon Northup, "Twelve Years a Slave: Narrative of Solomon Northup," in Osofsky, *Puttin' on Ole Massa*, p. 383.
17. William Wells Brown, "Narrative of William Wells Brown," in ibid., p. 193.
18. Bibb, "Narrative," p. 115.
19. Douglass, *Narrative*, p. 1.
20. Ibid., pp. 43, 58, 66.

21. Ibid., p. 74.
22. Louis R. Harlan, *Booker T. Washington: The Making of a Black Leader 1856−1901* (New York: Oxford University Press, 1972), p. 204.

Seven. "Who Gave You a Master and a Mistress?—*God Gave Them to Me*"

1. I am here recognizing the distinction between moralism and morality. Morality is the essential quality; moralism is the appearance, which may or may not reflect the essential. The distinction has long been recognized in English literature, as in the many examples from Shakespeare, such as Lady Macbeth's injunction to act the gentle flower but be the serpent under it. One might, in fact, begin a history of appearance at the point where the mythic simplicity of the organic village gives way to the complexity of urban and courtly life. Certainly the distinction becomes a way of life in the guidebooks written for chivalric and courtly etiquette. Richard Sennett sees the distinction as central to the advice Lord Chesterfield gives his son regarding how to act in the cityscape of eighteenth-century London: "The consciousness of a distance between oneself and one's traffic with the world became an overriding theme for many writers in the 1740's, of whom Lord Chesterfield was perhaps the most famous example. In Chesterfield's letters to his son the emphasis was all on learning to survive in the world by hiding one's feelings from others. . . . Chesterfield tells his son that he can survive the 'snares' of great cities like Paris and London only by wearing a mask. . . . Again and again Chesterfield cites his own mistakes as a youth, when sheltered from the realities of London, he grew up to think that directness and frankness were moral qualities; the price of these virtues was 'great harm done to myself and to others' when he began to live an adult life in London." Richard Sennett, *The Fall of Public Man: On the Social Psychology of Capitalism* (1977; repr. New York: Random House–Vintage Books, 1978), pp. 62, 63.

In America, the value of moralism is reflected in Governor Winthrop's sermon aboard the *Arbella*, in his recognition that the new colony would be as a beacon upon a hill. But this recognition of the public uses of morality sounds with sincerity over the centuries; Governor Winthrop was reflecting the Puritan assumption that Puritan appearance and reality were one, an assumption given prophetic energy by the Puritans' belief in their own election. It was Anne Hutchinson's subversive contention that sanctification (the appearance of salvation)

is no proof of justification (the reality of salvation), and it was this contention, along with others, that led to her ejection from the colony.
Governor Winthrop's mix of religious election and ordained nationalism (which is moralism at the national level) is a mix which recurs
through much of our history. But it is not until Benjamin Franklin's
Autobiography that we see an important recognition of the two levels
of appearance and reality and a willingness to manipulate them: "In
order to secure my Credit and Character as a Tradesman, I took care not
only to be in *Reality* Industrious and frugal, but to avoid all *Appearances* to the Contrary. I drest plainly; I was seen at no Places of idel
Diversion; I never went out a fishing or Shooting; a Book, indeed, sometimes debauch'd me from my Work; but that was seldom, snug, and
gave no Scandal: and to show that I was not above my Business, I sometimes brought home the Paper I purchas'd at the Stores, thro' the Streets
on a Wheelbarrow. Thus being esteem'd an industrious thriving young
Man, and paying duly for what I bought, the Merchants who imported
Stationery solicited my Custom, others propos'd supplying me with
Books, I went on swimmingly." Chester E. Jorgenson and Frank Luther
Mott, eds., *Benjamin Franklin* (1936; repr. New York: Hill and Wang,
1962), pp. 64–65. In some respects one might regard the autobiography
itself as the appearance of the man, designed to figure forth the public
persona for first his son William, later for the public; however, this
would seem to be too overtly revisionist and to ignore both the pressures of public roles and the fact that, historically, selective principles
had guided life writing from the first biographical accounts of the various Puritan divines. At the same time, Franklin's awareness of the various mixes of reality and appearance continues to intrigue. One of his
appeals to Europeans was his seeming rusticity; his coonskin cap was
the mannered appearance of the seeming unmannered.

2. Quoted in Ronald V. Sampson, *The Psychology of Power* (1965; repr.
   New York: Random House–Vintage Books, 1968), p. 150.
3. Boorstin, *The Americans: The National Experience*, p. 377.
4. Cited in Osofsky, *Burden of Race*, p. 39.
5. Cited in Osofsky, *Puttin' on Ole Massa*, pp. 32, 33.
6. Ibid., p. 33.
7. Lawrence W. Levine, *Black Culture and Black Consciousness: Afro-
   American Folk Thought from Slavery to Freedom* (London: Oxford University Press, 1977), p. 45. Some former slaves refused later to read the
   Pauline letters because of their injunction "Slaves, be obedient to your
   masters." Levine chronicles other responses: "In his autobiographical

Sketches from Slave Life, published in 1855, the black minister Peter Randolph wrote that when he was a slave in Prince George County, Virginia, he and his fellow slaves had the rather uninspiring choice of listening to the white Reverend G. Harrison who taught them: 'Servants obey your masters. Do not *steal* or *lie*, for this is very wrong. Such conduct is sinning against the Holy Ghost, *and is base ingratitude to your kind masters, who feed, clothe and protect you,*' or the white Reverend James L. Goltney who warned: 'It is the devil who tells you to try and be free.' " Ibid., p. 44.

The slaves were aware, too, that the Bible contained more than injunctions against disobedience, stealing, laziness, and lying—that the Bible, in fact, contained "subversive" teachings. Whites, too, were aware of this. Though no black may have been present during a debate in the South Carolina legislature in 1834, many blacks would have understood Whitemarsh B. Seabrook's declaration that anyone who wanted slaves to read the entire Bible was fit for a " 'room in the Lunatic Asylum.' " Quoted in ibid., pp. 46–47. John Dixon Long's experience bears on this point: "The Methodist minister John Dixon Long, who preached in Maryland from 1839 to 1856, was continually disturbed by the 'elementary and abstract preaching' he was forced to engage in and the 'adulterated Gospel' he was forced to embrace because of slavery. 'When you want to denounce sin,' he wrote, 'you must go to Adam and Eve, and to the Jews in the wilderness. You must be careful, however, when slaves are present, how you talk about Pharaoh making slaves of the Hebrews, and refusing to let the people leave Egypt. At any rate, you must make no direct application of the subject.' During one of his sermons on the conduct of Cain toward Abel, a slave asked him if he thought it was right for one brother to sell another. Long was at first confused and finally could do no better than to counsel: 'Colored friends, it is best for you not to discuss such questions here.' 'What preachers in the South,' he complained, 'can say with Paul that they have not shunned to declare the whole counsel of God?' " Ibid., p. 46.

8. In Osofsky, *Puttin' on Ole Massa*, p. 33.
9. Douglass, *Narrative*, pp. 117–119.
10. Cited in Eugene D. Genovese, *Roll, Jordan, Roll: The World the Slaves Made* (1974; repr. New York: Random House–Vintage Books, 1976), p. 261.
11. In Levine, *Black Culture and Black Consciousness*, p. 44.
12. Genovese, *Roll, Jordan, Roll*, p. 48. "Anderson Edwards, a black

preacher in Texas, was forced to preach what his master told him to: 'he say tell them niggers iffen they obeys the master they goes to Heaven; but I knowed there's something better for them, but daren't tell them 'cept on the sly. That I done lots. I tells 'em iffen they keep praying, the Lord will set 'em free.' " Levine, *Black Culture and Black Consciousness*, p. 48.

13. Levine, *Black Culture and Black Consciousness*, pp. 50–51.
14. Genovese, *Roll, Jordan, Roll*, p. 267.
15. I say "ostensibly" nonreligious forms of black literature for the simple reason that, as Levine has demonstrated, the sacred and the secular worlds have never, in the black experience, been so simply demarcated: "Neither the slaves nor their African forebears ever drew modernity's clear line between the sacred and the secular." Levine, *Black Culture and Black Consciousness*, p. 30. (The fact that drawing such clear lines is a modernist tendency generally is reflected in Jacob Burckhardt's statement that nineteenth-century religion was "rationalism for the few and magic for the many.") Anyone who attended black poetry readings during the sixties and seventies would have been struck by the mix of the secular and the sacred: by the moral thrust; the themes of exodus, bondage, and return; the sense of communion; the consciousness raising; the "audience" participation; the often direct address to the "audience"; the shouts of "Teach it!" "Preach it!"
16. Benjamin Quarles observes that slaves "believed English officers would give them their freedom," that like a "lamp unto his feet, the lure of freedom led the slaves to the camps of Clinton and Cornwallis." Quarles notes that "according to the Lutheran clergyman Henry Melchior Muhlenberg, the belief that a British victory would bring freedom was said to be almost universal in slave society." Benjamin Quarles, *The Negro in the American Revolution* (1961; repr. New York: W. W. Norton and Company, 1973), p. 115; see also pp. 68–93, 111–133. Despite the need for troops, however, it was not until the third year of the war that blacks were actively recruited as soldiers in any great numbers, and even then the states of Georgia and South Carolina refused to arm blacks, although employing them in war-related labor.
17. "Black leaders read the documents of American history carefully and knew them in detail; in sermons, editorials, orations, and pamphlets they reminded white men that they did not have [the civil rights guaranteed by the historical documents]." Nye, *Society and Culture*, p. 219.
18. The designations applied to black recruits during the Revolutionary

War provide a further instance of what might be termed the language of disappearance: "The typical Negro soldier was a private, consigned as if by caste, to the rank and file. Even more than other privates, he tended to lack identity. Often he bore no specific name; he was carried on the roles as 'A Negro Man,' or 'Negro by Name,' or 'A Negro name not known,' or 'Negro Name unknown.'" Quarles, *Negro in the American Revolution*, p. 74.

19. In employing the term *backstage* from Erving Goffman's *The Presentation of Self in Everyday Life*, I am altering its application: "A back region or backstage may be defined as a place, relative to a given performance, where the impression fostered by the performance is knowingly contradicted as a matter of course." Erving Goffman, *The Presentation of Self in Everyday Life* (New York: Doubleday and Company, Doubleday Anchor Books, 1959), p. 112.

20. Stephen Butterfield declares the major sources of ironical and satirical perception in the slave narrative to be "the contradictions between the official rhetoric of the American Promise and the actual treatment of black people, and between the theory that slaves were chattel goods and the fact that they were human beings. Underlying both contradictions are the larger ones between master and slave, pro- and antislavery religion, and the economic systems of North and South." He notes, too, that "the perception that sees the world in terms of irony and caricature is shaped by having to live with oppression, hypocrisy, contradiction, and double identity as daily conditions of existence." Butterfield, *Black Autobiography*, pp. 40, 42.

21. "The Negro is a sort of seventh son, born with a veil, and gifted with second-sight in this American world,—a world which yields him no true self-consciousness, but only lets him see himself through the revelation of the other world. It is a peculiar sensation, this double-consciousness, this sense of always looking at one's self through the eyes of others, of measuring one's soul by the tape of a world that looks on in amused contempt and pity. One ever feel his twoness,—an American, a Negro; two souls, two thoughts, two unreconciled strivings; two warring ideals in one dark body, whose dogged strength alone keeps it from being torn asunder." W. E. B. Du Bois, *The Souls of Black Folk* (1903; repr. Greenwich: Fawcett Publications, 1961), pp. 16–17.

22. Quoted in Butterfield, *Black Autobiography*, p. 39.

23. Gates, *Black Literature and Theory*, p. 291.

24. Osofsky, *Puttin' on Ole Massa*, p. 33.

25. Frederick Douglass's speech delivered at Rochester, New York on July 4, 1852 and titled "What to the Slave Is the Fourth of July?" is an example of the subverting of the seemingly universal.
26. Gates, *Black Literature and Theory*, p. 6.
27. Wright, *Black Boy*, pp. 248–250.

Eight. "A Spy in the Enemy's Country"

1. Simone de Beauvoir, *The Second Sex*, trans. H. M. Parshley (New York: Knopf, 1953), p. 542.
2. "Let us consider this waiter in the cafe. His movement is quick and forward, a little too precise, a little too rapid. He comes toward the patrons with a step a little too quick. He bends forward a little too eagerly; his voice, his eyes express an interest a little too solicitous for the order of the customer. Finally there he returns, trying to imitate in his walk the inflexible stiffness of some kind of automaton while carrying his tray with the recklessness of a tightrope-walker by putting it in a perpetually unstable, perpetually broken equilibrium which he perpetually re-establishes by a light movement of the arm and hand. All his behavior seems to us a game. He applies himself to chaining his movements as if they were mechanisms, the one regulating the other; his gestures and even his voice seem to be mechanisms; he gives himself the quickness and pitiless rapidity of things. He is playing, he is amusing himself. But what is he playing? We need not watch long before we can explain it: he is playing at being a waiter in a cafe." Jean-Paul Sartre, *Being and Nothingness*, trans. Hazel E. Barnes (New York: Philosophical Library, 1956), p. 59.
3. Wright, *Black Boy*, pp. 200, 203–204, 215.
4. Ellison, *Invisible Man*, pp. 118, 13–14.
5. Wright, *Native Son*, pp. 43, 64.
6. William Attaway, *Blood on the Forge* (1941; repr. New York: Macmillan Company, Collier, 1970), pp. 14–15.
7. Litwack, *Been in the Storm So Long*, p. 117.
8. Ibid., pp. 10, 138.
9. Ibid., p. 117.
10. Ibid., p. 165.
11. Ibid., pp. 154–155.
12. Ibid., p. 25.
13. Douglass, *Narrative*, p. 20.

14. Bibb, "Narrative," p. 66.
15. Osofsky, *Puttin' on Ole Massa*, p. 21.
16. Quoted in ibid., p. 9.
17. Ralph Ellison, *Shadow and Act* (New York: Random House, Signet, 1964), p. 70.

Nine. Introduction

1. The image recurs in Du Bois's *The Souls of Black Folk* where it assumes social-psychological significance, even when it is expressed almost mystically. For example, when Du Bois writes, "The Negro is a sort of seventh son, born with a veil, and gifted with second-sight in this American world," we can view it as an astute perception of the awareness of the outsider, not unlike the "sympathetic knowledge of the hidden sin in other hearts" that Hester Prynne manifests in *The Scarlet Letter*.

2. "Those features of the world outside which have to do with the behavior of other human beings, in so far as that behavior crosses ours, is dependent upon us, or is interesting to us, we call roughly public affairs. The pictures inside the heads of these human beings, the pictures of themselves, of others, of their needs, purposes, and relationships, are their public opinions." Walter Lippmann, *Public Opinion* (1922; repr. Toronto: Collier-Macmillan Canada, 1965), p. 18.

3. Ellison, *Invisible Man*, p. 268. His teacher is alluding to Stephen Dedalus's vaunting declaration at the close of *A Portrait of the Artist as a Young Man*: "Welcome, O life! I go to encounter for the millionth time the reality of experience and to forge in the smithy of my soul the uncreated conscience of my race." A comparison of the two exposes stark differences in relative situations. Stephen Dedalus expands in a luxury of rejection; Ellison's protagonist will learn how complex, painful, and long can be the process of self-knowledge if you are black in America. For further comparison, the reader might turn to the closing paragraphs of *Black Boy*, Richard Wright's portrayal of the black artist as a young man. For example, consider: "I was leaving the South to fling myself into the unknown, to meet other situations that would perhaps elicit from me other responses. And if I could meet enough of a different life, then, perhaps, gradually and slowly I might learn who I was, what I might be." Wright, *Black Boy*, p. 284.

4. Mr. Emerson's son asks the protagonist, "'Aren't you curious about what lies behind the face of things?'" To which the protagonist replies,

"'Yes, sir, but I'm mainly interested in a job.'" The son responds, "'Of course, . . . but life isn't that simple.'" Ellison, *Invisible Man*, p. 143.

5. Ibid., p. 438.

6. Paul Lawrence Dunbar, *The Sport of the Gods* (1902; repr. Miami: Mnemosyne Publishing, 1969), p. 25.

7. In William L. Andrews, *The Literary Career of Charles W. Chesnutt* (Baton Rouge: Louisiana State University Press, 1980), p. 78.

8. Charles W. Chesnutt, *The Marrow of Tradition* (1901; repr. Ann Arbor: University of Michigan Press, 1969), pp. 43, 44.

9. Charles W. Chesnutt, *The Colonel's Dream* (1905; repr. Upper Saddle River: Gregg Press, 1968), p. 153.

10. Saunders Redding, *The Lonesome Road: A Narrative History of the Black American Experience* (1958; repr. Garden City: Doubleday Anchor Books, 1973), pp. 165, 166.

11. "Six Mississippi men (three with families) had rented a 'plantation.' At the year's end, the landlord claimed that their debts far outbalanced the monies owed to them and took seven hundred bushels of wheat, fourteen fat hogs, some corn, and a wagon and a team of animals. After the blacks went to court without success, they told the landlord 'just what they thought of this wholesale robbery.' A few days later, 'masked Regulators' took the men from their beds, hanged them, and lashed their bodies to boards, which were floated down the Mississippi River with a white cloth fastened to each body. Each cloth had written on it, 'Any one taking up these bodies to bury them may expect the same fate.'" Herbert G. Gutman, *The Black Family in Slavery and Freedom 1750–1925* (New York: Random House–Vintage Books, 1977), p. 438. See also pp. 433–441.

     Even the image of the black man guarding his mistress's door while her husband was away fighting in the war must be drained of suggestions of manhood. His was not to be pictured as a manly, responsible act but more as an affectionate, loyal response as from a superior dog—the act called forth by the other rather than emanating from resources in the black self. In these instances the image often seems to turn in on itself. Rather than praising the actions of the slave, the act reflects the sterling qualities of mistress/master, who are able to evoke such loyalty from even so abject a creature.

12. Chesnutt, *Marrow of Tradition*, pp. 113–114.

13. Chesnutt, *The Colonel's Dream*, pp. 166–167.

14. Booker T. Washington, *Up from Slavery* (1901; repr. New York: Airmont Publishing Company, 1967), p. 136. Washington's address, while

speaking for separation, will also attempt to recall for his audience the old sentiments that had, in myth and in fact, interlinked black and white. Separation will be codified into law the following year by decision of the U.S. Supreme Court in the "separate but equal" doctrine of *Plessy* v. *Ferguson*.

15. Chesnutt, *The Colonel's Dream*, pp. 193–194.

16. This compliance had often rested on the personal relationship between slave and master, not on an abstract concept of duty. Eugene D. Genovese has considered this aspect of slave/master relations and has cited an example from the Sea Islands which suggests to what degree what might be termed *personal law* could exist on individual plantations: "Beyond racial dependency, a special sense of relationship to a particular person or persons emerges here. The abolitionists who went to the Sea Islands confronted this attitude immediately. When they told the freedmen that the government must be obeyed, they were met with blank stares. Persons, particular human beings, had to be obeyed. What was a government? The assassination of Lincoln stunned the freedmen not only because they had come to love him as a deliverer but because they had great difficulty in imagining that the government, which was protecting them, could survive or indeed had ever existed apart from his person." Genovese, *Roll, Jordan, Roll*, pp. 118–119.

17. In the 1840s Alexis de Tocqueville had been amazed at the depth of racial bias he had encountered in the North: "The prejudice of race appears to be stronger in the states that have abolished slavery than in those where it still exists." Quoted by C. Vann Woodward, *The Strange Case of Jim Crow*, 2nd rev. ed. (London: Oxford University Press, 1966), p. 20.

18. Quoted in ibid.

19. Cited in ibid., pp. 25, 14.

20. Ibid., pp. 26–27.

21. Jacqueline Jones, *Labor of Love, Labor of Sorrow: Black Women, Work and the Family, from Slavery to the Present* (1985; repr. New York: Random House–Vintage Books), p. 68.

22. Ibid., p. 69. "With school and freedom best clothes came out and ragged clothes were kept for the fields. Work and old 'raggedy' clothes were . . . closely associated in the minds of the large group of middle-aged Island folk." Quoted in ibid.

23. Ibid., p. 23.

24. Litwack, *Been in the Storm So Long*, pp. 258–259.

25. Ibid., p. 278.

26. Jones, *Labor of Love*, p. 63.

27. Litwack, *Been in the Storm So Long*, p. 263.

28. Frank Dumont of the Dumont's Minstrels Company regarded reddening the lips as unnecessary: "When you have applied the cork and left the lips in the natural condition they will appear red to the audience. Comedians leave a wider white margin all around the lips. This will give it the appearance of a large mouth, and will look red to the spectator." Frank Dumont, *The Witmark Amateur Minstrel Guide and Burnt Cork Encyclopedia* (Chicago: M. Witmark and Sons, 1899), p. 14.

29. Carl Wittke, *Tambo and Bones: A History of the American Minstrel Stage* (Durham: Duke University Press, 1930), p. 141.

30. Ellison, *Invisible Man*, pp. 241–242. Ellison's example of early Americana recalls the role playing of Shorty, the elevator operator in Richard Wright's *Black Boy* who manipulates the white men's perverse stereotypes. He bends over, in an often-repeated ritual, to pick up a quarter the white man has thrown on the floor of the elevator, whereupon the white man kicks him with all his strength. Shorty sings out but delays opening the door until he has popped the coin into his mouth: "'This monkey's got the peanuts,' he chortled," Later, in response to Wright's question, he responds, "'Listen, nigger . . . my ass is tough and quarters is scarce.'" Wright, *Black Boy*, pp. 249–250.

31. It is significant that the psychologically sensitive Marcus Garvey would single out dolls to comment on in the 1920s; he wanted black children to play with, and to love, black dolls rather than pale white dolls.

32. Quoted in Antonia Fraser, *A History of Toys* (London: Weidenfeld and Nicolson, 1966), pp. 178, 180. One is reminded of Hawthorne's description of the imitative play of the Puritan children: "She saw the children of the settlement, on the grassy margin of the street, or at the domestic thresholds, disporting themselves in such grim fashion as the Puritanic nurture would permit; playing at going to church, perchance; or at scourging Quakers; or taking scalps in a sham-fight with the Indians; or scaring one another with freaks of imitative witchcraft." Nathanial Hawthorne, *The Scarlet Letter*, in McMichael, *Anthology*, p. 1242.

33. Fraser, *History of Toys*, p. 178.

34. Janet Pagter Johl, *The Fascinating Story of Dolls* (New York: H. L. Lindquist Publisher, 1941), pp. 257–259.

35. Ibid., pp. 258–259.

36. Ms. Rosemarye Bunting, of the Pittsburgh Doll Club, informs me that the doll is still sold by Dean's Rag Book Company.

37. Margery Fisher, *Who's Who in Children's Books: A Treasury of the*

Familiar Characters of Childhood (New York: Holt, Rinehart and Winston, 1975), p. 122.

38. Fraser, *History of Toys*, p. 190.

39. Fisher, *Who's Who*, p. 123.

40. Dorothy B. Ryan, *Picture Postcards in the United States 1893–1918* (New York: Clarkson N. Potter, 1982), pp. 126–127.

41. Ibid., p. 75.

42. William Murrell, *A History of American Graphic Humor (1747–1865)*, vol. 1 (New York: Cooper Square Publishers, 1967), pp. 108–110.

43. Ibid., pp. 151, 190–191.

44. Harry T. Peters, *Currier & Ives: Printmakers to the American People* (Garden City: Doubleday, Doran and Company, 1942), p. 3.

45. Ibid., plate 157.

46. Ibid., plate 163.

47. Ibid., plate 158.

48. Walton Rawls, *The Great Book of Currier & Ives' America* (New York: Cross Rivers Press, 1979), pp. 152–155.

49. Peters, *Currier & Ives*, plate 133.

50. Ibid., plates 134, 132, 135, 183.

51. Ibid., p. 23. "The comics appealed to the sense of humor of many widely assorted types of people. The Duke of Newcastle, accompanying the then Prince of Wales on a tour of this country, was strolling through Nassau Street one day when he was attracted by the display in the window of the Currier & Ives store. The Darktown Comics so delighted him that he bought a full set (a hundred prints)." Ibid.

52. Henry T. Sampson, *Blacks in Blackface: A Source Book on Early Black Musical Shows* (Metuchen: Scarecrow Press, 1980), p. 6.

53. Murrell, *History of American Graphic Humor*, vol. 2, p. 105.

54. Rawls, *Great Book*, pp. 45–46. The occasions for the humorous depiction of black failings seem to have been unlimited. Eugene Levy cites an example from the 1893 World's Columbian Exposition in Chicago: "The unofficial exposition humor magazine, *World's Fair Puck*, mercilessly lampooned 'Darkies' Day at the Fair,' with a cleverly devised double-page cartoon depicting how a 'Georgia coon, named Major Moon' failed in his efforts to corner the watermelon market on 'Darkies' Day.'" Eugene Levy, *James Weldon Johnson: Black Leader Black Voice* (Chicago: University of Chicago Press, 1973), p. 40.

55. "Though minstrelsy had its roots in northern urban soil, it quickly branched out into every corner of the nation. Between the 1840s and the 1870s minstrelsy was the dominant form of American popular art.

Within twenty years after the early successes . . . there were more than a hundred professional troupes in blackface. New York alone boasted ten resident companies by 1860, and professional troupes held forth at various times in Boston, Hartford, Washington, Richmond, Charleston, Savannah, Mobile, New Orleans, St. Louis, Cincinnati, Columbus, Cleveland, Chicago, St. Paul, and San Francisco." Gary D. Engle, *This Grotesque Essence: Plays from the American Minstrel Stage* (Baton Rouge: Louisiana State University Press, 1978), pp. xix–xx. "In 1870, Dan Bryant opened Bryant's Opera House on Twenty-third Street, near Sixth Avenue. Bryant's Minstrels played continuously for nine years at Mechanics Hall, eight months in San Francisco, and then returned to other New York theatres for a total run of sixteen years, a record which it would be difficult to duplicate in all the annals of the American stage. Wood's Minstrels played at one hall or another in New York City for a total of fifteen years, and Hooley's Minstrels played in Brooklyn for a decade." Wittke, *Tambo and Bones*, pp. 69–70.

56. Robert C. Toll, *On with the Show* (New York: Oxford University Press, 1976), p. 109.
57. Ibid., p. 86.
58. Carl Wittke, *Tambo and Bones*, pp. 7–9. Wittke had quoted from Francis Pendleton Gaines, *The Southern Plantation: A Study in the Development and Accuracy of a Tradition* (New York: 1925), p. 3.
59. Ibid., pp. 121, 135.
60. Cited in ibid., p. 31.
61. Russel Crouse, *It Seems Like Yesterday* (Garden City: Doubleday, Doran and Company, 1931), p. 140.
62. Constance Rourke, *American Humor: A Study of the National Character* (1931; repr. Garden City: Doubleday and Company, Anchor Books, 1953), p. 86. Rourke's discussion of the blackface minstrel is imaginative but unconvincing. Her misreadings grow out of her tendency to merge three types: Yankee, backwoodsman, and Negro. But it is the difference between such types as backwoods humor and black folklore that is so revealing. The inflation so central to the backwoods tall tales is a reflection of the "space" available. The indefiniteness of the West permitted inflation in both tales and language. Imaginatively, its parallel can be seen in the bestiaries of the Middle Ages, which filled the unknown world with grotesque and composite creatures. The American stress on freedom, in combination with the open and relatively unknown West, encouraged inflation in character, language, and narrative structure. But the cities did not easily breed the tall tales, nor did

the plantations, where the naturalistic press of circumstance kept the imagination from such exotic efflorescences. The West provided the setting (as it did later for the more formal work of such humorists as Mark Twain), the city the market.

63. Dumont, *Witmark Amateur Minstrel Guide*, p. 1.

64. Dailey Paskman and Sigmund Spaeth, *"Gentlemen, Be Seated!": A Parade of Old-Time Minstrels* (Garden City: Doubleday, Doran and Company, 1928), p. 80.

65. Wittke, *Tambo and Bones*, p. 42.

66. Toll, *On with the Show*, pp. 86, 86–87.

67. Engle, *This Grotesque Essence*, pp. xxvii–xxviii, xxvii.

68. Toll, *On with the Show*, p. 68.

69. Richard Moody, *America Takes the Stage: Romanticism in American Drama and Theatre, 1750–1900* (Bloomington: Indiana University Press, 1955), p. 59.

70. Wittke, *Tambo and Bones*, pp. 19, 34.

71. Cited in Sampson, *Blacks in Blackface*, p. 105.

72. Engle, *This Grotesque Essence*, p. xxvi.

73. Billposters and sheet music were not considered in this discussion of graphic forms since they were mostly a product of the minstrel stage. The billposters advertised forthcoming performances and usually included representations of the blackface minstrel; sheet music generally included some of the most popular songs sung by a particular minstrel company as well as representations of the minstrel performers. Both forms were, of course, widespread and reinforced the prevailing graphic stereotypes. For examples, see Toll, *On with the Show*, and Paskman and Spaeth, *"Gentlemen, Be Seated."* In his performance guide, Jack Haverly asserted the importance of billposters: "Nothing succeeds so well as judicious advertising. First prepare your programme of just such acts as you intend presenting for the opening night, using as much display as possible and also, if procurable from your local printer, get humorous darkey cuts to insert upon it—thereby making it attractive or something that will not be immediately thrown away. Then proceed to bill your town, carefully covering every house, store, shop, etc., including surrounding territory of at least five miles. Start these circulars out not less than twenty days before the performance." Jack Haverly, *Negro Minstrels: A Complete Guide* . . . (1902; repr. Upper Saddle River: Literature House, 1969), p. 8.

74. James Weldon Johnson, *Along This Way* (New York: Viking Press, 1933), p. 160.

75. Paul Laurence Dunbar, "The Poet," in *The Complete Poems of Paul Laurence Dunbar* (New York: Dodd, Mead and Company, Apollo Editions, 1913), p. 191. All subsequent references are to this edition.

76. William Dean Howells, "Introduction to *Lyrics of Lowly Life*," in Dunbar, *Complete Poems*, p. ix.

77. Jean Wagner, *Black Poets of the United States from Paul Laurence Dunbar to Langston Hughes* (Urbana: University of Illinois Press, 1973), p. 111. In fairness, Wagner's response is more complex than the quote might suggest: "Paul Laurence Dunbar is probably the black poet it is most difficult to evaluate fairly. . . . But to the poet's credit is a certain integrity in his presentation of the subject. This sets him off markedly from the plantation school and is something that, to the best of our knowledge, has not hitherto been stressed. . . . Dunbar tended to tone down the more outrageous features of the plantation school's portrait, particularly by inserting brief evocations of slavery's abominations." Ibid., pp. 73, 85, 86.

78. James M. Whitfield, "America," in Benjamin Brawley, ed., *Early Negro American Writers* (1935; repr. New York: Dover Publications, 1970), pp. 228–229.

79. Arnold Rampersad, *The Art and Imagination of W. E. B. Du Bois* (Cambridge: Harvard University Press, 1976), p. 104.

80. Eugene B. Redmond, *Drumvoices: The Mission of Afro-American Poetry* (Garden City: Doubleday, Anchor Books, 1976), p. 124.

81. The conventions were embedded in the forms Dunbar appropriated. As Peter Revell has argued, "The popular magazines from northern publishers established the style of Negro dialect and plantation subject matter as firmly in verse as in the short story, and even earlier." The popular magazines printed what "the times" preferred: "It was an age which, seeking respite from the gathering momentum of economic, social, and industrial change, looked to its writers and artists for reassurance, the reassertion of traditional values, and the nostalgic, often sentimental and idealized recall of a past world of lost content. It inclined toward traditional forms and conventional language and characterization in its literature." Peter Revell, *Paul Laurence Dunbar* (Boston: Twayne Publishers, 1979), pp. 77, 19.

82. In *Lyrics of Love and Laughter* (1903) the stereotyped master-slave relationship almost disappears, despite the increase in the number of poems written in black dialect. However, in "Fishing" (172) the master tells the slave to, yes, go fishing, because the weather's too bad for working. In "The Visitor" (177) ol' Miss sends down a basket of food to a

rheumatic black, who will in turn tell a story to little Miss.

83. For which, Redmond adds, "black critics will not forgive him." Redmond, *Drumvoices*, p. 122.

84. Peter Revell, after quoting Wagner's criticism that "Dunbar's dialect is at best a secondhand instrument irredeemably blemished by the degrading themes imposed upon it by the enemies of the black people," responded: "But there is more to the dialect poems than the stereotyped appeal of the plantation tradition and the comic buffoonery of the minstrel show, though elements of these latter qualities are certainly present on occasion. The redeeming feature, leaving aside the lyricism of the language, is the genuine warmth and humanity of the love poems. It was this that constituted their appeal for Paul Robeson. The simple and artless words of praise for black beauty are frequently eloquent beyond any artificiality." Wagner, *Black Poets*, p. 111; Revell, *Paul Laurence Dunbar*, p. 84. Darwin Turner has criticized Dunbar's standard English on the grounds that its "imagery, if particularized at all, is a copy-book imitation of sights and sounds familiar to the English lyricists who were his models, but foreign to the Ohio-born Dunbar." Darwin T. Turner, "Paul Laurence Dunbar: The Poet and the Myths," in Jay Martin, ed., *A Singer in the Dawn: Reinterpretations of Paul Laurence Dunbar* (New York: Dodd, Mead and Company, 1975), p. 59.

85. "Paul Laurence Dunbar came over from Dayton and read to us. I had known his work but was astonished to find that he was a Negro." W. E. B. Du Bois, *Dusk of Dawn* (New York: Harcourt, Brace and Company, 1940), p. 57; Redmond, *Drumvoices*, p. 121.

86. James Weldon Johnson apparently stressed the limitations of dialect poetry during Dunbar's 1901 visit: "The thing that I was sure of and kept repeating to him was that he had carried traditional dialect poetry as far as and as high as it could go; that he had brought it to the fullest measure of charm, tenderness, and beauty it could go. We agreed that the public still demanded dialect poetry, but that as a medium, especially for the Negro poet, it was narrow and limited." Johnson, *Along This Way*, p. 161. The view that dialect poetry was a limited form is suggested, too, by a response from Dunbar's model, James Whitcomb Riley: "When Howells . . . asked Riley for contributions to the *Cosmopolitan*, Riley replied, 'But do you want dialect—or serious work—or both?' " Revell, *Paul Laurence Dunbar*, p. 92. Some of Redmond's remarks seem to reflect a questioning of the form: "But it is generally agreed that, especially since he used ridicule-directed white models, he saw the black man as a subject for either humor or pity." Redmond, *Drum-*

voices, p. 122. Dickson D. Bruce, Jr., among others, has challenged this critical approach: "The harshness with which more recent critics have viewed Dunbar's dialect poetry does not seem to have been present in the criticism appearing during his lifetime, nor were there any apologies for the dialect verse. Dunbar's critics could have chosen to condemn his dialect writing by silence if they did not choose to attack the man directly, but, in fact, all went to great pains to proclaim not only its depth and breadth, but also the accuracy with which the poet had portrayed at least some part of black-American life." Dickson D. Bruce, Jr., "On Dunbar's 'Jingles in a Broken Tongue': Dunbar's Dialect Poetry and the Afro-American Folk Tradition," in Martin, *A Singer in the Dawn*, p. 97.

87. Wagner, *Black Poets*, p. 76.
88. Elkins, *Slavery*, particularly pp. 81−87.
89. Gutman, *Black Family*, pp. 625, 8, 9.
90. Daniel Patrick Moynihan, *The Negro Family* (1965), in Lee Rainwater and William L. Yancy, eds., *The Moynihan Report and the Politics of Controversy* (Cambridge: Massachusetts Institute of Technology Press, 1967); see esp. chap. 4, "The Tangle of Pathology," pp. 75−91.
91. Wright, *Black Boy*, p. 83.
92. Baldwin's criticism first appeared in his 1949 *Partisan Review* article "Everybody's Protest Novel," later reprinted in *Notes of a Native Son* (1955). The criticism will be elaborated in "Many Thousands Gone," where he stresses the absence from Wright's *Native Son* of the shared experience that creates the black identity; but his criticism of identity-as-reaction is already articulated in his 1949 statement: "For Bigger's tragedy is not that he is cold or black or hungry, not even that he is American, black; but that he has accepted a theology that denies him life, that he admits the possibility of his being sub-human and feels constrained, therefore, to battle for his humanity according to those brutal criteria bequeathed him at his birth." Later, but only after Wright's death, will Baldwin consider that element in his criticism which might be viewed as symbolic acts of parricide: "I had used his work as a kind of springboard into my own. His work was a road-block in my road, the sphinx, really, whose riddles I had to answer before I could become myself. . . . he had been an idol. And idols are created in order to be destroyed." James Baldwin, *Notes of a Native Son* (Boston: Beacon Press, 1955), pp. 22−23; and *Nobody Knows My Name: More Notes of a Native Son* (New York: Dell Publishing Company, 1961), pp. 22−23. Ralph Ellison's criticism of Wright is expressed in his article "The World and the Jug," his reply to Irving Howe's article in *Dissent*,

"Black Boys and Native Sons," later published in Howe's *A World More Attractive*. Ellison asserted, "No, Wright was no spiritual father of mine, certainly in no sense I recognized," and criticized *Native Son* for its concentration on environment: "In *Native Son*, Wright began with the ideological proposition that what whites think of the Negro's reality is more important than what Negroes themselves know it to be. Hence Bigger Thomas was presented as a near-subhuman indictment of white oppression. He was designed to shock whites out of their apathy and end the circumstances out of which Wright insisted Bigger emerged. Here environment is all—and interestingly enough, environment conceived solely in terms of the physical, the non-conscious." Ellison, *Shadow and Act*, pp. 124, 121. The popularity among historians of the "victimization model" and its rejection by them is discussed in August Meier and Elliott Rudwick, *Black History and the Historical Profession 1915–1980* (Urbana: University of Illinois Press, 1986), pp. 248–254.

93. Litwack, *Been in the Storm So Long*, pp. 56–57, 59.

94. Jones, *Labor of Love*, pp. 107–108.

95. Cited in Gutman, *Black Family*, p. 3. Lawrence W. Levine has written: "Upon the hard rock of racial, social, and economic exploitation and injustice black Americans forged and nurtured a culture: they formed and maintained kinship networks, made love, raised and socialized children, built a religion, and created a rich expressive culture." *Black Culture and Black Consciousness*, p. xi.

96. Jones, *Labor of Love*, p. 43.

97. Gutman, *Black Family*, pp. 303–304. See also pp. 31–32.

98. Litwack, *Been in the Storm So Long*, pp. 229–230, 232. "Thomas Calahan, who commanded black Mississippi troops, said they had 'an almost universal anxiety . . . to abide by first connections. Many, both men and women with whom I am acquainted, whose wives or husbands the rebels have driven off, firmly refuse to form new connections, and declare their purpose to keep faith to absent ones.' " Gutman, *Black Family*, p. 21.

99. Gutman, *Black Family*, pp. 13, 14.

100. Ibid., pp. 135, 138.

101. Ibid., pp. 86–87.

102. Jones, *Labor of Love*, p. 36.

103. Ibid., pp. 12–13, 63.

104. Ibid., pp. 64, 58.

105. Ibid., pp. 36–37.

106. Genovese, *Roll, Jordan, Roll*, pp. 489–490. Genovese has observed

that even in the absence of the father there were other slave models: "Even when a slave boy was growing up without a father in the house, he had as a model a tough, resourceful driver, a skilled mechanic or two, and older field hands with some time for the children of the quarters." Ibid., p. 493.

107. Jones, *Labor of Love*, p. 84.
108. Gutman, *Black Family*, pp. xviii, xix.
109. Higginson, *Army Life*, p. 253.
110. Genovese, *Roll, Jordan, Roll*, pp. 237, 238.
111. Jones, *Labor of Love*, p. 102.
112. Maya Angelou, *I Know Why the Caged Bird Sings* (1970; repr. New York: Bantam Books, 1971), pp. 107, 108.
113. Cited in Litwack, *Been in the Storm So Long*, p. 459.
114. Cited in ibid., pp. 461−462.
115. Levine, *Black Culture and Black Consciousness*, pp. 30−31.
116. Ibid., pp. 40−41.
117. Ibid., p. 33.
118. Ibid., pp. 33, 80.
119. Jones, *Labor of Love*, pp. 99−100, 101−102.
120. Cited in ibid., p. 65.

Ten. Charles W. Chesnutt

1. Du Bois, *Souls of Black Folk*, p. 23.
2. Cited in Andrews, *Literary Career*, p. 13.
3. Ibid., pp. 4, 5, 6. Andrews has argued that "throughout his essays and fiction Chesnutt rebutted the charge that the mulatto was, in the words of one white man whom Chesnutt remembered, 'an insult to nature, a kind of monster.'" Ibid., p. 5.
4. Ibid., p. 77.
5. Writers in the "plantation tradition," whether the setting was rural or urban, contributed images, characters, and plots to the ideology of restoration: "When 'new Negroes' of the new generation failed to adhere to the advice which their old-time betters gave them, then most popular writers met the threat of black upward mobility in their fiction with ridicule, caricature, and at last resort, force. . . . the lazy, 'wuthless,' pretentious, self-indulgent New Negro, drunk on his undeserved political 'recognition,' became a stock character in post−Civil War American writing. Most often he was caricatured and dismissed with a horse laugh, but when his political and social climbing seemed to unbalance

the racial status quo, southern writers seized on him as the enemy of the reconciliation which they so assiduously sought to propagandize through their fiction. . . . The few stories of the Page-Harris school which pictured the criminal 'bad Negro' regularly traced his antisocial behavior back to his corruption by ideas of self-determination, equal opportunity, and equal worth. . . . freedom for the Afro-American was perceived as license and licentiousness, ambition as aggressiveness, dignity as 'uppityness,' while the deferential hangers-on from the old days were ritually celebrated as the norm of the black man's behavior and the acme of his aspiration." Ibid., pp. 79, 80, 81. As late as 1929, so sensitive a writer as William Faulkner will employ in *Sartoris* the stock strategy of applying a piece of stovewood to the hard "haid" of the black Caspey in order to restore civil balance and the old relationships.

6. Charles W. Chesnutt, "Her Virginia Mammy," in *The Wife of His Youth and Other Stories of the Color Line* (1899; repr. Ann Arbor: University of Michigan Press, 1968), p. 38.

7. Charles W. Chesnutt, "The Wife of His Youth," in ibid., p. 7.

8. Victorian domestic spaces were often formal, staged, and aseptic, places where the family acted out highly crafted roles; where, for example, books may not be set out that might bring a blush to the cheek of the fairest of maidens, as William Dean Howells at one point cautioned. Edith Wharton's experience is perhaps extreme, but it still provides a glimpse into the possible dimensions of formality. In her twelfth year, R. W. B. Lewis reports, she had decided to write a story, beginning with the lines, "'Oh, how do you do, Mrs. Brown?' said Mrs. Tomkins. 'If only I had known you were going to call I should have tidied up the drawing-room.'" Lewis records that "when she shyly brought the pages to her mother, Lucretia Jones gave it only a swift glance before handing it back with the chilling observation that 'drawing rooms are always tidy.'" R. W. B. Lewis, *Edith Wharton: A Biography* (1975; repr. New York: Harper and Row, Harper Colophon Books, 1977), p. 30.

9. Andrews, *Literary Career*, p. 44. Baker views the tales as a contest between Western philosophical rationalism and African conjure spirituality: "In effect, he presents a world in which 'dialect' masks the drama of African spirituality challenging and changing the disastrous transformations of slavery. . . . What moves through Chesnutt's collection is the sound of a southern black culture that knew it had to *re-form* a slave world created by the West's willful transformation of Africans into chattel." Baker, *Modernism*, pp. 44, 47.

10. Andrews, *Literary Career*, p. 36.

11. Charles W. Chesnutt, "The Sheriff's Children," in *The Wife of His Youth*, p. 76.

12. Charles W. Chesnutt, "The Web of Circumstance," in ibid., pp. 312, 316, 322–323.

13. Andrews, *Literary Career*, pp. 98, 98–99.

14. Ibid., pp. 117–118.

15. Chesnutt, "Her Virginia Mammy," p. 37. Regarding those attending the ball sponsored by the "Blue Vein Society" in "The Wife of His Youth," the author observes, "These were colored, though most of them would not have attracted even a casual glance because of any marked difference from white people." "The Wife of His Youth," p. 18.

16. This was, for some critics, the balance Kate Chopin achieved in her "immoral" novel *The Awakening* by the death of Edna Pontellier; and it was the balance Theodore Dreiser failed to achieve when he permitted Carrie Meeber to remain "unpunished" at the close of *Sister Carrie*.

17. Andrews, *Literary Career*, p. 173.

18. Charles W. Chesnutt, *The House behind the Cedars* (1900; repr. New York: Macmillan Company, Collier Books, 1969), pp. 116–117. All subsequent references are to this edition.

19. Sidney Lanier, on duty in Chesnutt's North Carolina during the Civil War, attended such a tournament as Chesnutt describes. The role of such tournaments is described by Clement Eaton: "While he [Lanier] was stationed at Kinston, North Carolina, he attended on January 7, 1864, a grand tournament, followed by a coronation ball. The tournament was a peculiarly Southern manifestation of the romantic movement that the war did not stamp out. Southern aristocrats dressed as medieval knights would engage in a contest of skill in riding swiftly by a suspended ring, trying to pierce it with long shafts resembling medieval lances. On this particular occasion the 'Knight of Dixie' with a helmet made of pasteboard won the prize of the tournament. Southern belles, dressed as queens and princesses, awarded tokens of their favor to brave and skillful 'knights.'" Clement Eaton, *The Waning of the Old South Civilization* (1968; repr. New York: Pegasus, 1969), p. 100.

20. In an unpublished, undated essay in the Chesnutt Collection at Fisk University, Chesnutt suggests guidelines for successful passing, which include "very limited communication with black relatives, complete breaks with Afro-American friends, no discussion of race matters, and avoiding the limelight." Cited in Sylvia Lyons Render, *Charles W. Chesnutt* (Boston: Twayne Publishers, 1980), p. 90.

21. William L. Andrews notes Chesnutt's manipulation of assumptions and

his strategy of indirection but does not consider in any detail the techniques employed by Chesnutt in this complex process. Andrews, *Literary Career*, pp. 159–160.

22. James Weldon Johnson, *The Autobiography of an Ex-Coloured Man* (1912; repr. New York: Hill and Wang, 1960), p. xii. All subsequent references are to this edition.

23. George S. Schuyler, *Black No More* (1931; repr. New York: Macmillan Company, Collier Books, 1971), p. 118.

Eleven. James Weldon Johnson

1. "The Goophered Grapevine," published in *Atlantic Monthly* in 1887, is "believed to be the first fiction by an Afro-American to appear in the most prestigious magazine of the period, although Chesnutt's ethnic identity was not publicized until 1899." Render, *Charles W. Chesnutt*, p. 27.

2. Ellison, *Invisible Man*, p. 248. The phenomenon I am discussing is more limited than that general sense of the white other included in the "double-consciousness" described by Du Bois: "It is a peculiar sensation, this double-consciousness, this sense of always looking at one's self through the eyes of others, of measuring one's soul by the tape of a world that looks on in amused contempt and pity." Du Bois, *The Souls of Black Folk*, pp. 16–17.

3. Wilson Jeremiah Moses, *The Golden Age of Black Nationalism 1850–1915* (Hamden, Conn.: Archon Books, 1978), p. 40.

4. Ibid., pp. 71, 101, 71, 72, 73.

5. Ibid., p. 126.

6. Ibid., p. 131.

7. Johnson, *Along This Way*, pp. 119–120.

8. Levy, *James Weldon Johnson*, pp. 34, 35.

9. Ibid., pp. 35–36.

10. Du Bois's experience with rural school teaching in Tennessee is recounted in "Of the Meaning of Progress" in *The Souls of Black Folk*. Toomer's experience in rural Georgia breathes through *Cane*; ambivalence is present throughout the novel and is central to the turmoil experienced by the northern-educated schoolteacher Ralph Kabnis.

   Du Bois's response to the black masses found expression in two different attitudes. On the one hand he advocated racial uplift, as described above; but he also expressed an attitude toward the "folk" that can best be described as "romantic racialism." Moses has written that "romantic racialism on the European continent has signified the idea that every national group manifests distinctive talents and peculiar traits of personality which may be spoken of as its racial genius." Moses, *Golden Age*, pp. 48–49. This element of Du Bois's thinking can be related to Arnold Rampersad's discussion of the appeal to Du Bois of Heinrich von Treitschke's "romantic authoritarian nationalism," absorbed during Du Bois's studies in Germany: "The romantic vision of the state, with its stress on the authentic *geist*, spirit, or soul of the nation, appealed for a long time to DuBois, as it tends to appeal to someone who is obsessed by his people's historic deprivation and disunity and who yearns for a greater national or racial future." Rampersad, *Art and Imagination*, p. 45.

The very title of Du Bois's book, *The Souls of Black Folk*, implies a "romantic" impulse different from that exhibited in his earlier, more consistently "scientific" studies. His emphasis on black spirituality/white materialism is a recurring theme. The opposition is established in the first essay, "Of Our Spiritual Strivings": "We the darker ones come even now not altogether empty-handed: there are to-day no truer exponents of the pure human spirit of the Declaration of Independence than the American Negroes; there is no true American music but the wild sweet melodies of the Negro slave; the American fairy tales and folk-lore are Indian and African; and, all in all, we black men seem the sole oasis of simple faith and reverence in a dusty desert of dollars and smartness." Du Bois, *The Souls of Black Folk*, p. 22.

"Romantic racialism" will mix with exotic primitivism, hedonism, and sensuality/sexuality to produce the complex public aura of Harlem in the 1920s. And Du Bois will respond by praising the work of such writers as Jessie Fauset and Nella Larsen, whose characters are middle class, mulatto, and much like "white folks," and condemning such a book as Claude McKay's *Home to Harlem*, whose portrayal of the lower-class world of work, street life, and night life he will state, "For the most part nauseates me, and after the dirtier parts of its filth I feel distinctly like taking a bath." W. E. B. Du Bois, "'Home to Harlem' and 'Quicksand'" (*Crisis*, June 1928), in Theodore G. Vincent, ed., *Voices of a Black Nation: Political Journalism in the Harlem Renaissance* (San Francisco: Ramparts Press, 1973), p. 359.

11. Levy, *James Weldon Johnson*, pp. 45, 47.
12. Ibid., pp. 93, 93–94. "Jim Johnson's reaction to ragtime showed a similar ambiguity. In 1905 a national magazine asked him to write a short article on Negroes in contemporary music. In the course of the article

Johnson gave his highest praise to those composers and performers whose music was least identifiably black. At the top of his list stood Samuel Coleridge-Taylor in England and Harry T. Burleigh in the United States—composers who made their reputation chiefly in conventional classical music." Ibid., pp. 92–93.

13. James Weldon Johnson, *The Second Book of Negro Spirituals* (New York: Viking Press, 1926), p. 20.

14. E. Franklin Frazier has written on the "pre-eminence" of Washington "society" in the period prior to the first World War: "Washington became, in fact, the center of Negro 'society' and retained this distinction until after the first World War. This was owing partly to the fact that until the mass migrations of Negroes to northern cities, Washington with around 90,000 Negroes had a larger Negro community than any city in the United States until 1920. The pre-eminence of Washington as the center of Negro 'society' was due more especially to other factors. Because of its relatively large Negro professional class, including teachers in the segregated public school system, doctors, dentists, and lawyers, and large numbers of Negroes employed in the federal government, Negroes in the nation's capital had incomes far above those in other parts of the country. This enabled Washington's 'colored society' to engage in forms of consumption and entertainment that established its pre-eminence among American Negroes." E. Franklin Frazier, *Black Bourgeoisie: The Rise of a New Middle Class* (1957; repr. New York: The Free Press, 1965), pp. 197–198.

15. W. E. B. Du Bois, in a passage from *The Souls of Black Folk* (1903), sounds very much like Johnson's doctor; Du Bois's comments, in fact, throw light on post–Civil War class divisions within the black community: "One thing, however, seldom occurs: the best of the whites and the best of the Negroes almost never live in anything like close proximity. It thus happens that in nearly every Southern town and city, both whites and blacks see commonly the worst of each other. This is a vast change from the situation in the past, when, through the close contact of master and house-servant in the patriarchal big house, one found the best of both races in close contact and sympathy, while at the same time the squalor and dull round of toil among the fieldhands was removed from the sight and hearing of the family." Du Bois, *The Souls of Black Folk*, p. 125. See also p. 136.

16. Eugene Levy notes that Johnson "wrote to George Towns shortly after the publication of the novel that the task before black Americans was

twofold: 'one, to fit ourselves; the other to prove to the great and powerful majority that we are fit.' " Levy, *James Weldon Johnson*, p. 137.

17. Addison Gayle, Jr., notes that the protagonist's "willingness to surrender his cultural artifacts" begins as early as during his trip to Europe:
"The protagonist makes his great discovery: 'I sat amazed. I had been
turning classic music into rag-time, a comparatively easy task; and this
man had taken rag-time and made it classic. The thought came across
me like a flash—it can be done, why can't I do it?' " Gayle observes,
"Thus black art and the black artist alike disappear as distinct entities,
as individuals, become American artists, and their productions, American ones." Addison Gayle, Jr., *The Way of the New World: The Black
Novel in America* (Garden City: Doubleday, Anchor Books), p. 114.
Stepto sees this pattern of rejection as beginning in the protagonist's
childhood attempt to dig up the colored glass bottles used as borders for
beds of flowers, which Stepto relates to an African burial survival: "To
be sure, the front yard of the Ex-Coloured Man's first home is not a
burial ground, but is a ritual space in that it is the place of his birth—
a spatial expression of community into which he is born. When the
Ex-Coloured Man digs up the bottles—ironically, in order to 'know
whether or not the bottles grew as the flowers did'—he performs an
innocent yet devastating act of assault upon a considerable portion of
his heritage. That act prefigures his misdirected attempts to approach,
let alone embrace, black American culture, including most obviously
his desire to render the 'old Southern songs' in 'classical form.' " Robert
E. Stepto, *From Behind the Veil: A Study of Afro-American Narrative*
(Urbana: University of Illinois Press, 1979), pp. 100–101. Cooke sees a
lifelong pattern of rejection which ultimately turns on the rejecter:
"The ex-colored man, understandably but unwisely looking to immu-
nize himself against circumstances, immures himself out of existence.
From a child he is all calculation, and the final sum of his calculations
with circumstance is near zero. . . . he is left without an identity, without realized or articulate human relationship. His whole life has depended on enclosures, but ambivalently so: he loves the nightclub but
hates the risk it entails, loves the millionaire's apartment but resents
its obligations. Finally he has enclosures he can count on, in his narrow
protected home and then, with the loss of his wife, in his even narrower,
secret, autobiographical box. But he is ultimately deceived, betrayed.
That box is his cryptic casket, the proof that he is surviving in a living
death." Michael G. Cooke, *Afro-American Literature in the Twentieth*

Century: The Achievement of Intimacy (New Haven: Yale University Press, 1984), pp. 51−52. Nathan Huggins notes: "Although different in many ways, it is interesting to compare *The Rise of David Levinsky*, 1917, with *The Autobiography of an Ex-Coloured Man*. In both novels acceptance and success in American society come at the cost of a rich cultural heritage." Nathan Irvin Huggins, *Harlem Renaissance* (New York: Oxford University Press, 1971), p. 318. The Nashville *Tennessean*, in its review of *The Autobiography of an Ex-Coloured Man*, provided what is perhaps the incomparable summing up: "The Southern paper condemned *The Autobiography* as a 'lie' and an 'insult to Southern womanhood.' There was no such thing as 'an ex-colored man,' the paper claimed; 'once a negro, always a negro.'" Levy, *James Weldon Johnson*, p. 127.

Twelve. Wallace Thurman

1. "Although mulattoes were not always treated better than the blacks, as a rule they were taken into the household or were apprenticed to a skilled artisan. Partly because of the differential treatment accorded the mulattoes, but more especially because of general degradation of the Negro as a human being, the Negro of mixed ancestry thought of himself as being superior to the unmixed Negro. His light complexion became his most precious possession. Witness, for example, the typical case of the mulatto slave begging Frances Kemble that she 'be put to some other than field labor because hoing in the field was so hard on her *on account of her color*.' Concerning the prestige which white 'blood' conferred, Miss Kemble observed that the slaves accepted the contempt of their masters to such an extent that 'they profess, and really seem to feel it for themselves, and the faintest admixture of white blood in their veins appears at once, by common consent of their own race, to raise them in the scale of humanity.'" Frazier, *Black Bourgeoisie*, pp. 135−136.

2. Ibid., p. 14. "Being primarily the offspring of the white planter class, the mulattoes were the privileged group of the slave regime. Eye-witnesses give ample testimony to this fact, as do the statistics showing that the overwhelming majority of the free Negroes were mulatto, along with the general prevalence of mulattoes among the domestics and the artisans. They were the ones who interacted most with whites during slavery and who assimilated white mores and lifestyles. . . . The small free Negro community of Charleston [South Carolina] was extremely in-

bred. Most free Negroes considered it demeaning to marry a slave, and one scholar has discovered that 'rigid caste lines were followed rather closely in the selecting of one's mate. Color, economic and cultural status, and free ancestry played an important part in in-group relations.'" Thomas Holt, *Black over White: Negro Political Leadership in South Carolina during Reconstruction* (Urbana: University of Illinois Press, 1977), pp. 61, 64.

3. Wallace Thurman, *The Blacker the Berry...* (1929; repr. New York: Macmillan Company, Collier Books, 1970), p. 179. All subsequent references are to this edition.

4. Levine cautions the reader against oversimplifying—that the folklore includes songs and verses denigrating yellow and brownskin women and praising black men and women, though the praise is often a veiled recognition of the greater steadiness and reliability of the less socially desirable black men and women. This is the folk wisdom of Miss Curdy in Claude McKay's *Home to Harlem*: "Miss Curdy had been very emphatic to Susy about 'yeller men.' 'I know them from long experience. They never want to work. They're a lazy and shiftless lot. Want to be kept like women. I found that out a long, long time ago. And that's why when I wanted a man foh keeps I took me a black plug-ugly one, mah dear.'" Claude McKay, *Home to Harlem* (New York: Harper and Brothers, 1928), p. 61.

5. James A. Farabee, *A Guide to Beautiful Skin for Black Men and Women* (Garden City: Doubleday and Company, 1983), p. 1.

6. Frazier, *Black Bourgeoisie*, p. 198; Gerri Majors (with Doris E. Saunders), *Black Society* (Chicago: Johnson Publishing Company, 1976), p. 3; Abram Kardiner and Lionel Ovesey, *The Mark of Oppression* (1951; repr. New York: World Publishing, Meridian Books, 1962), p. 47.

7. Gwendolyn Brooks, *Maud Martha* (New York: Harper and Brothers, 1951), pp. 53, 54.

8. Toni Morrison, *The Bluest Eye* (1970; repr. New York: Simon and Schuster, Pocket Books, 1972), pp. 139, 61, 61–62. Psychiatric studies have provided considerable data on the impact of color consciousness. The case of R.R., included in Kardiner and Ovesey, *Mark of Oppression*, though perhaps extreme, reveals the complexity of responses that color prejudice can induce:

> "They grew up with a superior feeling toward us. All my cousins are almost white. My sister and I are darker. My wife is light like my cousins. Grandma accepted my wife. Grandma is very color-conscious. She speaks constantly of dark Negroes as 'black bastards.' She has a terrific prejudice against darker

people. My father can pass. He has blue eyes and blond hair. He had high goals for his children. We could go only with certain crowds. There are only two crowds among Negroes—light and dark. He wanted us to go with the light. He always objected if he saw me with a dark Negro. All my girl friends were of one type, one color—light and fair."

He dwells on the color theme again and again: "My wife's hair is straight and she doesn't look colored. Where we go on the beach we go purposely to avoid the colored. We go to Jones Beach. It's not like Rockaway where there are blocks and blocks of Negroes. It's awful, but the conversation in any group I'm in seems always to drift to this color business. So many of my friends are fair and feel so superior and really are not. I was brought up in this clique. Shades to them are the most important thing. I've had some of my friends rejected because they weren't light enough. One of my wife's girl friends was over last night. She wants to get married but her family doesn't like the fellow. Her family are all very fair with straight hair and sharp features. The fellow doesn't conform to the family looks. He is of my complexion with soft features. The concern is with the quality of the hair and nothing else. He doesn't have nice hair—straight hair—but just colored (Negro) hair. It's just ordinary colored (Negro) hair. The quality of the hair is more important to them than the color of the skin. It's a strange thing, but the majority of the families in my community think the same way when matching up the kids. They don't look into their backgrounds. They are not interested in that. They only care about the looks. They must have some outstanding Caucasian feature. If not color, then hair; if not hair, then blue eyes—or something like that."

Kardiner and Ovesey, *Mark of Oppression*, p. 188. More recently, Robert Coles, recording the lives of migrants in the cities, included the meditations of Thomas James Edward Robinson, a young man who had benefited from black consciousness-raising sessions, in his *The South Goes North*:

"I'd look at my skin. I'd look at my nose and my lips and my hair. I'm not ashamed to talk about it; no, I'm glad I can talk about it. Over at the office we make each other talk about how we look. We tell each other how we used to talk and what we used to say to ourselves in front of the mirror and what we say now. I used to think that if I could just hold my nose in, it would look different, thinner. I'd practice, tightening my lips up. My aunt said a lot of women get their hair straightened. She's never done it, but my other aunt, you can bet she does—for the white man! Today I can admit it! I used to think I'd look great if I had straight hair and if I could change my face. I wanted to be white. I didn't dare admit it then, even to myself. Once, though, I did. My friends here really make me admit it every day; but before I joined up, I admitted it to myself for a few minutes. I was in her room, my aunt's. I looked in her mirror. It's the only one we have. She keeps it beside her bed in a drawer. . . . I looked in the mirror and I saw the same old face, and all of a sudden I thought it would be great if I looked like the kid my aunt talks about—he's in the place she works, the white woman's house. He's the white woman's son, and he's my age. I've never seen him. I've never seen a picture of him. All I know is that she says he's blond; so, when I looked in the mirror I dreamed I was him. I was a white boy with blond hair! I didn't really believe I was, but for a few seconds I almost did convince myself. I tried walking like I thought he would—fancy-like. I swung my hands. I tried to make myself bigger. I tried to talk white. Then I heard my aunt. I put the mirror away."

Robert Coles, *The South Goes North* (vol. 3 of *Children of Crisis*) (Boston: Little, Brown and Company, 1971), p. 71.

9. Huggins, *Harlem Renaissance*, p. 55; David Levering Lewis, *When Harlem Was in Vogue* (New York: Alfred A. Knopf, 1981), p. 4.

10. E. David Cronon, Introduction to E. David Cronon, ed., *Marcus Garvey* (Englewood Cliffs: Prentice-Hall, 1973), p. 8.

11. Jervis Anderson, *This Was Harlem: A Cultural Portrait 1900–1950* (New York: Farrar, Straus and Giroux, 1982), p. 126.

12. Claude Brown will ask, where do you go once you've reached the "promised land"? Wallace Thurman's 1929 play *Harlem* closed on the cry of Ma Williams: "'Tell me! Tell me! Dis ain't de City of Refuge?'"

13. Wright, *Lawd Today*, pp. 111, 109. The connections between streets and power and manhood are suggested in an observation by David Levering Lewis: "Southern newspapers editorialized ghoulishly about the fate awaiting any Afro-American veteran daring to come home uniformed, bemedalled, and striding up main street like a white man." Lewis, *When Harlem Was in Vogue*, p. 14.

14. Claude McKay, *Harlem: Negro Metropolis* (1940; repr. New York: Harcourt Brace Jovanovich, Harvest, 1968), pp. 150, 154.

15. McKay, *Home to Harlem*, p. 85.

16. Anderson, *This Was Harlem*, pp. 94–98; Marianna W. Davis, ed. *Contributions of Black Women to America*, vol. 1 (Columbia: Kenday Press, 1982), pp. 339–341.

17. Wright, *Lawd Today*, pp. 112–113.

18. Lewis, *When Harlem was in Vogue*, pp. 36–37.

19. John Daniels, *In Freedom's Birthplace: A Study of Boston Negroes* (1914; repr. New York: Johnson Reprint Corporation, 1968), p. 163.

20. Rampersad, *Art and Imagination*, p. 16.

21. Quoted in Wilson Jeremiah Moses, *Black Messiahs and Uncle Toms:*

Social and Literary Manipulations of a Religious Myth (University Park: Pennsylvania State University Press, 1982), p. 134.

22. Lewis, *When Harlem was in Vogue*, p. 37.

23. Du Bois was certainly sensitive to the problem: "Du Bois nevertheless saw danger in the negation of race pride. It was dangerous when an audience of blacks could guffaw at a speaker's suggestion that a child might be as black as the night and yet be beautiful, as the *Crisis* reported in October 1920, or when the magazine received angry objections from blacks to pictures of dark-skinned women on its covers." Rampersad, *Art and Imagination*, p. 147.

My focus on the psychological impact of Garvey's appeal is in no way intended to oversimplify the political realities of the period but to stress the emotional appeal of those qualities cited by Nathan Huggins: "Most of Harlem's Negro leaders were relieved to see Garvey removed from the scene; he was disruptive. But most, like DuBois, also sounded a note of regret at his exile, because Garvey personified a spirit and genius for touching and moving men's souls to dream, a quality of leadership that they, in their aloofness, lacked." Garvey could reach men's souls by cutting through the welter of ambiguity produced by an American society that both beckons and excludes, idealizes and damns, provides and abandons: "It was Garvey's ability to reduce complexities to their most simple formulation that made him a charismatic leader. He could induce people to share his dream because his fantasies were untroubled by the kind of paradoxes that perplexed men like Du Bois, Johnson, and Randolph." For an excellent discussion of the practical political difficulties posed for the black "leadership" by white indifference, consider Huggins's chapter 1, "Harlem, Capital of the Black World." After discussing white indifference to the political leverage of the black vote, Huggins considers the "epiphenomenal" nature of the black leadership:

> But this Harlem leadership was weakened too because of its peculiar relationship to its following. All of them except Garvey—DuBois, Owen, Randolph, and James Weldon Johnson—had been weaned on traditional middle-class reform. Like their white progressive brothers they were committed to reason and truth and enlightened democracy to bring about desired change. Their magazines were filled with the same exposé literature that the muckrakers had used to reform trusts and the meatpacking industry, abolish child labor, and so on. And like their white counterparts, they were an elite, removed from the masses. A. Philip Randolph, of course, turned to organizing the sleeping car porters. But neither DuBois nor Johnson could have affected the political machine that in these same years had been winning minor con-

cessions for immigrant masses in the cities. They were not involved in the block and precinct work that might have given them the kind of political leverage that the American political system understood. They, like other middle-class reformers, rejected that alternative as corrupt. It meant that Harlem intellectual leadership was epiphenomenal. It had no grass-roots attachments. Its success depended on its strategic placement, not its power. These leaders made themselves into conduits of Negro thought to white men of influence, and they attempted to channel white good intentions into effective reform. Except as white power could be inflected through them, they had no reason to believe that they could command black people's actions. Without mass support they were mere emblems of leadership, impotent to force change.

Huggins, *Harlem Renaissance*, pp. 47, 45, 48.

24. Quoted in Cronon, *Marcus Garvey*, pp. 45–46. "During this period [around 1914], and for some time afterward, the pages of black newspapers were crowded with the advertisements of beauty culturists and manufacturers of beauty products. Black-No-More was a cream for 'bleaching and beautifying' the complexion. Fair-Plex Ointment made the 'skin of women and men . . . bright, soft and smooth.' The makers of Cocotone Skin Whitener advised, 'Don't envy a clear complexion, use Cocotone . . . and have one.' And—as if replying to Cocotone's claim—an ad for Golden Brown Ointment declared, 'Don't be fooled by so-called "skin-whiteners." But you can easily enhance your beauty, lighten and brighten your dark or sallow skin by applying Golden Brown. . . . It won't whiten your skin—as that can't be done.' . . . As had happened with skin-lighteners, the advertising columns of black newspapers were loaded with information about anti-kink ointments, hair-growing preparations, special soaps and shampoos, combs, wigs, beauty parlors, and competing hair-dressing schools and systems." Anderson, *This Was Harlem*, pp. 92–93, 94. George S. Schuyler will title his satirical novel of passing *Black No More* (1931).

25. Lewis, *When Harlem Was in Vogue*, p. 235.

26. Jessie Fauset, *Plum Bun* (New York: Frederick A. Stokes, 1928), p. 277.

27. Quoted in Arnold Rampersad, *The Life of Langston Hughes*, vol. 1 (New York: Oxford University Press, 1986), p. 140. Hughes has commented frequently on the connections between his poetry and black music. In *The Big Sea* he noted that "I tried to write poems like the songs they sang on Seventh Street [in Washington, D.C.]—gay songs, because you had to be gay or die; sad songs, because you couldn't help being sad sometimes. But gay or sad, you kept on living and you kept on going."

Langston Hughes, *The Big Sea* (1940; repr. New York: Hill and Wang, 1963), p. 209. He discussed the emotional quality of the blues in notes he sent to Carl Van Vechten: "I know very little to tell you about the Blues. They always impressed me as being very sad, sadder even than the spirituals because their sadness is not softened with tears but hardened with laughter, the absurd, incongruous laughter of a sadness without even a god to appeal to. In the Gulf Coast Blues one can feel the cold northern snows, the memory of the melancholy mists of the Louisiana low-lands, the shack that is home, the worthless lovers with hands full of gimme, mouths full of much oblige, the eternal unsatisfied longings." Quoted in Rampersad, *The Life of Langston Hughes*, p. 111. David Levering Lewis has commented on the reaction of the black "elite" to the music that Hughes's poetry both evoked and cherished: "Afro-American music had always been a source of embarrassment to the Afro-American elite. The group continued to be more than a little annoyed by the singing of spirituals long after James Weldon Johnson and Alain Locke had proclaimed them America's most precious, beautiful, and original musical expression. Its feelings about urban spirituals— the blues—and about jazz sometimes verged on the unprintable." Lewis, *When Harlem Was in Vogue*, p. 173.

28. Wagner, *Black Poets*, p. 211.

29. Lewis, *When Harlem Was in Vogue*, pp. 226–227.

30. George S. Schuyler, "The Negro-Art Hokum," in Michael W. Peplow and Arthur P. Davis, eds., *The New Negro Renaissance: An Anthology* (New York: Holt, Rinehart and Winston, 1975), pp. 467, 469.

31. Langston Hughes, "The Negro Artist and the Racial Mountain" in ibid., pp. 471, 471–472, 475, 476. Hughes's reaction to the black bourgeoisie was a reaction, in part at least, to the elite of Washington, D.C.: "Introduced to the world of the black bourgeoisie—nowhere more exclusive than in Washington—Langston found it, on the whole, insufferable. The younger blacks were obsessed by money and position, fur coats and flashy cars: 'their ideals seemed most Nordic and un-Negro.' Light-skinned women coolly snubbed their darker acquaintances; college men boasted of attending 'pink' teas graced by only 'blue-veined' belles almost indistinguishable from whites." Hughes's response was to turn to black Seventh Street, the street whose vitality Jean Toomer will celebrate in *Cane*: "There the plainest, blackest folk in the city lived, sang the blues, shot pool and one another, guffawed and hollered out tall tales, and devoured watermelon and greasy barbecue without apology. On grimy Seventh Street, Hughes would write, poor blacks 'looked at

the dome of the Capitol and laughed out loud.' " Rampersad, *The Life of Langston Hughes*, pp. 99–100, 102.

32. W. E. B. Du Bois in Rampersad, *The Life of Langston Hughes*, p. 193. Du Bois concluded: "I read 'Nigger Heaven' and read it through because I had to. But I advise others who are impelled by a sense of duty or curiosity to drop the book gently in the grate and to try the *Police Gazette.*"

33. Lewis, *When Harlem Was in Vogue*, p. 194.

34. Rampersad, *The Life of Langston Hughes*, p. 135.

35. Lewis, *When Harlem Was in Vogue*, p. 195.

36. Rampersad, *The Life of Langston Hughes*, p. 140.

37. Ibid., pp. 144, 145.

38. Lewis, *When Harlem Was in Vogue*, pp. 238, 236–237, 237. Richard Bruce Nugent, later Thurman's friend, initially reacted against the black Thurman and revealingly recalled, "He was black . . . in a way that it's hard for us to recognize that people ever had to be black." Ibid., p. 236.

39. Not surprisingly, perhaps, "Blue Vein Society" was described earlier in fiction by Charles Chesnutt in "The Wife of His Youth," published in the *Atlantic* in July 1898: "The original Blue Veins were a little society of colored persons organized in a certain Northern city shortly after the war. Its purpose was to establish and maintain correct social standards among a people whose social condition presented almost unlimited room for improvement. By accident, combined perhaps with some natural affinity, the society consisted of individuals who were, generally speaking, more white than black. Some envious outsider made the suggestion that no one was eligible for membership who was not white enough to show blue veins. The suggestion was readily adopted by those who were not of the favored few, and since that time the society, though possessing a longer and more pretentious name, had been known far and wide as the 'Blue Vein Society,' and its members as the 'Blue Veins.' " Quoted from Chesnutt, *Wife of His Youth*, pp. 2–3. Holt has described the Brown Fellowship Society, which was founded in Charleston, South Carolina among free mulattoes on November 1, 1790: "The organization was an instrument for maintaining the boundaries of a largely independent and self-conscious class that saw itself threatened from above by 'the dominant race' and from below by 'the backward race.' . . . It was clear that, to enjoy the white ruling class's protection, mulattoes 'had to be in accord with them and stand for what they stood for.' . . . Their exclusion of blacks fostered destructive enmities and distortions

in the Negro community, encouraging the free blacks to form their own society." Holt, *Black over White*, pp. 65, 66.

Thirteen. Nella Larsen

1. Cited in Huggins, *Harlem Renaissance*, p. 47.
2. Frazier, *Black Bourgeoisie*, pp. 198–199.
3. Cedric Dover, *American Negro Art* (1960; repr. New York: New York Graphic Society, 1965), p. 33.
4. This is the "comic" theme of a 1924 *Happy Hooligan* episode; as late as 1935 the *Katzenjammer Kids*, first published in 1897, is exploiting the theme. Stephen Becker, *Comic Art in America* (New York: Simon and Schuster, 1959), pp. 19, 48.
5. Alain Locke, "The Legacy of the Ancestral Arts," in Alain Locke, ed., *The New Negro* (New York: Albert and Charles Boni, 1925), p. 261.
6. Alain Locke, "The New Negro," in ibid., p. 15. After noting his race's "strange, child-like capacity for wistfulness-and-laughter," Claude McKay writes: "No wonder the whites, after five centuries of contact, could not understand his race. How could they when the instinct of comprehension had been cultivated out of them? No wonder they hated them, when out of their melancholy environment the blacks could create mad, contagious music and high laughter." McKay, *Home to Harlem*, p. 267.
7. Lewis, *When Harlem Was in Vogue*, p. 162.
8. Albert C. Barnes, "Negro Art and America," in Locke, *The New Negro*, p. 20. For Moses, both Du Bois and Garvey saw the black as redemptive: "At the peak of his career, during and immediately following World War I, DuBois believed strongly in the power of black Americans to redeem the United States. . . . Garvey, along with the traditional leadership, was still clinging to the myth of the old, suffering Christlike Negro who had a mission to redeem the world." Moses, *Black Messiahs*, pp. 113, 115.
9. Countee Cullen, "A Song of Praise," in Peplow and Davis, *New Negro Renaissance*, pp. 358–359.
10. Waring Cuney, "No Images," in ibid., pp. 358–359.
11. Dover, *American Negro Art*, p. 33.
12. Langston Hughes, "When Sue Wears Red," in Rampersad, *The Life of Langston Hughes*, p. 37.
13. Langston Hughes, "To the Black Beloved," in Peplow and Davis, *New Negro Renaissance*, pp. 366–367. James Weldon Johnson considered the stereotypes in his autobiography: "I saw strong men, capable of sus-

tained labor, hour for hour, day for day, year for year, alongside the men of any race. I saw handsome, deep-bosomed, fertile women. Here, without question, was the basic material for race building. I use the word 'handsome' without reservations. To Negroes themselves, before whom 'white' ideals have so long been held up, the recognition of the beauty of Negro women is often a remote idea. Being shut up in the backwoods of Georgia forced a comparison upon me, and a realization that there, at least, the Negro woman, with her rich coloring, her gayety, her laughter and song, her alluring, undulating movements—a heritage from the African jungle—was a more beautiful creature than her sallow, songless, lipless, hipless, tired-looking, tired-moving white sister." Johnson, *Along This Way*, p. 121.

14. Langston Hughes, "Poem," in Rampersad, *The Life of Langston Hughes*, p. 78.

15. McKay, *Home to Harlem*, pp. 289–290, 320. Du Bois has recorded his own response to the "extraordinary colors" of his people, viewed in the South while attending Fisk University: "I was thrilled to be for the first time among so many people of my own color or rather of such extraordinary colors, which I had only glimpsed before, but who it seemed were bound to me by new and exciting and eternal ties. . . . Into this world I leapt with enthusiasm. A new loyalty and allegiance replaced my Americanism: henceforward I was a Negro." Quoted in Rampersad, *Art and Imagination*, p. 12.

16. Nella Larsen, *Quicksand* (1928; repr. New York: Macmillan Company, Collier Books, 1971), p. 108. All subsequent references are to this edition.

17. Later, in Denmark, when her Danish aunt and uncle make of her person an esthetic and exotic object, Larsen reveals Helga Crane's consciousness of her feet: "And she knew that she had lovely shoulders, and her feet *were* nice" (122).

18. Her "small oasis in a desert of darkness" suggests both the discrimination and selection but also comments upon her setting: both Naxos and most of her associates. Naxos is a barely masked Tuskegee Institute: "This great community, she thought, was no longer a school. It had grown into a machine. It was a showplace in the Black Belt, exemplification of the white man's magnanimity, refutation of the black man's inefficiency. Life had died out of it. It was, Helga decided, now only a big knife with cruelly sharp edges ruthlessly cutting all to a pattern, the white man's pattern" (28). Washington's practice of having his students fall into formation and march to such activities as meals becomes, in Helga Crane's viewing, "massed phalanxes increased in size and number, blotting out pavements, bare earth, and grass" (40).

19. Even the small Alabama town she will later live in with the preacher will stir such feelings: "There was a recurrence of the feeling that now, at last, she had found a place for herself, that she was really living" (196).

20. The adjective "pale" recurs in her consciousness. Interestingly, Du Bois too employs the adjective at the very beginning of *The Souls of Black Folk*—in terms of the "pale world about them," the world of whites that bears down heavily upon the consciousness of black youth. Du Bois, *The Souls of Black Folk*, p. 16.

21. Although Robert Bone takes note of the problem of identity, he believes the "dramatic tension of the novel can be stated in terms of a conflict between Helga's sexuality and her love for 'nice things.'" Robert Bone, *The Negro Novel in America*, rev. ed. (New Haven: Yale University Press, 1965), p. 104. Gayle, on the other hand, stresses the problem of identity, and that the search for it "in a world, race mad, must produce serious psychological problems of the spirit and soul." Gayle, *Way of the New World*, p. 133.

22. Nella Larsen, *Passing* (1929; repr. New York: Macmillan Company, Collier Books, 1971), p. 178. All subsequent references are to this edition. Irene Redfield is, of course, not entirely frank. "Their own best good" is at least in part a mask for her self-interest, as Larsen indicates: "It was only that she wanted him to be happy, resenting, however, his inability to be so with things as they were, and never acknowledging that though she did want him to be happy, it was only in her own way and by some plan of hers for him that she truly desired him to be so" (107).

23. Mary Helen Washington has written: "'Passing' is an obscene form of salvation. The woman who passes is required to deny everything about her past: her girlhood, her family, places with memories, folk customs, folk rhymes, her language, the entire long line of people who have gone before her. She lives in terror of discovery—what if she has a child with a dark complexion, what if she runs into an old school friend, how does she listen placidly to racial slurs? And more, where does the woman who passes find the equanimity to live by the privileged status that is based on the oppression of her own people?" Mary Helen Washington, "The Mulatta Trap: Nella Larsen's Women of the 1920s," in Mary Helen Washington, ed., *Invented Lives: Narratives of Black Women 1860–1960* (New York: Doubleday and Company, Anchor Press, 1987), p. 164.

24. Her tragic yearning suggests a scope larger than that implied by my earlier comment relating her to the id; she seems almost to embody

traits that suggest "romantic racialism," just as Irene Redfield—in her Puritanism and inhibitions—seems to become representative of the white world. In terms of my earlier formulation, the "struggle" could be viewed as psychological; from this altered perspective, it can be seen as cultural. Both perspectives illumine qualities of the conflict and probably comment upon the element of ambivalence and irresolution in the texts—an irresolution as well, perhaps, in the life of the author. Mary Helen Washington has asked of Nella Larsen: "What happens to a writer who is legally black but internally identifies with both blacks and whites, who is supposed to be content as a member of the black elite but feels suffocated by its narrowness, who is emotionally rooted in the black experience and yet wants to live in the whole world, not confined to a few square blocks and the mentality that make up Sugar Hill?" Washington, *Invented Lives*, p. 162.

25. Adelaide Cromwell Hill, Introduction to Larsen, *Quicksand*, p. 15.

Fourteen. Jean Toomer

1. Arna Bontemps, Introduction to Jean Toomer, *Cane* (1923; repr. New York: Harper and Row, Perennial, 1969), p. xiii. All subsequent references are to this edition. Nellie McKay observes that Toomer, recalling his feelings while he was in Georgia, wrote that "at times I identified with the whole scene so intensely that I lost my own identity." From "Why I Entered the Gurjieff Work," included in the Jean Toomer Special Collection at Fisk University and quoted in Nellie Y. McKay, *Jean Toomer, Artist: A Study of His Literary Life and Work, 1894–1936* (Chapel Hill: University of North Carolina Press, 1984), p. 87. Others who consider Toomer's search for his identity include Wagner, *Black Poets*, pp. 260–264, and Fritz Gysin, *The Grotesque in American Negro Fiction* (Basel: Francke Verlag Bern, 1975), pp. 37–38.

2. Darwin T. Turner has commented: "At his best, he did not tell stories; he sang and painted, and his subject was Woman." *In a Minor Chord: Three Afro-American Writers and Their Search for Identity* (Carbondale: Southern Illinois University Press, 1971), p. 27. Jean Toomer, in correspondence with Sherwood Anderson included in the Jean Toomer Special Collection, commented that "the Georgia sketches lacked complexity and described them as 'too damn simple for me.'" Quoted in McKay, *Jean Toomer, Artist*, p. 83. My own approach focuses on the female figures of the Georgia sketches as the embodiment of a young man's wish and ignores the world in which the women walk and which

limits their ability to fully realize their role. McKay's interesting study considers this world in more detail and explores the tragic qualities which limit these women. Of Karintha, for example, she comments: "'Karintha' incorporates symbolic and realistic details of one humiliating aspect of the lives of southern black women: sexual oppression. . . . The tension between the positive and the negative aspects of the narrative rests in the conflict between what nature generates and what human beings subvert." Ibid., pp. 91, 96. See also pp. 97–124 for McKay's reading of the other Georgia sketches in Part One of *Cane*. My own discussion becomes a detailed analysis with my examination of the urban pieces in Part Two.

3. Sinclair Lewis's characterization of Gopher Prairie as "dullness made God" seems almost benign in comparison to such a world as that of "Box Seat," which is more like some child of *Main Street, 1984*, and *The Waste Land*.

4. Toomer's Moses lacks the power to lead anyone out of Egypt: "Suppose the Lord should ask, where was Moses when the light went out? . . . Oh come along, Moses, you'll get lost; stretch out your rod and come across. LET MY PEOPLE GO!" (117, 125).

5. Roots for Toomer, as for a number of other black writers of the Harlem Renaissance, includes the African heritage (as in the often-quoted "The Dixie Pike has grown from a goat path in Africa" [18], but Toomer's focus is more immediately on the South, specifically on Georgia. Other allusions to Africa can be found on pp. 23, 49, 229.

6. It was the old writer's view, in his "The Book of the Grotesque," that there were many truths and that these were beautiful, but that "the moment one of the people took one of the truths to himself, called it his truth, and tried to live by it, he became a grotesque and the truth he embraced became a falsehood." Sherwood Anderson, *Winesburg, Ohio* (New York: Random House, Modern Library, 1919), p. 5.

7. On the influence of Anderson on Toomer, McKay writes that "Anderson helped Toomer particularly in his own formulations of a literature of social analysis. In a letter to Anderson in 1922, he wrote: 'The beauty and full sense of life that these books contain are natural elements, like the rain and sunshine of my own sprouting. . . . Roots have grown and strengthened. They have extended out. I sprang up in Washington. *Winesburg, Ohio* and *The Triumph of the Egg* are elements of my growing. It is hard to think of myself as maturing without them.'" McKay examines the influence: "The close thematic relationship between the sketches in *Winesburg, Ohio*, the sympathy and understanding that the

author brings to the portrayal of the lives of defeated people, and the growth and maturity of George Willard are aspects of this book that can be compared with Toomer's *Cane*. In his book, Toomer struggled with the problems of the cultural failure of a society that is unable to facilitate meaningful relationships between people. . . . Despair, human isolation, frustration, and hopelessness are vividly portrayed by both men, and the hope for richer, fuller possibilities in human experience." Mckay, *Jean Toomer, Artist*, pp. 30–31.

8. This is most clearly suggested in the lines in which she dismisses the man she was with: "The man whom she was with, and whom she never took the trouble to introduce, at a nod from her, hailed a taxi, and drove away. That gave me a notion of what she had been used to. Her dress was of some fine, costly stuff. I suggested the park, and then added that the grass might stain her skirt. Let it get stained, she said, for where it came from there are others" (85).

9. I am alluding here to Robert Musil's *The Man without Qualities*. Wylie Sypher, in his *Loss of the Self in Modern Literature and Art*, has identified Musil's protagonist, an "individual vanishing behind the functionary," as a symbol of the loss of self in modern literature and art. I will be considering the relevance of Sypher's approach in my concluding chapter.

10. "In a letter to [Waldo] Frank, he points out that he is the source of both Lewis and Kabnis, Lewis with 'the sense of direction and intelligent grip on things that Kabnis lacks, Kabnis with the sensitivity and emotion Lewis does not have.' " McKay, *Jean Toomer, Artist*, p. 84.

Fifteen. Conclusion

1. Wylie Sypher, *Loss of the Self in Modern Literature and Art* (New York: Random House–Vintage Books, 1962), p. 28. All subsequent references are to this edition.

2. Christopher Lasch's recent, and sensitive, study of the self is also a study of the self in its diminished state after the fall: "Emotional equilibrium demands a minimal self, not the imperial self of yesteryear." Christopher Lasch, *The Minimal Self: Psychic Survival in Troubled Times* (New York: W. W. Norton and Company, 1984), p. 15. For blacks, of course, the imperial self has not been a possible self, just as many of the myths typically identified as American to which a self might respond—American dream, melting pot, movement westward—have not typified the black experience.

3. By Hughes Mearns, quoted in S. I. Hayakawa, *Language in Thought and Action*, 4th ed. (New York: Harcourt Brace Jovanovich, 1978), p. 171.

4. Included in Osofsky, *Burden of Race*, p. 78.

5. One of the manifestations of this consciousness of the look of the other—the look that is appraisal, discrimination, judgment—is the preoccupation in black literature with the shading of one's skin, that container of one's being. I have discussed this above in chapters 12 and 13, but though this sensibility first appears among the early modern black writers, it persists in the literature in response to the persistence of attitudes. As recently as 1979, Baldwin's *Just above My Head* casually includes, within the first nine pages, such descriptive passages as "Ruth's a big chick, with a color somewhere between mahogany and copper," and "people probably take me as a pleasant-enough-looking dude, dark-brown-skinned." James Baldwin, *Just above My Head* (1979; repr. New York: Dial Press, Dell, 1980), pp. 19, 21. Blacks may be simply blacks in the perceptions of a racist; in the sensibility of blacks the complexity reflects a history of the consciousness of difference.

6. Quoted in Hoyt Fuller's Introduction to *Passing*, p. 13.

7. Psychiatrists William H. Grier and Price M. Cobbs will argue as late as 1968 that "permeating the thinking of all Negroes remains the connection between status and beauty and fair skin." William H. Grier and Price M. Cobbs, *Black Rage* (1968; repr. New York: Basic Books, Bantam, 1969), p. 71.

8. My inclusion of Booker T. Washington in this grouping may seem somewhat perverse, but Du Bois's response to the Atlanta address should alert us to the need to weigh carefully the impact of an act in its time. Wilson Jeremiah Moses has considered the similarities, along with the differences, between Douglass and Washington, as well as the positions taken by the American Negro Academy and Du Bois. He concludes that "not only could the Tuskegee rhetoric parallel that of the American Negro Academicians, at times it sounded more militant" and that "the issues surrounding the Washington-DuBois controversy are often oversimplified." Moses, *Golden Age*, p. 101. Washington will no doubt remain a controversial figure. In his autobiography *Up from Slavery* he observes how the slaves gradually "threw off the mask" (25), but it is questionable whether, or when, Washington threw off *his*. Louis R. Harlan's metaphor of the onion is a possible, and provocative, way of imaging this complex figure: "The complexity of Booker T. Washington's personality probably had its origin in his being black in white America. He was forced from childhood to deceive, to simulate, to wear the mask.

With each subgroup of blacks or whites that he confronted, he learned to play a different role, wear a different mask. He was so skillful at this that it is no wonder his intimates called him the 'wizard.' . . . Perhaps psychoanalysis or role psychology would help us solve Booker T. Washington's behavioral riddle, if we could only put him on the couch. If we could remove those layers of secrecy as one peels an onion, perhaps at the center of Washington's being would be revealed a person with a single-minded concern with power, a minotaur, a lion, a fox, or Brer Rabbit, some frightened little man like the Wizard of Oz, or, as in the case of the onion, nothing—a personality that had vanished into the roles it played." Louis R. Harlan, *Booker T. Washington: The Making of a Black Leader 1856–1901* (New York: Oxford University Press, 1972), pp. viii, ix.

9. Ellison's *Invisible Man* is, of course, a primary document in the assessment of this awareness of complexity, an awareness further extended by his sensitive collection of essays *Shadow and Act*. He has posed, for example, one of the most important questions regarding the nature of the black self: "Can a people . . . live and develop over three hundred years simply by reacting? Are American Negroes simply the creation of white men, or have they at least helped to create themselves out of what they found around them?"

10. "But I was beginning to learn something about the blankness of those eyes. What I was learning was beginning to frighten me to death. If you look steadily into that unblinking blue, into that pinpoint at the center of the eye, you discover a bottomless cruelty, a viciousness cold and icy. In that eye, you do not exist: if you are lucky." James Baldwin, *If Beale Street Could Talk* (1974; repr. New York: Dial Press–Signet, 1975), p. 211. Consider, too, Pecola Breedlove and the storekeeper: "How can a fifty-two-year-old white immigrant storekeeper with the taste of potatoes and beer in his mouth, his mind honed on the doe-eyed Virgin Mary, his sensibilities blunted by a permanent awareness of loss, *see* a little black girl? Nothing in his life even suggested that the feat was possible, not to say desirable or necessary." Morrison, *The Bluest Eye*, p. 42.

INDEX